UNIVERSITY VILLAGE

THOUSAND OAKS

CALIFORNIA

i

Cover Photographs reproduced from Public Domain sources

All other photographs are courtesy of authors and their families

University Village Thousand Oaks
3415 Campus Drive
Thousand Oaks, CA 91360

Printed in USA

Tales of Challenge and Courage

Growing up in the Great Depression

By

UVTO Residents

These stories collected and published
By
"The Memoirs Committee"
Dr. James Birren, PhD
Barbara Warkentien
Jennifer Zobelein
Charles Kircher
John Bardgette
Tom Simondi

University Village Thousand Oaks (UVTO)

ACKNOWLEDGMENTS

One of the advantages of living in a retirement community such as University Village Thousand Oaks is the great resource of having a large group of people readily available with a myriad of abilities and information. Desirous of sharing this knowledge, especially with the younger generation, retired Professor of Psychology and Gerontology, Dr. James Birren, put out a call for volunteers to consider publishing a book. From the original group, those named below formed the Memoirs Committee and combined their talents to complete this publication.

Chairman

James E. Birren, PhD, originated the idea of inviting UVTO residents to write their experiences from the Great Depression and/or World War II for publication. He secured the support of UVTO management and guided the committee's focus.

Editor

Jennifer Zobelein maintained the roster of all authors and created copyright release forms. She revised the World War II manuscripts by offering suggestions and making changes as needed. She developed one manuscript from video tapes and took excerpts from a previously published book. She proofread every page for typing errors.

Editor

Barbara Warkentien revised The Great Depression manuscripts, making changes similar to those done by Jennifer. She created the title for the book. She also revised the Introduction and wrote the Book Cover Comments.

Layout and Format Designer

Charles "Chuck" Kircher was responsible for the overall book design including selecting fonts and font sizes, scanning and embedding pictures, and reformatting and combining individual stories to create an attractive, readable product that met the printer's requirements. He also created the lead-in pages and the Table of Contents as well as converting the text to PDF format.

Cover Designer and Facilitator

Tom Simondi created the photo montage for the cover, worked with the Director of Accounting to establish funding and assisted Chuck in expediting the account set-up and submission of files to the online publisher.

Proofreader

John Bardgette inspected the book draft for format consistency and general appearance to ensure a quality product.

UVTO Management

The Memoir Committee sincerely appreciates UVTO Management's financial funding, legal assistance and enduring support for this publication. Their significant contributions have been vital to *Tales of Challenge and Courage* becoming a reality. Scott Polzin, Former Executive Director; Ryan Exline, Executive Director; Warren Spieker, Vice President of Sales and Marketing; Bob Bouchard, Vice President of Design and Development

INTRODUCTION

The real life accounts presented in this book, *Tales of Challenge and Courage*, were written by the residents of **University Village Thousand Oaks**, a continuing care retirement community in California. The purpose of these memoirs is to share the important life experiences of these UVTO residents with family members, friends and others. The details of their life experiences provide a perspective on two major historic events, the Great Depression and World War II.

There is a growing interest in hearing and reading the life stories of people who lived during those times. Some of this curiosity may stem from the fact that our society is more efficient but less personal. For instance, when the current elders grew up, the stores where they shopped were small and they knew the owners. Clerks in grocery stores, butcher shops, and bakeries might offer advice while wrapping purchases. Today a shopper can go to a large mega store, fill a cart with items, do a self-checkout and walk away without talking to a single employee.

Cell phones, computers, and e-mail have contributed to a more efficient, but sometimes less friendly society. Now neighbors pass by talking on their cell phones without acknowledging others or asking how they or their children are doing. Face-to-face interaction is reduced as people rely on electronic devices for communication.

Nevertheless, thoughtfully-written life stories reveal the impacts on daily lives created by wide-ranging changes in society in one or two generations. Differences dominate every era. Astonishingly, American society has gone through the agricultural age to the industrial age into the information age during the lifetime of a single person of the older generation. Has the knowledge been passed on to the younger generation about these changes and how they affected lives and how people adapted to them? The authors, through their stories, have attempted to answer such questions by providing a more complete picture of the transformations they faced.

James E. Birren, PhD

GROWING UP IN THE GREAT DEPRESSION

LIVING THROUGH WORLD WAR II

SECTION ONE

GROWING UP IN THE GREAT DEPRESSION

THE GREAT DEPRESSION BY JEAN BARDGETTE

One of my earliest memories in the early 1930's was looking out of the second story window of my father and my mother's office overlooking Main Street in Pecos, Texas. By the time I started first grade, my father had closed his insurance company. After all, who could afford insurance in such hard times? My mother's business was moved into our home. This was The Retail Merchants Association, which checked credit worthiness of people for local merchants. After a few years of school, I was able to help her with the filing and operating the mimeograph machine.

Dad bought some acreage on the edge of town, constructed a very simple house and bought some dairy cows and chickens. The government had a program to help low income people by providing them with milk and eggs. Dad received one of these government contracts and received payment for delivering milk and eggs to eligible people. He also provided milk, butter and eggs to others in town. By the time I was in third or fourth grade, it was my job to do most of the washing and sterilizing of the glass milk bottles. We did not have running water; all of our hot water was heated on the kerosene stove. There was also the churning of milk to make buttermilk and butter, eggs to be gathered and cleaned before packing. My older sister was away at college; my two brothers were still at home. They helped Dad take care of the cows and chickens, do the milking and carry in water. My older brother was a pretty good mechanic and kept the old Model A Ford running. He also worked at one of the local service stations through his high school years before going off to college.

Times were tough and when the provisions for supper were low, my mother would ask my brother to take his 22 rifle and go shoot a couple of cottontail rabbits. There were plenty of these around in the pasture. This was not what is usually thought of as pastures, just West Texas land with a lot of mesquite bushes and scrub grasses. We ate a lot of fried rabbit during those years. It's really quite tasty.

Our property was next to a major highway, US 90, going from east to west with railroad tracks on the other side of the highway. Many trains stopped at the many stock pens and the tall water tank. The water was used for both cattle and the trains. This was near enough to our house that my younger brother and I would often go there to climb and play on the fences, sometimes with cattle milling below us waiting to be shipped. At this time many men went across the county hitchhiking or hopping a ride on freight trains trying to find work. Cars were convoyed across country to the west coast, one being driven while pulling another. There would be many of these traveling together. I expect a large number of the men I saw hitchhiking were headed east to pick up more cars to drive west. Many times one of these men would come to our back door asking for a meal. My mother always fed them. She would ask them to go chop some wood for her at our always present wood pile and she would fix them eggs and toast, potatoes if we had them and milk and coffee to drink. They were always grateful and never any trouble. Those were different times; we didn't even have keys to our house. I frequently would walk the mile and a half to and from school, much of it across the open pasture or by the side of the highway when it was raining with no concern about who was along the road.

Another memory of this time was the terrible dust storms we had. This was the period during the thirties known as the "Dust Bowl" when the central plains states had such a severe drought that it felt as if the entire country would blow away. I would walk home from school with my head covered and a handkerchief across my nose and mouth sometimes wondering if I were making any progress. When the storm passed, I would have to help Mother clean the house, we had no vacuum or modern cleaning supplies then, just the broom, dust and wet mops and rags.

Times changed in the late 1930's. The United States started to prepare for war, or at least to supply materials for the British and French. Suddenly there were jobs in the defense industry. My father found work with a contractor building arsenal plants. This required occasional moves. As the remaining child at home I went to live with my sister and her husband in Midland, Texas, freeing my mother to join Dad. I finished high school, worked a year at a law office and was then accepted in the Cadet Nursing Corps and left for The University of Texas School of Nursing at Galveston, Texas, to become a Registered Nurse. I completed my schooling following the end of WWII but loved my profession and felt an obligation to work at nursing for many years.

MEMORIES OF THE GREAT DEPRESSION BY JOHN BARDGETTE

I was a boy during the years of the Great Depression, and don't have any memories of the hard time that I've read and heard about. My father was killed in Saint Louis, Missouri in 1924, when I was just two years old. During the depression years my Mother and I lived in Galveston Texas. In retrospect, I believe that different areas of the country had very different experiences during the Depression. Those that lived in industrial cities felt the effects much more that those that lived in smaller, non-industrial cities or small towns.

In contrast, during my childhood, I was never hungry. We had three meals every day and I frequently had a second helping of anything that was a favorite, like fried chicken. We had an icebox and the iceman delivered ice regularly. We kids followed the ice delivery truck to get chips of ice as the iceman cut off another block. There was also a milk delivery of narrow-neck glass bottles with cardboard seals. The cream rose to the top and was poured off for coffee.

I always had clothing suitable for each season, hot humid summers and cold, and often, wet winters. As a boy I never wore an undershirt and most of the time my shirttail was hanging out. In the summer I always went barefoot, and in the winter I mostly wore rubber sole tennis shoes. I always had a bed to sleep in, in a house with a good roof, but there wasn't any central heating. During the winters the houses that I lived in had radiant gas heaters in the living room and dining room. The cook stove kept the kitchen warm, and it was usually the warmest place in the house. None of the bedrooms were heated, but we had enough quilts to keep us warm. I don't remember having blankets in those years, probably because they cost more than homemade quilts.

I also remember a remark that I heard Uncle Porter say more than once, "It's cheaper to rent than it is to own, and it's cheaper to move than it is to rent". This probably accounts for the fact that we lived in three different houses in Galveston, where Mother and I lived with Uncle Porter and Aunt Leck, Mother's sister. At one time several families, all relatives, lived in a large two-story house, Uncle Porter, Aunt Leck, Tommie and Betty Lou, and Uncle Chet, and Ralph, Rosalie, Orland and Robert, and Mother and I. Uncle Porter had a good, steady job as an automobile mechanic at Dow Chevrolet and Uncle Chet was a carpenter foreman at the U.S. Government's Fort Point shipyard, and Ralph Batchelder worked at Todd Shipyard.

Many of my toys were homemade, or were very inexpensive. I made a gun that shot rubber bands, which I played with quite a bit. It had a long barrel with a pistol grip handle. A spring-loaded clothes pin was attached to the backside of the handle. A rubber band was clamped into the clothes pin and stretched to and over the end of the barrel. I would aim the gun at a target and squeeze the clothes pin, opening it to release the rubber band and it would fly toward the target. It wasn't a very accurate gun but I had a lot of fun with it. I built my own skateboard scooter. The base was a 2x4 with a skate nailed to the bottom, and the post for the handle was a 1x4 nailed to the front end. I separated the skate into its two pieces and removed the shoe-toe clamps, then nailed these in place.

I played several games, jacks, pick-up-sticks and hopscotch, with my cousins, Betty Lou and Tommie, and other kids in the neighborhood. Besides my cousins, I played with Charles and Clarence, two brothers that lived a few doors down the block. One of the games we enjoyed playing was marbles and I collected a goodly quantity of them. Besides playing regular marbles, we and other neighborhood boys, played a game called "holey" that was played with marbles and a smoothly rounded hole in the ground. The hole was about three inches in diameter at the top and about two inches deep. The player took an even number of marbles in his hand, two of his and two from one of the other players, and threw them down at the hole in the ground. If an even number stayed in the hole, he won and all of the marbles were his. If an odd number stayed in the hole, the other player won.

Mother and I frequently visited Aunt Cora and Aunt Stella, first cousins of my maternal Grandmother. They lived in a small house. It was a two-story building that they heated with kerosene space heaters in the winter months. These heaters gave off a distinctive odor that was somewhat unpleasant. The house did have electricity for lighting and a flush toilet, but it was in a small building about ten to fifteen feet away from the back door. Both of my "Old Maid" aunts were seamstresses, who made clothes to order. They each had a treadle sewing machine and an adjustable clothes dummy that could be expanded or reduced to the dimensions of their customers. This allowed them to pre-fit the dresses on the dummy before the customer came in for a final fitting.

Besides the western movies that I went to in my grade school years, I went to various types of movies in my high school years. I remember that bedroom scenes always had the men and women fully clothed in pajamas and robes. They had twin beds and as soon as they got out of bed, they would put their robes on. This was in compliance with the "Hay's Code", the film industry's 1930 voluntary moral regulation guidelines, that controlled the production of movies in those days. There were also "Adult Only" movies, but I never saw any of those until I was eighteen. They wouldn't sell me a ticket before then. Common in all of the movies of that era were the actors smoking. All of the men and many of the women were shown smoking. This was certainly a factor in encouraging teenage boys to smoke; however, I didn't start smoking until after I had graduated from high school and started to work with young men that did smoke. Camel and Lucky Strike were the most advertised and popular cigarettes at that time, but I mostly smoked Wings because they were much cheaper. If I remember correctly, they cost 5 cents a pack.

I graduated from Ball High School in 1940, about the end of the Great Depression. World War II had started in Europe and just over a year later the United States entered the war.

© 2012 John Bardgette

DANCING AWAY THE GREAT DEPRESSION BY SKIPPY BATES

I, Janice Annetta Lyen, was born in Chicago on August 15, 1925. My father, C. Franklin Lyen, was a concert violinist; my mother, Madge Ferris Burgh Lyen, a concert pianist. My sister, Edith Euretta Lyen and I were given ballet and tap dancing lessons at age three and four. My first performance was at the Navy Pier in Chicago when I was three and a half. My memory of that debut was going around collecting ticket stubs from the stands at the doors. By 1929, Dad was selling vacuum cleaners, and Mom was cleaning other people's houses.

We lost our home, packed everything we could save and loaded it into an old bus that Dad bought.

We headed for Iowa, where my grandmother lived. My sister and I sat on a portable kitchen cabinet that Mom wanted to keep, all the way to Oakaloosa.

We left most of our furnishings at grandma's and started for Colorado to my father's folks. My father tuned pianos on the way, in exchange for eggs or whatever. My sis and I even got a ride on a horse from one of the farmers. We ate dandelion greens, wild asparagus growing in streams, and lots of wild rabbit, always filled with a lot of buckshot. In Tulsa, Oklahoma, we parked our old bus at the back of a Safeway store. There was a huge dump, which my sis and I had to explore. We found oranges, apples, grapefruit and lettuce that had brown or rot spots on them, but for the first time in weeks, we had something in our tummies besides bread with melted lard or pancakes with sugar water. We did have hamburger once in a while because it was 10 cents a pound.

We made it to Cortez, Colorado. We lived in a one-room unit in a motel next to the hospital, where Mom got a job cleaning. Dad taught violin and electric guitar and did odd jobs. When the little town found out that we were a musical family, they began to invite us to grange hall meetings, PTA affairs etc. and we would dance and sing.

Dad would play the violin, and mom, an extraordinary child impersonator, would do some skits. My sis and I played the violin, piano, and my specialty, the xylophone.

After the show, the town folks would pass the hat. By the time I was six-years old, we began the life of "show biz."

We traveled all over the country until my mom at age forty got pregnant, which was unheard of at that time. Our show biz days ended when she was six months along.

We ended up in Fullerton, CA, having previously been out to California in 1939 to learn new tap routines and find additional talent for our show. We had grown to theater work by then.

In 1941 when I was sixteen, I enrolled in Fullerton Jr. College and became a drum majorette for our band. We were invited for the first time in FJC history to march in the Pasadena New Year's Rose Parade. I was ecstatic! THEN, Dec 7th and Pearl Harbor. The parade was cancelled, my heart broken. We did the best we could for the war effort.

I remember my Mom adding her rubber girdle to the donation trash bin in downtown Fullerton at a big rally, and saving bacon grease etc. I tried to join the WAVES because their uniforms were so nifty, but I was too young. My sister and I volunteered to go to the Fullerton Railroad Station and pass out coffee and doughnuts to the Japanese, who were being moved to internment camps. In my sixteen-year-old mind, I did not comprehend the magnitude of what was going on and we would just smile and try to be nice to a very tearful group of people.

I graduated at seventeen and because I wasn't eighteen, I needed parental consent to get a job. With the necessary approval of my parents, I was employed at Knott's Berry Farm from 1942-43. I not only earned a salary, but I also gained the name, Skippy. The kitchen was one large room, including the cooking area, dishwashing area, and an area for completing the food orders for delivery. There was no public address system, so our orders were called out by our names. Over the noise it was hard to distinguish--Lynn, Annette, Janice Annetta (me) etc. I was asked if I had a nickname. I told of my boyfriend, who called me "Skipper." He was crazy about boats and said that someday when we owned a boat, I could be his skipper. It was shortened to Skippy and I've used it ever since.

Then I left home, found a dance studio on Robertson Blvd. in Beverly Hills. I walked in and talked to the head dance teacher, who hired me. Later, we became roommates. When I turned eighteen the next August, I went to work on graveyard shift at Lockheed Vega Aircraft plant in Van Nuys. That left my days to pursue my theatrical career, BUT one night just a few weeks after I went to work there, a pair of blue eyes peered over the wing I was working on, and the owner of those eyes became by husband, Frank Mathes, Jr. in 1945. An interesting tidbit--On the way to get our marriage license, Frank turned to me and said, "By the way, Skippy, what is your real name?"

We lost a son, in October, 1946, so I again went back to the only thing I knew--"Show Biz." I started working at Eagle Lion Studios and later worked for Fox, Metro, and RKO. When I became pregnant again in 1949, I gave up working and became a full time mom. That was law by my husband. While our two daughters, Wendy Lee and Debra Linn, and our son, Frank D. Mathes, III, were at home, I stayed home.

Finally, when all were in high school, I told my husband that I was either going to become an alcoholic or he had to let me get a job. I went into real estate in l969. I had my own office for many years; but when my husband got really sick, I sold my office, working only part time. I was widowed in 1989.

In 1992, I bought a place in Palm Desert. I was wasting away. I took up golf, started playing bridge again, having lunches with the girls, etc. In 1994, I met Lee Bates. We married in May, 1996. 2007 found us here at UVTO. Living it and Loving it.

© 2012 Janice L. Mathes

GROWING UP IN THE GREAT DEPRESSION BY JAMES BIRREN

There were long lines of people waiting to get into the banks with locked doors when the banks closed in the Great Depression. I remember clearly the long lines of depositors whose money was frozen. I was about eleven years old and didn't quite understand what was going on. My father, August Birren, told me banks had lent money to people to buy houses and then the Depression and loss of jobs resulted in many people not being able to pay back their mortgages that the banks held.

My father taught my brother and me how to earn money by selling him cigarettes. He had us buy a carton of cigarettes at the local drug store. They were $1.25 for a carton. We sold the packs back to my father and made 25 cents on each carton. My brother and I alternated each week buying a carton. As a smoker my father died, having lost his lungs to cancer at age seventy-two.

My father had my brother and me put our money into postal savings accounts at the local post office, so we didn't lose the few dollars we had saved. In the Depression we didn't lose any money in the closed banks. My brother and I were taught about earning and saving money at an early age.

When my brother and I were young, we would get some Christmas money from my father's employer. On the day before Christmas my brother and I would go to the laundry where our father worked and get admitted to the boss's office. There he gave each of us a silver dollar or later a small gold coin that we both saved. Gold was then $35 an ounce. Today (2012) it is about $1,795 per ounce. What a change! This, like many other things, leaves me with the puzzle of how costs and inflation always seem to be sneaking up behind me.

Food costs were low in the Depression years. When I was in fifth and sixth grades in elementary school, my mother sent me to shop on Saturday mornings. I went to the local shops about a half mile from our rented house to buy the food for our family of four for the weekend. I took my coaster wagon to bring home the bags of things I bought. The shops were all small; there was a butcher shop, a bakery, a green grocery next to one another. Inside the shops were the proprietors and I got to know them. The prices were low, 7 cents for a quart of milk, a nickel for a loaf of bread, 10 cents for salad greens that included a tomato. At the bakery I bought two coffee cakes for a week-end treat. They were expensive, 25 cents each. As a carry forward from the Depression, I sometimes recall these low prices when I shop today. It is not easy to forget what things cost then, and it does influence my attitude towards saving more and spending less—a Depression legacy.

I don't recall any members of my mother's and father's families being short of food in the Great Depression. My mother had two siblings and my father had five. Family gatherings always involved food, which the women cooked. My grandmothers and mother never worked outside of the home and I recall only one unmarried aunt who worked and five who didn't. Each spring in his garden, my paternal grandfather put up a small smoke shed, where he smoked some meats and sausages for later eating by all the family including the growing grandchildren like me. In the area of Chicago where he had built his house, the garden was small. Perhaps there was only space about 50 by 50 feet for the small smoke shed to share space with planted tomatoes and other vegetables.

Other memories of the Great Depression involved banks selling the houses they foreclosed. In 1937 my father bought a two-bedroom brick house with a garage for $7,000. It had been foreclosed and originally sold for $8,500 with a $1,000 second mortgage and a $7,500 first mortgage. Who lost their money when the house was foreclosed? I believe the first mortgage holder was a bank that lost $500, but the second mortgage was held by a private investor who lost $1,000.

My memories of the Great Depression include seeing veterans from World War 1 selling apples for a nickel on Michigan Boulevard in downtown Chicago. One of my father's brothers-in-law lost his job and my father passed on a few dollars a week to him. This caused some tension with my mother about weekly budgets.

My father had a stable income during the Depression managing a laundry. That was before washing machines were invented and commercial laundries were the seventh largest business in the USA. My father got my brother and me to deliver laundry advertising handbills on Saturdays to houses and flats and we earned $2.00 a day. We put one-page laundry ads under the doors of apartments and houses. It was very tiring and I had to sleep a bit before I could eat dinner after a day of pedaling.

My father's early emphasis on saving money persisted with me and I kept putting my money into a postal savings account. By the time I was in my third year of college, I had saved $400. Next came the opportunity to lease and operate a gas station from the Shell Oil Company. I was twenty-years-old and two friends about the same age joined me in renting the gas station. Since I had saved the most money, I signed the lease for the station. Two of us worked the station on alternate evenings as well as on weekends. The other friend went to night school so he ran it during the day. What did we earn? We paid ourselves 27 ½ cents an hour from the profit we made selling gasoline for 15 cents a gallon. At that price the service to our customers included washing the windshield and checking the tires. When the Shell Oil truck delivered the gasoline, we paid for it in cash. Later we opened a checking account, so we could pay by check. We did have to hustle over to the bank to deposit our cash receipts from our customers, many of whom we knew. There were no credit cards in those days.

One evening a young man came into our small gas station to use the toilet. When he came out, he was holding a 45 caliber gun and waved it at me. He told me I had to give him all the money I had. I gave him the folding bills and then he told me to empty my coin holder that was on my belt. I took it off and gave it to him not wanting to face his waving gun any longer. He left and I sat down very shaken up.

Other money issues come to mind. In 1940, 25 cents would buy a hot roast beef sandwich with mashed potatoes and gravy in a restaurant across the street from the gas station. A cup of coffee cost 5 cents. Cars could be bought for a few dollars. I bought a second hand Model A Ford for $50 and used it to drive to college. I charged my school friends who rode with me the fares that they might have spent on busses and elevated trains. I remember my father buying a new Dodge four door sedan for $733 during the Depression. Things were not very expensive but our income was quite low.

Many things were different in those years, for example, security. In 1932 I went to downtown Chicago for my local school to pick up slides at the main library. Walking along Michigan Avenue, I saw an open automobile coming by with one motorcycle in front and one motorcycle behind it. The man waving from the car was Franklin Roosevelt. He was coming to Chicago to accept the Democratic Party's nomination for the Presidency. Now, security is a major issue and I am sure no presidential candidate would be going by waving from an open car, protected by only two escorting motorcycles.

What did I learn during the Great Depression? I learned to earn money, save money, and be careful about what I did with my money. What came next were many things that changed my life.

When I was in the Chicago Teachers College finishing work on my bachelor's degree, I took a course in the psychology of reading with Professor David Kopel. The professor asked me why I didn't plan to go on to graduate school. Why not, I asked myself? I applied in the spring of 1941 and entered graduate school in psychology at Northwestern University. What followed were many surprises.

© 2012 James Birren

LIFE IN NEBRASKA BY MICKEY BISHOP

In the 1920's I had a Nebraska playground of 160 acres. I was born on May 31, 1922, to Louis and Alma Schwartz. I was the second oldest of their six children.

My family worked the ground to feed the world and did a pretty darn good job of it. My sister and I made music practicing the piano until one day Dad said we would have to quit taking lessons because the banks had closed. We continued playing and Dad joined us, playing the concertina.

So began the 1930's and the Great Depression. We heard of people in cities who didn't have enough to eat. That didn't worry me much because we had the land on which to grow the food. What I forgot was successful farming required lots of water. One year the well ran dry. Our cattle, hogs, horses and chickens were in jeopardy until the well was dug deeper. The only one who made money that year was the well digger.

The crops were poor. Grasshoppers came in hordes. I remember my dad looking at the mounds of dirt along the fences and saying, "Oh no, there goes all my top soil". No rain – just dust. It seems all we did those years was pray for rain. Come to think of it, I've prayed for rain ever since. I made the mistake of moving to Southern California, and I'm still praying for rain.

In 1940 it rained and the crops were good. The day before Dad planned to cut the oats, it rained and then it hailed the size of golf balls. I remember standing at the window crying and saying, "God, you can't do this to us again." He did! By 1941, I had grown up. It was time to make my life. My sister Lillian, who had chronic kidney disease, had spent a lot of time in hospitals, and

her contacts were mostly doctors and nurses and she told me about them. So, nursing became my goal. I earned an R.N. and served in the Army Nurse Corps. Afterwards, I became a TWA flight hostess.

My youngest brother married and took over our parents' farm. They moved to a smaller farm nearby, for they were a part of the land.

In 1950 I married George Bishop and we had three sons. After our sons were older, I returned to nursing. I was Director of Nursing in convalescent homes, retiring at age sixty-five, but I continued to work part time until I was seventy-four. George passed away in 1977. I moved to University Village in September 2007.

© 2012 Mickey Bishop

MEMORIES OF THE GREAT DEPRESSION ERA BY ELEANOR BROWN

My name is Eleanor Brown. I was born July 11, 1918, in a hospital in Crookston and went home to McIntosh, a small town in northern Minnesota. I am the youngest of seven children born to Everett and Martha Webster. World War I, the "War to End all Wars," was over. My oldest brother, Leslie, came home from serving in the Occupation Army in France when I was three-years old. One year later my father died from an injury resulting from an automobile accident. During the next four years, my oldest sister, Marie, finished college. My brother, Tom, moved to Chicago, where he found work and a wife. My brother, Carl, had died at age three almost seven years before I was born. That left my mother, my brother John, my sister Betty and me. Leslie had tuberculosis and died in a veterans hospital. He was buried at the Los Angeles National Cemetery.

When I was eleven-years old, we moved to California and settled in Long Beach in August of 1929. When I think of the Great Depression that began with the stock market crash in 1929, I have happy memories and sad ones. There was so much which I didn't understand--so many things I questioned. Why did they dump oranges into empty fields, pour gasoline on them and set them on fire? Government officials said it was to keep the price of oranges up for the farmers. There were so many hungry people who could not afford to buy oranges at any price. To a fourteen-year-old, it seemed a better idea to give the oranges to the poor people. And, why was the government paying the farmers not to grow crops when there was so much hunger? Again, I was told, "We have to keep the prices up for the farmers."

President Franklin Delano Roosevelt started the WPA, Works Progress Administration, to provide jobs, to build roads and to build bridges. The WPA also upgraded many national parks and created some other interesting jobs as well. For a short time, my widowed mother was employed by the WPA to make men's shirts. I recall that she earned $60 per month or about $2.50 a day. It took her a whole day to make a shirt. The retail price of a shirt at the store was $2. Another wasteful use of tax dollars, which I recall, was the time my brother-in-law, then in his early 20's, came home from his WPA job quite angry. He, along with his fellow workers, had been told to dig holes in the ground. When they were finished digging the holes, they were then told to fill up those holes which they had just dug. He was a good worker and wanted to do something constructive, not just kill time by digging and then filling up holes in order to bring home a paycheck.

In the fall of 1932, we moved to Carrington, North Dakota, where my sister, Marie, was teaching. The plan was for me to complete my freshman year of high school there. However, circumstances combined with the 20 to 30 degree weather changed our plans. After losing his job in Chicago, my older brother, Tom, joined us on our return to California.

We arrived in Long Beach on Sunday, March 5, 1933, and began the process of settling into our apartment. Suddenly, on Friday, March 10 at 5:55 p.m., a 6.4 magnitude earthquake struck. We were advised not to stay inside our home the first night. Our landlord allowed her residents to take their 9 by 12 living room carpets to the parking lot behind the apartments to sleep on. Tom and my sister opted to stay inside until a 4 point after shock brought them out. We slept outside two nights.

Fortunately, the city gas was turned off with the first quake; so fires were not a problem. The Navy provided martial law one-half hour after the first quake. With no gas, cooking was a problem. The city provided electric stoves in some garages. However, carrying our food a block to cook it, was not too easy. Some of the residents in our apartment court were innovative. They built a stove from the plentiful supply of loose bricks from fallen buildings. A Coca-Cola sign was used as a cooking surface. About 4 p.m. each day, someone would start a fire so that it would be hot enough for people to cook dinner at 5 p.m. We used this cooking method for the three weeks we were without gas.

Newer buildings survived the earthquake well with little or no damage. Older buildings including two high schools, nine junior highs and twenty-two elementary schools were destroyed. Only five-to-seven schools were salvaged. The loss of life was 120, but it would have been much worse if school had been in session. Six students were killed in the Woodrow Wilson High School swimming pool.

The schools had been poorly constructed, as the contractors had used little or no mortar to keep the bricks in place. My brother and sister cleaned bricks for $1 a day. One good outcome of the Long Beach earthquake was the passage of The Field Act by the California Legislature April 10, 1933. This act mandated earthquake-resistant construction of schools K-14. No Field Act school has failed in earthquakes since then.

We had no school for three weeks. Then we started meeting our teachers each morning on the playground of my school, Franklin Junior High, reduced to just a pile of bricks. The playground was marked off in squares for each teacher. Our teachers gave us our daily assignments, and we returned them the next day.

We were living in a small apartment. Finally, my brother, John, and my mother were able to buy a small house with a living room, dining room, kitchen, bathroom and two bedrooms. My brother, my mother, my sister Betty, her husband Bill and their two-year-old and I all lived there. Betty and Bill and their toddler shared one bedroom. Mother and I shared the other bedroom. John, slept on a day bed in the dining room. This continued even after Betty and Bill brought their second child home from the hospital. (Our home in Minnesota, where we had lived prior to coming to California, was a five-bedroom, two-story house with lots of space.) This little house did seem a bit crowded. But it was a step up from the apartment. That's for sure!

For three years, I attended Long Beach Poly High in tent bungalows, since the buildings had been destroyed by the earthquake. When the usual two-week February rainy season arrived, the worn canvas tents had many holes, and everyone scattered to get a seat out from under the holes. By my senior year, only two buildings (the chemistry and business ones) had been rebuilt. The auditorium was retrofitted. We didn't have a gym for dances. So, on Thursday nights, the Cinderella Ballroom had dances for high school students that cost 25 or 35 cents for the whole evening. Most of the teachers didn't assign homework on Thursdays.........unless they forgot it was dance night!

Dances were about the only social activity in those days. Before World War II, a forerunner of the USO sponsored dances for servicemen stationed in the Port of Long Beach. Hostesses were needed to dance with the servicemen. My friend and I became hostesses. I met Lee Brown one Sunday afternoon. We danced, played shuffleboard, and then talked over donuts and coffee. As he put me on the bus to go home, he said, "I'll see you on Tuesday." I broke a date with another young man to keep the one with Lee. He was pretty sure of himself for an eighteen-year-old. I was a senior in high school. At seventeen, I knew what I wanted, too.

I finished high school and attended Long Beach Junior College for two years. Then I transferred to Bishop Johnson College of Nursing located at the Good Samaritan Hospital in downtown Los Angeles. I graduated with my R.N. Lee was honorably discharged from the Marines after serving four years including a tour with the expeditionary forces in Shanghai, China. He then attended Long Beach Junior College, where he served as the editor of the school's newspaper. After graduating, he went to work for Douglas Aircraft, but the work was monotonous. When the opportunity arrived to work for the civilian branch of aeronautics as a radio operator, he jumped at it. During this time we were married.

Lee often shared his memories of the Great Depression with me. He was raised in Pittsburgh, Pennsylvania. After the steel mills and companies like Westinghouse closed their doors, the men were not only out of work, but out of any prospects. My mother-in-law told me that, before the Depression, women had to wash their steps every day and their curtains every week because of the soot spilling out of the steel mill chimneys. Then came the Depression. Scrubbing steps daily and washing curtains weekly was not necessary for three years or more because the mills had closed. When the steel mills reopened, the women were mighty glad to scrub steps and wash curtains again since it meant that their husbands had gone back to work. My father-in-law wouldn't take welfare. Since he was a foreman at Westinghouse, he and one other man went to the factory each Saturday and put Cosmolene, a type of oil, on the Westinghouse machines to keep them from rusting.

A one-day-a-week job didn't pay much, so he also rented a hall on Friday and Saturday nights. There he ran a BINGO game on Fridays with flour, sugar, etc as prizes. On Saturday nights, he ran a square dance. My husband Lee, who was then in high school, helped with both.

When school was out for the summer, Lee and a friend caught a freight train and headed for wherever it went. They kept their parents informed of their whereabouts with post cards. His buddy's mother knew that when it was about time for school to start, there would be the sound of pebbles hitting the window and her son, John, would be home.

Lee told me many stories about his travels. He saw most of the country. At fifteen, he was in Seattle, where he and John were caught by the "bulls," security people who made life difficult for hobos. He wired home for money to get back to Pittsburgh. His father wired back, "You got yourself there. You can get yourself home." (Tough love didn't start in the 1990's!) Lee said that although the "bulls" were hard on hobos, some railroad companies reserved freight cars for "families only." He did some hitchhiking when he couldn't catch a freight train. He remembered some wonderful meals prepared for him by kind women after he offered to split wood or mow a lawn. He was a skinny kid with an honest face. Lee's stories were always welcome to his children and friends. He was a Scotsman and told his stories well.

There were no jobs for the men in Pennsylvania; so Lee enlisted in the Marine Corps, after graduating Salutatorian of his high school class. He went to radio operations school and was stationed on the USS *Louisville*, whose home port was Long Beach.

Lee and I were married for sixty-seven years and had four children. Our son, Dan, died in 1993. He was followed in death ten years later, in 2003, by our son, Bob. When Lee died in 2006, I lost the last of my men. Our two daughters remain. Barbara, lives in Camarillo, while Elizabeth lives in the Palo Alto area.

We enjoyed our careers and after retirement traveled extensively in the United States and Canada. Lee and I had planned to retire to UVTO, but he died before it was finished, and so I moved in alone in October 2007. I'm happy we made the decision to move, and I'm glad Lee chose a two-bedroom apartment. I've enjoyed my life here at UVTO and was pleased to share Lee's poems with the village by reading them at the talent shows.

HARD TIMES MEMOIR BY XIE CRANMER

I was born November 17, 1919, in Washington, D.C., and baptized with the unusual name of Xie (pronounced XC) Katrina Storey. It is really a Chinese name; and when I go to my ophthalmologist, his Chinese technician always calls me Shay. I was named for my

mother's aunt, a model for Lewis Carroll, famous author of *Alice in Wonderland.* He had a whimsical nature and thought the exotic name, Xie, fit my great aunt. He was also famous for his photography of little girls, and many thought his pictures were pornographic. His photographs including some of my great aunt can be found in museums all over the world.

Most of my life I lived in Washington, D.C., and I practically grew up on the Capitol steps. I treasure those days. Remembering this historical city and the events I was able to participate in, makes me very nostalgic. My family was very political, and I remember going to the presidential inaugurals from Herbert Hoover to George W. Bush. I was very disappointed that I could not get to the historic inaugural of Barack Obama.

I was the eighth child and had six brothers and a sister. Our grandparents lived across the street from our home. Our grandfather's name was Michael, thus we children called him Papa Mike and our grandmother Mama Mike. When I was about six-years old, I remember my brothers and me sitting in my grandmother's parlor. I was probably stringing beads that she kept in a Baker's Cocoa can, while my brothers worked on Erector Sets. Mom Mike was stitching at the quilt frame that was always up in her parlor. Sometimes an incubator was there too, and we waited for the eggs to hatch into furry little yellow chicks. When they hatched, our grandmother would let us take them out and play with them on the parlor rug. Sometimes disaster resulted when the chicks ran off the paper she put down for them. If our mother was there, she scolded our grandmother for getting the rug dirty. There were no electric vacuum cleaners then, so my brothers had to take the rugs into the yard to beat them clean.

One evening we asked Mom Mike why she had all the large portraits hanging on the wall. They were very large, formal portraits placed high on the wall. Dressed in formal clothes, their stern faces with long beards or moustaches appeared to be looking at us in a most intimidating manner. She told us it was to remember her loved ones. "What do you remember about them" we asked? Then she would tell us a story about her brother, whom she called "Bunny" and that made my brothers and me laugh. How did the grim-looking man in the portrait get to be Bunny? My brothers and I started calling each other Bunny

Rabbit and made fun of the man in the picture, and Grandmother would not tell us any more about him.

I wish our grandmother had told us the stories of her brothers and the historic times in which they lived. She lived during the Civil War; and in fact Dr. Samuel Mudd, who set John Wilkes Booth's broken leg after he assassinated President Lincoln, was her neighbor. My grandparents were tobacco farmers as was Dr. Mudd. They were friends and went to the same church. In later years when we went to the "country" as we called the thirty-mile excursion from our home in Washington to visit our relatives, she would point out the house but would never tell us the story of that sad event. Mother would tell us not to ask about Dr. Mudd because it upset our grandmother. As we grew older, we believed that our relatives, who were tobacco farmers, probably were divided about freeing the slaves.

When Mom Mike was 75-years-old the portrait of Uncle Bunny and the portraits of the other relatives were disposed of; my mother did not want any of them. It was not the fashion then to hang large portraits of family ancestors on the wall. None of my brothers and their wives were interested in them. It might be a different story today, although I doubt if any of my nieces or nephews would want to hang those big-framed portraits of stern looking ancestors they never knew.

My childhood home was in Washington, D.C., and my mother's relatives still lived in nearby Southern Maryland. We had access to so much history. My mother was born in Surrattsville, and her mother was born in nearby Port Tobacco. These towns were prominent in their day. Surrattsville was named after the Surratt family. Mary Surratt was hanged because she was found guilty of collusion with John Wilkes Booth in the assassination of President Lincoln. My father was a resident of the nearby town of Port Tobacco, the second largest river port in Maryland. It declined in later years when it was cut off from Chesapeake Bay as silt and tidal action changed the river and the large ships transporting the tobacco could no longer navigate the river.

Living in Washington, D.C., we saw history unfolding before our eyes, especially since my family was very involved in the events of the day. My father took us to see the thousands of marchers who came to Washington to claim payment for the bonus that was promised them after WWI. We saw the tents and the shacks that war veterans constructed on the Capitol grounds; we witnessed the hardships of their terrible poverty. Our church was involved in providing food and clothing to help them. I heard the sermons and the controversial conversations of my parents and their friends disagreeing on the issue of the bonus. I clearly remember seeing the veterans' shacks burned. The names of General MacArthur and Eleanor Roosevelt were prominent figures in this dispute. MacArthur was under orders to burn the campsites, and Eleanor Roosevelt visited the camps and tried to help the veterans. My father did not like what was happening to the veterans.

I remember my childhood as a mostly happy, leisurely time. Today, I think children live in frenetic times; whereas in my childhood, we walked to school, to church, the library and to our friends' homes. We played impromptu baseball games in neighborhood vacant lots with just a bat and a ball whenever enough players showed up to play.   The calendar in my day just hung on the wall.   On Sundays we knew we were going to church.   My mother was the organist and choir director, and my older brothers pumped the organ.   Our play times were not scheduled.   We walked to the public library and were proud of having cards that allowed us to take home as many books as we could carry.   I walked to the nearby park with my best friend, Pauline, still a dear friend these eighty years later.   We read *The Yearling*,   by Marjorie Rawlings while sitting in the park. I would read a chapter and then she would read a chapter.   Later we promised each other not to read another chapter until we met in the park the next day.   However, I couldn't wait and did read; finishing the book at home, but I still enjoyed our reading together at the park.

Only two or three neighbors had automobiles.   Because there were six boys in my family who all loved cars, we seemed to have several cars around all the time.   My parents never drove a car, but they provided cars for the boys.   As children we walked to school and to our other activities. Usually, my friends and I walked to school together.   But sometimes one of us needed to go on ahead, so we developed a code.   If one of us did go ahead, she would put a chalk mark of an X on the sidewalk.   A friend seeing the X would know not to wait.   We lived on the bus route and used the Washington, D.C. transportation system.   My brothers did drive to high school because the school was not in our area.   We all walked to grammar school and came home for lunch. There were no cafeterias in the schools until our high school days, and even then we took our lunches to school.   My mother always had homemade soup and made most of the bread we ate.   Always we had homemade jam to spread on the bread.   We enjoyed pears and apples picked from the trees in our yard.   Our jams and jellies were made by Mom Mike and my mother from the fruit trees in our yard.   When we heard about frozen fruit and vegetables, we were afraid to try them, not trusting the advertising that they were frozen and would taste as if they were fresh.   We had a big ice box in our kitchen and hanging in the window, a sign telling whether we wanted a ten-cent block of ice or would need twenty-five or fifty-cent blocks.   It was a treat to get a big block of ice and use a scraper to make snowballs and flavor them with vanilla or fruit syrup.   On Sundays we always had homemade ice cream, and my brothers took turns turning the paddle.   My family all marveled when a big electric refrigerator was installed in our kitchen.

In winter I remember my brothers and me looking out the window and wondering if the rain would stop, so we could go skating.   When it snowed, the big hill on Newton Street would be blocked off and all the neighborhood would turn out with sleds for exciting rides downhill, where a bonfire would warm us before climbing the hill to slide down again.   In spring we opened our baseball season and played ball on the vacant lot on our street.   We had a dedicated coach, the father of one our neighborhood friends, who kept us all together and taught us the rules of the game.

We walked to the Young Peoples Fellowship (YPF) at our Episcopal church.   In fact, we also participated in the activities at the Presbyterian Church.   My first real boyfriend, Raymond, and I attended both groups.   It was fun walking home holding hands and talking about our futures.   We discussed many subjects at YPF, and I know my life was enriched by my participation in these youth groups. We had time to think and talk. Sometimes, we rolled up the rugs in the dining room and moved the big table into the parlor to make room to dance. My brother Ben had taken lessons at the Arthur Murray Dance School, and would guide us around the floor showing us the latest steps. We learned to do the Big Apple and, of course, the Charleston and The Lindy Hop.

Our school work and church activities kept us busy, but we had responsibilities at home too. However, I must admit that I did not have many household tasks. I think my mother was raising me in the old Southern tradition to be a lady. Also, I was painfully skinny in the days when it was not fashionable to be a string bean, as I was called. My mother worried about my health, and I needed to drink a lot of milk fortified with "Bosco," a kind of chocolate drink, which I hated and my brothers loved. But I did take care of my clothes-- washing and ironing them and keeping them in perfect shape. I set the table, a big task in our household, for we usually had twelve or more people at out dinner table. (No eating in front of the TV in those days.)

I was a companion to my grandmother, who lived with us in the winter. In the summer she lived with my aunt on a farm in Southern Maryland. My mother would not let my grandmother do any household chores except the mending which was always in the sewing box. In those days, women darned socks and with six boys that was an ongoing task. Mom Mike always seemed content to sit in her rocking chair, although she often said she missed her cats. When she came to live in our home, my mother would not allow her to bring her cats.

My brothers kept busy with chores and neighborhood jobs. They mowed the lawn and cut the big hedge around our yard. They also picked blackberries in the nearby fields for my mother to using in baking pies and making jam. Our neighbors were pleased to buy them for 25 cents a basket. They also delivered papers. We had a big grape arbor and a kitchen garden that needed maintenance. My brother Richard was a talented, self-taught automobile mechanic. In fact, he knew how to repair anything. As a boy, he took old watches, examined the works and put them back together again. He fixed bicycles and even put together a beautiful two-wheel bike for me. On Saturdays he worked in the local hardware store. Richard put the knowledge he learned at the hardware store to good use all of his life. He learned to be friendly, greet people, help them with all kinds of mechanical things, and became known as a great raconteur.

Ben was a gifted pianist and our neighbors enjoyed hearing the tune, "Stormy Weather," wafting from our house. Mother went to Murphy's Five and Ten Cent Store, where their pianist played all the new tunes for sale. Mother wanted me to learn to play, but when I saw my brother Ben sitting on the piano stool with Mother sitting beside him practicing for hours, I knew I would have none of that. I enjoyed twirling around on the piano stool. I still have that stool in my home today, and it brings back many family memories.

I grew up in a very political household. My father was a Mason and my mother belonged to Eastern Star. They attended their lodges faithfully. I recall occasions when they went to balls at the Mayflower Hotel. My mother would always want my father to purchase a tuxedo; and although he liked to dress up, he always rented the tux. His argument was that his size would change as he aged. However, my father and my brothers were always slim.

My father was very involved in the presidential race between Herbert Hoover and Alfred Smith. During that campaign, the windows of our house were papered with big posters of Hoover. My father had a keg of the pins, and we plastered them on our clothes. When my aunts and uncles visited, they would sit in the living room and talk for hours about politics and religion. Of course as children, we considered ourselves bound to the politics of our parents. Until I was about eight-years old, we lived just about a mile over the District line in Maryland. To curtail my father's political involvement, my mother walked across the line into the District of Columbia and purchased a new house. District of Columbia residents were unable to vote in presidential elections until the twenty-third amendment ratified March 26, 1961, gave them that right. We were not able to exercise that right until 1964, when President Lyndon B. Johnson defeated Senator Barry Goldwater. Unfortunately, my father had died before he ever had the opportunity to vote again.

My Grandmother was born in Port Tobacco, MD and lived most of her life on the family's tobacco farm. This town has a very historical story. Early inhabitants came from England during the religious turmoil. They established the first Anglican (Episcopal) Church in 1683. My family developed strong ties to the Episcopal Church. Tobacco farming was very profitable in those days, especially the crop grown in Maryland because it was a special leaf that blended well with other tobaccos. When we visited our relatives; we had fun sliding down the hay stacks, playing hide and seek in the barn, and pumping a cold drink of water from the well. We also saw what hard work it was to grow, cut, hang and strip tobacco as well as maintain the entire farm. These farms were not "gentlemen's" farms, for they required diligent physical effort day after day.

While the men worked with the tobacco, the women tended their kitchen gardens and their egg business. They had cows and my aunt made butter as well as bread and, of course, jams and jellies. When the tobacco was ready to be stripped in the fall, itinerant workers were hired creating extra work for the women as they had to fix three large meals a day for the workers as well as feed the family. My mother always felt sorry for her sister who lamented that her work was so hard managing and feeding all the workers. Her job was not recognized nor was she paid. It was just her role as a wife to do it. This was before equal rights, and women were not recognized as earning a living and having a share of the profits to spend as they wanted. (Later in my career I was an executive in the Equal Rights Program for women and worked for recognition for women and payment for their services.) In addition to going to the country to visit our relatives, my father and older brothers went to purchase whiskey. It was the days of Prohibition and bootleg whiskey was readily available. I think many of the farmers enjoyed making more money off the whiskey with much less work than they made from the tobacco. This income disappeared in 1933 when the 18th Amendment was repealed.

In the early 1930's when the banks failed, my aunt would come up from the country to visit my mother and would actually cry that their savings were gone. They needed the money to buy the seed and supplies for the tobacco crop, their money crop. Fortunately, they had food for the table from their garden and the chicken and egg business. There was no FDIC insurance in those days and no welfare programs either. They survived, but only one of the five children chose to remain on the farm and grow tobacco. Tobacco was a very profitable crop, but proximity to Washington, D.C., and the expanding jobs in government, science and research were luring people to the area. The real estate market flourished and the old farms were sold to establish new neighborhoods. New roads and highways had to be built and my Aunt and Uncle's acreage was taken by the government by eminent domain to build Highway 301, which opened up the route from Delaware to Florida. A few farms with their old barns were preserved for historical purposes.

When I go to Washington these days, I like to visit my old haunts. The families living there now are in upscale homes built on the old tobacco farm lands. I visit the old cemeteries and find the graves of my relatives. I think of the women who died in childbirth. I linger by the grave of my uncle George, who had inherited the farm from his father. He first married my grandmother's sister who was named Xie (my name) and she and her newborn son died in childbirth. Then Uncle George married another one of my grandmother's sisters. She, too, died in childbirth, but the baby boy survived. My grandmother sent her teenage daughter, Gertrude, to the farm to take care of the baby. She then became his third wife. Yes, George married two of my grandmother's sisters and then her daughter. Looking at all the gravestones, it was sad to see how many women died in childbirth in those days. The sentiments engraved on the headstones bring tears to my eyes. Most have endearments, but some I don't like such as "God's garden has need of little flowers." I heard this same sentiment at a funeral of a young nephew and I don't agree with it.

Now I am the oldest living member of my family. My six brothers and sister are long gone. I am blessed to have lived a long, good life and as I write this I am 91-years old. I have had a loving marriage celebrating fifty-one years married to Episcopal Priest, Andrew Keady. He served at St Albans parish church on the grounds of the National Cathedral. We moved to Thousand Oaks, where he served the local St Patrick's Episcopal Church. After his death, I had another loving marriage for more than sixteen years to Ben Cranmer, president of the local Security Pacific Bank. Ben passed away a year after we moved to UVTO in 2008.

© 2012 Xie Cranmer

MEMORIES OF THE DEPRESSION YEARS BY EUGENE HANNEMANN

My father was a businessman in Fredericksburg, Texas. By 1928, he had lost his business due to debts owed to him by customers who could not pay. He went to work for someone else, so our family was all right financially. However, in 1929, he died suddenly of a heart attack. My mother was a young widow of thirty-three with eight children, and another on the way.

She refused to let any of us go to live with relatives, as was often the case when a father died. We owned a big house on four acres of land. There was a large barn with three milking stalls and several cows, so she started a dairy business. This was to be the family income for the next four years. At one time, we were milking eight cows, twice a day. Mother, a sister and one brother were the milkers. We leased a grazing field about a half-mile from our house, and we drove the cows back and forth each day. The older children did this, but we all had to pitch in and do our chores. I was six at the time. There was a milk house where the bottles were washed and sterilized by the younger kids. Bottles were placed into two large vats - one with chlorine and one with clear water - then placed on a shelf to air dry. After the bottles were filled, paper caps were placed on top. The milk was sold to a dairy in town, and also delivered to customers each day.

We had a donkey, Anton, and a four-wheel cart to make the deliveries. One drove the cart and two walked along, put the milk in a box outside the houses and picked up the empty bottles. That donkey had a mind of his own, so it was quite a project for young kids. Once, when the son of a customer rattled rocks in a tin can, that donkey took off, lickety-split, and turned the cart over. Fortunately there were no bottles in it at the time. Later the older boys were able to have other jobs, but the younger ones continued with the dairy. All of us were willing to drive the cows because we took turns riding the donkey. Sometimes as many as three rode it at once. That was our favorite way to get to our grandparents' house. Speaking of Grandfather, he was a Lutheran pastor, as well as a medical doctor, so we had free medical care and free lectures on behavior!

At one time when the dairy business was checked by the state health department, our milk was declared to be the best in town. However, when I was about ten, we had to give it up; we couldn't compete when the local commercial dairy expanded.

Our mother was never idle. Besides taking care of the house and family, she managed the dairy farm, cleaned our church, sold cosmetics (an Avon lady) and worked as a cook in various places in town. She was really a great cook. Feeding so many boys had given her lots of experience! We all had friends around, so when she made doughnuts, she made a dishpan full. And there were never any leftovers.

She had another use for that dishpan. Once, some boys were fighting in the backyard. She didn't say a word - just filled the pan with water, took it out the back door, and threw it over the scuffle. The fighting stopped! Mother had us so well-organized, each child had a special chore for cleaning up after a meal. Our school was about six blocks away and we had an hour for lunch. We could get home, eat lunch, clean up, and get back to school for a short time on the playground.

The older boys took over a paper agency. They had papers from three cities. It became quite a thriving business, so we younger ones joined the company. I had my first paper route when I was nine years of age. We had a car, a motorcycle, and four bicycles. (Mother helped me get my first driver's license when I was twelve.) Our day began at 5 a.m. First, all of us rolled the newspapers, then we headed out in all directions to deliver them – and still got to school by 8 a.m. in all kinds of weather, of course. As soon as school was out, we repeated the procedure for the second shift.

Some of us would help Mother clean the church. Then, in the winter, we got up at four o'clock on Sunday mornings and went to church to start a fire in the wood heater. After the papers were delivered, one of us would stop by the church and stoke the heater. We all went home to put on our best clothes, then went to Sunday School and Worship. One chore we really enjoyed was ringing the bell for services. We loved to swing on the rope!

In today's age, Mother would probably have been accused of child abuse and we would have been put in foster homes, or on welfare. She was a truly amazing woman. What an example she set for us. She had five sons in the military during World War II and encouraged them to use the GI Bill to attend college. She was very proud of all her children, but especially that two had continued on to Seminary to become pastors. By the time of her death at the age of 57 in a car accident, she had also managed restaurants and owned two. Caecilia Hannemann, who had only an elementary education, the daughter of a German immigrant, was known, loved and respected by the whole community. More people were at her funeral than had ever attended a service in our church.

MY MEMORIES OF THE GREAT DEPRESSION BY MARGARET HANNEMANN

I actually do not have memories of the earliest years, just what I heard from my parents. My father, Cassius Lafayette Burnette, grew up in the mountains of western North Carolina. For about seventy years, I have wondered how parents could give an innocent little baby such a name! As a young man, he heard about 'homesteading' possibilities in Montana. When he was about twenty-one years old, he boarded a train and headed west. He stayed there for over twenty years. He built his log cabin in Gallatin, and worked as a ranger in the Montana side of the Yellowstone National Park. He loved his life there – but never married. Then the really good news came! Silver was discovered on his land. The government, very kindly, bought his property.

So with his pockets full, he returned home on a vacation in 1924. He met Lucy Bryson, a young widow with two small children. She was taking care of her elderly father who rented rooms to boy students at a nearby college. I do not know how Cash and Lucy met, but Father said that the minute he saw her, he knew he was never going to return to Montana. They were married and lived with Grandfather in Webster, North Carolina, where I was born. Three years later, in 1929, just after my sister Ellen was born, they bought another house. Then the Depression hit. Within months, they lost everything – both houses and the money in the bank. I do not know if Father had a job. If he did, it would have been something out-of-doors.

Because there was news that a Dutch Company had built a rayon factory in Buncombe County and was hiring hundreds of employees, we moved again. The factory, the America Enka Corporation, chose this mountain area because of the abundant water supply. Many of the jobs required women's skills. My mother, who was already a very independent person, became a working mom. A company bus provided transportation. My older half-sister quit high school to take care of my younger sister and me. My older half-brother was hired as a mechanic.

The Enka Corporation owned thousands of acres and had built over a hundred bungalow-type houses. Another village of finer homes for the plant officials was built around a lake and included a Clubhouse. All employees could use the lake facilities, but not the Clubhouse - unless, you were a couple of little girls whose best friend's mother was the manager. The land included property which was a former YWCA camp. It was converted into a very nice park with several cabins. Since my father did not have any mechanical training needed for working in a plant, he was offered a house for us in exchange for his work as a caretaker of the property. Our home was a rustic log cabin, of course. I didn't like it, because it made me feel poor. Mother pointed out that Abraham Lincoln had also lived in a log cabin, but that didn't help much. One of the buildings was a big dance hall, with a huge rock fireplace and a balcony. It was only used once by the Company, so my sister and I turned the whole thing into a giant playground. Mother bought roller skates for us, and after only a few scrapes and bruises we were whizzing around daily on our own private skating rink. One empty cabin was our paper doll house, and another was an orphanage for our poor dolls. Children from the village came up to skate in the dance hall and to wade in the streams. Adults came to walk the trails and we would 'tag along'. Otherwise, we were not allowed to roam the woods by ourselves. There was also an apple orchard and many different berries for anyone to enjoy.

The Company had a gym and provided all kinds of sports and other activities. We were able to take dancing lessons for $1.00 a week. There was also a wonderful library right in the plant. Children's books were abundant. There were stores where anything we needed could be purchased, as well as a post office. At Company Christmas parties, each child would receive treats, along with an appropriate gift from Santa, chosen by the parent.

Mother had bought a green roadster with a rumble seat. What fun to take a Sunday outing! But since our brother was the only one who could drive, he took the car with him when he married. The biggest drawback was the distance. We had to walk a couple of miles from our house to everything, including the school bus. So we grumbled about that, especially in bad weather. But looking back, those were actually wonderful years, with delightful memories. That Dutch Rayon Company provided a very good life for residents in and around this area in western North Carolina, during the worst years of the Great Depression.

In 1937, our "dance hall" skating rink was torn down. Father was able to buy the lumber and used it to build a house in a nearby location. So, we had brought our converted skating rink with us, in a way. Unfortunately, Father died three years later. My older sister began working at the plant, so she and Mother were very proud to be able to pay for Ellen's and my college education. That plant also provided summer office employment for me during my college years. About twenty years ago, with better fabrics being developed, production gradually began to decrease. Soon the plant was sold to another company. Just last year, I sadly watched a video clip on the computer showing the famous landmark Enka smokestack being demolished. It marked the end of an era.

I am happy that I have, and can share, good memories of the Great Depression.

© 2012 Margaret Hannemann

MY GREAT DEPRESSION EXPERIENCES BY ARTHUR DANIEL JONES, Jr.

I was born in a farmhouse in Mitchell County, Georgia, on April 18, 1928. My parents had five children: Loulie Amiel, Lillian Margaret, Marcus Samuel, Evelyn Loyce and myself, Arthur Daniel, Jr. As my father, Arthur Daniel Jones, Sr., was a farmer; we raised most of the food we consumed. We did not go hungry.

My mother, Altee Judith Goare, always had a vegetable garden in one of the fields near our home, and she also raised chickens for marketing at the nearby co-operative market in Camilla, Georgia. My father grew many different crops, including cotton, oats, corn, peanuts, tobacco, watermelons, cantaloupes and a small patch of sugar cane.

We also had a pecan orchard and about a dozen other fruit trees. When I needed spending money, I would pick up a few small bags of pecans and sell them to the local grocery store in Cotton, a small unincorporated town with a population of ninety-six. Until I graduated from high school and went off to college, I worked at all the jobs on the farm, as did my brother and sisters, since raising and harvesting several crops required a considerable amount of manual labor. All cotton was picked by hand, stored until we had enough to take to the local cotton gin where it was "sucked' into the gin via a big 12-inch metal tube, removed from its seeds and "squeezed" into a bale about 5 feet tall.

Like cotton, tobacco was selectively plucked from stalks as it ripened and was thrown into a mule-drawn sled that was pulled between the rows of tobacco plants. When the sled was full, it would be taken to the tobacco barn, placed on a platform where "stringers" would place it on sticks about 4 feet long. The stringer would take "hands of tobacco" consisting of three leaves from each of two "handers" in succession. (A "hander" was a worker who gave the "hands" of tobacco to the "stringer.") When each stick was full, other workers would then hang the stick on a set of rails inside the tobacco barn. One barn could contain rows of 300 to 500 sticks.

When the barn was completely full, we would close the barn doors, and seal any openings in preparation for the curing process. Next we started a fire in the furnace using slabs of scrap lumber for fuel. A series of 12-inch pipes connected to the furnace distributed gases to the tobacco and vented to the atmosphere through the roof.

Curing the tobacco occurred in stages. We would start with low heat, about 99 degrees, to change the color of the tobacco leaves and raise the temperature over the next three to five days to cure first the leaves and then the stems. When the stems were cured, the fire was extinguished, and the barn opened so that moisture could return to the tobacco leaves. During the curing process, temperature regulation was a manual process as we had no automatic temperature controls. During the four to five days it took to cure the tobacco leaves, we entertained ourselves playing card games, boiling raw peanuts inside the furnace or roasting ears of corn in their husks.

After curing was complete, the tobacco was taken from the curing barn, removed from the sticks by hand, then graded according to leaf color and quality, and tied up in 4-foot by 4-foot burlap sheets. The sheets of tobacco were next taken to a large warehouse and placed in rows and then auctioned off to tobacco companies.

My father raised produce, mostly cantaloupes, corn and tomatoes. He specialized in "exotic" cantaloupe varieties that he allowed to ripen on the vine. One variety was named "Queen of Colorado." During the harvest season, we would pick a truckload of ripe melons, carefully pack them in straw and truck them overnight to the Farmers' Market in Columbus, Georgia, about 125 miles from our farm. The ripe cantaloupes were quickly sold as they were more popular than the typical "Hale's Best" variety that could be picked as early as two weeks before it ripened.

Another major crop we raised was peanuts. To harvest peanuts we used a mule-drawn plow that would loosen the plants. We manually pulled the plants from the ground, shook away the dirt and stacked them on a pole with the nuts on the inside of the pole. A pair of 4-foot slats nailed about 12 inches above ground level kept the peanut plants from touching the ground to accommodate the drying process. To protect the nuts from the weather, a cap of grass diverted the rain water during the drying process.

After about eight weeks, depending on the weather, the peanuts were sufficiently dry for harvest. Using the front wheels of a wagon, hitched to a pair of mules, the stacks were dragged to a tractor-driven peanut picking machine. Using pitchforks, two men would feed the peanut vines to the intake side of the picking machine, which would separate the peanuts from the vines. We then collected the nuts in a tub and placed them into a truck for transport to the local market. The vines were kicked out the back of the picking machine and stuffed into a hay-baling machine. The hay was used to feed our livestock. I recall I made $1 per day shaking and stacking peanuts. I also would join the share-croppers in picking cotton. The pay was $1 per hundred pounds. I could work all day and not make $1 picking cotton.

Life on the farm was difficult especially during the Great Depression of the early and mid-1930's. My father usually had to borrow money in the spring to purchase seed and fertilizer, and hopefully collect enough money from harvests to pay off the loan in time to repeat the process the next year. Living in the country, I never saw bread-lines. Occasionally, someone would stop by and ask for food. I recall that we took in a young man who needed work and a place to live temporarily until he could earn enough to move on to another farm.

I graduated fourth in a class of forty-four from nearby Pelham High School in 1945 and was selected to give a speech at graduation. I attended the University of Georgia in Athens, Georgia, during the summer semester of 1945. In February 1946 I joined the Navy and entered boot camp in Norfolk, Virginia. While I was in boot

camp, the Navy announced it would be selecting candidates to attend the U.S. Naval Academy Preparatory School (NAPS) located at the Naval Training Center in Bainbridge, Maryland, in 1943. (Note: The Center opened for recruits October 11, 1942, by order of President Roosevelt, who named the Center Bainbridge in honor of Commodore William Bainbridge, Commander of the U.S. Navy Frigate *Constitution* during the War of 1812. It closed March 31, 1976. At that time NAPS was moved to Newport, Rhode Island.)

I was unable to take the test as I was en route to Japan. After working three months at the U.S. Naval Hospital in Yokosuka, I was ordered to proceed to NAPS. After NAPS, I spent four years at the U.S. Naval Academy in Annapolis, Maryland, graduating in 1951. During my years at the Academy, I met Marion Jane Almy. We were later married on March 10, 1953.

My first tour of duty was for three years on the USS *Cotten* (DD-669), a WWII 2100-ton Fletcher Class destroyer. After completing a round-the-world deployment, including the last month of hostilities in Korea, we returned to Newport, Rhode Island. My next duty station was a two-year tour on the USS *Fearless* (MSO 442), a minesweeper. I transferred from Active Duty to Naval Reserve in 1956.

On entering civilian life, I was employed as an armament engineer by the Martin Company in Middle River near Baltimore, Maryland. In 1964 I was transferred to a new division of Martin, Bunker Ramo in Canoga Park, California. Later I worked for Litton Data Systems in Van Nuys. I retired from Litton in April, 1992.

Jane and I are the parents of four sons: Arthur Daniel, III, William Everett, Randolph Marcus and Robert Phillip. While traveling with our sons to the National Parks, we had great times. We were active members of St. James Presbyterian church in Tarzana. Since I loved singing, I was glad to sing tenor in the church choir. We enjoyed playing bridge with our friends for many years.

I was active in the Naval Reserves for thirty years, retiring as captain. For more than ten years, Jane and I sought for the perfect retirement community. We found it in 2004, when we signed up for UVTO. We moved in 2007. A special bonus was that we lived near our beloved grandchildren, residents of Newbury Park. It has been a joy to attend their sporting, musical and school events. Our friends and activities here at UVTO have added much pleasure to our lives.

© 2010 Arthur Daniel Jones, Jr.
(Since this was written, Dan passed away February, 6, 2010

MY EARLY YEARS BY CHARLES KIRCHER

I am a native Californian born October 3, 1923. My birthplace, the San Fernando Valley, was in those years a rural area. It was before the Great Depression and life was good. A developer had subdivided a section between Ventura Blvd. and the Los Angeles River. He paved a few streets, put in curbs and sidewalks, sold individual lots and left it up to the buyers to build whatever they wanted. This resulted in a very eclectic mix of styles. My father, a plumber, bought a lot and built our small two bedroom house himself. We had a few neighbors but mostly open fields with the river on one side of the tract and Ventura Blvd. on the other. There was a small grocery store on the boulevard but the nearest town, Van Nuys, was several miles away.

My father, mother, brother and I were very happy but my memories are hazy. I do remember playing in the big front yard, fruit trees of various kinds in the back, chickens in a small chicken house, a goat for milk and my mother watering the flowers, vegetable garden and trees. One of my memories is of having an ice box instead of a refrigerator. The ice wagon, drawn by a horse, would come once a week I think. Later it was mounted on a Model T truck. The ice company provided a square sign with a hole in each corner and a number that designated the size of the block of ice that was wanted and a hook that mounted in the front window. Most houses had a back porch where they kept the ice box and the delivery man, with a leather apron over his shoulder, using ice tongs would bring up the ice and put it in the ice box. I also remember the bread wagon, usually Helms Bakery with all kinds of baked goods. We also had a milk man that delivered milk bottles right to our door. We had a goat and so didn't use his services.

My father had plenty of work and then the stock market crash of 1929 brought a change to my little world. I, being only six, was not aware of it and I don't think that it affected my father's world right away either. I do know that he had a 1931 Ford truck and we also had a 1931 Buick sedan so 1930 could not have been too bad for us. My memories of the financial morass that the world had dropped into began about 1932 when my father announced that we were selling our house for 1000 dollars. We could rent a small house around the corner for 25 dollars a month and we needed the cash to keep our heads above water. This was before the days of construction loans, credit cards and easy credit. There were few ways of financing construction. It seems that my father and a friend of his, a carpenter, acting as general contractors, agreed to build a big house for a movie mogul. They were using their own money but the lot was in the Mogul's name. After the crash, the Mogul went broke and filed for bankruptcy. The partially completed house and lot were lost and my father and his friend lost everything. This was not an isolated instance. Many people were either declaring bankruptcy or just plain disappearing. They just ignored what they owed knowing that most people didn't have the money to sue. They left disasters in their wake.

My earliest memories of a political nature began about this time. I remember the election of 1932 with Hoover running for re-election and Roosevelt running on a change platform much like Obama has done. Radios were fairly new and it was the first election carried on the airwaves with minute by minute coverage of the candidates. My parents were Republicans and very much out of favor. I, age nine, listened to all the broadcasts fascinated by all the rhetoric. I remember Hoover, shortly before the election, saying "If Roosevelt is elected then grass will grow in the streets of a hundred cities and weeds will overrun a thousand farms". Meanwhile Roosevelt was promising a New Deal and complete repudiation of the Republican platform that he claimed had brought us to rack and ruin. I remember Roosevelt's promise to help the common man and his references to his "Brain Trust".

As it turned out, both were right. Our country did continue to spiral into one of the worst depressions of history. Thousands were out of work and weeds did grow on a thousand farms. Roosevelt brought forth program after program and some worked while others were either failures, declared un-constitutional or, while working, had no effect. If we ignore various political statements we realize that the Depression, for the common man, wasn't really over until we started re-arming our country in 1939 when Hitler began to threaten world peace.

So how did this affect my little world in 1932? First, we did sell the house and moved around the corner to a house and lot that backed up to the Los Angeles River and I was now old enough to explore, if not alone, at least I could tag along with my older brother. The river then was a magical place. It was a couple of hundred yards across with the banks about 15 or 20 feet deep. The actual river then ran along the center of this wide area with willow trees, pussy willows and other unknown growth filling the sandy floor of this greater river area.

My brother and I spent many happy hours in the summer time down in this river bottom. We would catch Sun Perch with a willow pole, string and a homemade hook. If we could get a nickel, we could buy a big piece of liver at the little grocery and tie a small piece on a string and troll for crawdads. They could smell the liver and rushed across the bottom to try to get a piece. We would pull up the liver with usually two or three crawdads attached. We could get a small bucket full in a couple of hours. My mother would fry the Sun Perch for us and would break off the tails of the Crawdads, clean them and cook them and make a salad, (like shrimp salad) for dinner that evening. In the spring and summer before the hot Santa Ana winds of fall dried up the river we could go swimming with other neighborhood kids in the large swimming hole down by Woodman Avenue. No one that I knew of ever drowned even though we very seldom had any supervision. Cowboys and Indians was a favorite game among the growth and willows. My mother had a large bell that she would ring from the river bank when she wanted us.

My brother and I had many chores around our home. We raised rabbits to sell as people ate a lot of rabbit in those days. I learned how to skin and dress a rabbit at an early age. We would stretch the skins on a wire frame and scrape and cure them with salt and sun. I'm not sure but I think that people paid 50 cents apiece for a skinned and dressed rabbit. We had to make sure our goat had feed and water (my brother and I were raised on goat's milk). We also raised chickens and planted a garden each year. Most of the time, I had only one pair of school pants and a couple of shirts. Money was always short but at that age I never missed it.

School was a couple of miles away and in inclement weather my mother drove us; otherwise we walked. Meanwhile, my father was too proud to go on the "dole" as he called it and would not enroll in any of Roosevelt's programs such as "PWA" or "WPA" or "CCC" and went out each day bidding on jobs and getting a few and finding work wherever. Most of my parent's friends were in the same boat with the city dwellers having the hardest time. We, at least, could always kill a chicken or a rabbit and either had fresh vegetables in the summer or canned in the winter and so never starved. I now realize my mother and father were probably suffering terribly while my brother and I were protected and happy.

After a couple of years like this, my father was forced to strike a deal with a man who had purchased a large chicken farm off Haskell in the West Valley. The man knew nothing about raising chickens, egg production or anything else as near as I could tell. Where he got the money to buy the chicken ranch I never knew. Anyway, he hired my father to run the chicken ranch for him. The deal didn't include much money but the ranch did have a small house for us to live in and we could raise some of our own chickens primarily for meat production. His were laying hens for egg production. The owner had a number of eccentricities such as buying everything in bulk and only what he could get at a special price. If he found a special price on canned string beans, then his family ate string beans everyday for a month or until they were gone. He had two sons about our age and he beat them vigorously with a stick and didn't allow them to play with my brother or me. My brother and I had to change schools, had a lot of chores and our whole family was miserable. We stuck it out for two years.

In the spring of 1936 my father ran into a man who four years earlier had declared bankruptcy while owing my father a good amount of money. Even though he no longer legally owed the money, he was in much better shape financially and was now a land developer. He signed over title to a two-and- one-half acre unimproved lot to settle the old debt. This lot was alongside the Big Tujunga Wash, poor sandy soil, on a dirt road, no neighbors, not worth much but to us, Heaven. It provided a way to get off the chicken ranch. In the evenings, sitting at the kitchen table, my father and mother drew up a plan for a three bedroom house and a large 30 by 30 foot garage for my father's plumbing business. We didn't dare let the owner of the chicken ranch know what we were planning as we feared he would boot us off summarily. My father had a slab poured and he built the garage in such a fashion that we could move into it. It had a large room across the front with a Murphy bed for my parents, my brother and I slept behind the couch. A kitchen and eating area and a small bathroom completed the structure. He had it completed by the time school let out for the summer and we gave notice and moved off the chicken ranch.

Before I go on into my teenage years I should explain that this period of my life from about age eight through age twelve was when I really became aware of the Depression and what it took to survive. I learned about money or the lack of it anyway. I learned about taking responsibility for a job and completing it as promised. I learned cooperation and how a joint effort made any job easier. I don't think I really enjoyed learning these lessons but learn them I did. School also was difficult. In my old school I had friends and enjoyed learning. In the school near the chicken ranch, I just never fit in and was miserable most of the time. Now, things changed with a new home, a new school and a new life.

That summer a number of things happened. My father signed a contract to do plumbing for Roscoe Hardware, which acted as general contractor in the building of new houses. Building of large tracts of houses hadn't started yet and most homes were built by individual contractors on a one by one basis. Roscoe Hardware had independent carpenters, electricians, plumbers and roofers as subcontractors. The agreement required that each of these subcontractors had to purchase all of his supplies through Roscoe Hardware. Using this method they were able to underbid the average general contractor and so had plenty of work. I will always have a debt of gratitude to Roscoe Hardware for what they meant to my family then and later, when my father passed away, how they helped my mother.

I can probably pass over my teen years fairly rapidly. On our land we built another building that housed a brooder house, a chicken run, a rabbit house and a garage. We never did get around to building the original three bedroom house my parents designed. We planted fruit trees, a garden, and raised chickens and rabbits mainly but occasionally some ducks or a pig. All of this was to supplement what my father could earn as a plumber. My brother and I moved into the brooder house after we stopped raising our own chicks. We built wooden bunks and my mother made feather beds for us. No springs. We had a wood burning stove in the middle of our 20 by 20 foot room. As our room was separated from the main house by about 30 feet, we could pretty much do whatever we wanted. At one point we built a small darkroom and developed our own films and made contact prints. At another time we built a bench and sink across one wall and did all kinds of chemistry experiments when we were involved in high school chemistry.

As soon as we were able, we went on jobs with my father and learned how to dig ditches, thread and cut pipe, lead cast iron drain pipes and a variety of other jobs. Both my brother and I attended San Fernando Junior and Senior High schools. At that time both schools shared one campus adjacent to downtown San Fernando. Neither of us participated in sports or other after hour activities as we always had chores awaiting us at home.

All in all it was a pleasant time. I still fondly remember Sunday evenings sitting around the radio listening to Sunday's programs and playing board games. Inasmuch as there was no 911 or help facilities close by, my parents taught both my brother and me to drive as soon as we could reach the pedals. This was in a big old '31 Buick with wooden spoke wheels, no power steering, no power brakes, with a stick shift on the floor. There were only dirt roads with no drainage ditches so it was really hard to get into trouble. My dad had a full choke 12 gauge double barreled shotgun and a 22 rifle. He taught us to shoot and to practice gun safety. We would go rabbit hunting in the wild area along the wash and the few times we were able to hit a rabbit, my mother would fry it for breakfast the next morning. My mother worked in downtown Los Angeles and so my brother and I did have a lot of time to spend by ourselves. We had to learn to cook, clean the house, do the laundry as well as our chores with our livestock and land.

High school in those days had a variety of career paths: Academic, Commercial, Shop, or Home Economics. Both my brother and I took academic courses even though we had no hope of attending college. There was no money for higher education. In February of 1940 my brother turned eighteen and also graduated from high school. He set about trying to find a job, any job not in the construction business. He certainly did not want to become a plumber. He could not find a job. My father was pressuring him to work for him in the plumbing business and, to escape the pressure, my brother left home, hitchhiked to San Francisco and found employment there. In the fall disaster struck and my world changed again.

One morning in the fall of 1940 my father was ill. He had been under the weather for a couple of days but had continued to work. As I was getting ready for school, I realized that my father was very ill and had trouble breathing. My mother insisted on taking him to the Sawtelle Veterans Hospital on her way to work as she felt that he was too ill to drive. I caught the school bus. She dropped him off on the steps of the hospital and continued on to her job. As soon as she was out of sight, my father collapsed. He never regained consciousness and died that night. My brother quit his job in San Francisco and came home. He found work at Lockheed. This was in 1940, no Social Security, no 401K, no savings but luckily we owned the house and lot. My brother and mother had jobs but their wages were low.

In the spring I found a job that would let me finish high school. I worked in a local hardware store where I earned fifteen dollars a week as a delivery driver and sometime clerk. I drove our old Model A work truck to and from the job. My girlfriend who lived a couple of blocks away agreed to bring home the homework assignments for the few classes I needed to graduate. My physics teacher agreed to act as my advisor and to administer any tests that were required. He did this on Saturday mornings. I did graduate with my class although I didn't actually attend my last semester. I don't think students could do that today.

All thoughts of college were gone and I anxiously awaited my eighteenth birthday when I could get a job at Lockheed and earn more money. After my birthday I rushed to the Vega plant in Burbank as it was advertising for workers. I was hired but before starting work I was given a physical examination to verify fitness for work on the factory floor and a hernia was found. I guess I had acquired one carrying large bundles of fencing to an upstairs storage room at the hardware store. An operation was required. I had the operation at a doctor's office and the wound immediately got infected and took several months to heal.

While almost recovered, on a clear sunny Sunday morning, December 7, 1941, I was out for a drive with a friend when we heard on the car radio that the Japanese had bombed Pearl Harbor. I had grown up among Japanese truck farmers, had school chums who were Japanese and now I felt confused and betrayed. A couple of weeks later, the Vega doctors felt I was well enough to go to work. After a few weeks of training I found myself on the factory floor working the graveyard shift as a riveter. I started at 50 cents per hour but quickly advanced until with my shift bonus I was making $1 per hour. This was big money for an eighteen-year-old especially since only a couple of years before, there were no jobs of this type to be had for a young person. My old Ford Model A truck was very tired; it no longer had a top and when it rained, I covered up with a tarp while driving. It wasn't long before I purchased a 1933 Ford three window coupe. It was a V8 and very hot!

So there I was, my country now involved in a war both in the Pacific and Europe, with my patriotic instincts saying go to war while on the other hand, I had a great job, was making great money, had a hot car and was not anxious to give up this great life to become a private in the infantry. My solution was to do nothing. Eighteen-year-olds weren't being drafted yet and besides I and my partner Rich had been designated "Instructors" which carried a draft deferment. We continued this happy life-style for about six months; we were living the good life while feeling guilty about not joining up.

One night my partner Rich was late to work and told me that he had car problems and asked if I could provide transport for a few days while his car was repaired. I, of course, agreed. He then sprung something new when he disclosed that he had planned to go downtown the following morning to the Federal Building and apply for Naval Aviation Training. It seems that the Navy had just relaxed its qualification requirements and no longer required completion of at least two years of college before acceptance into this program. I agreed to take him to downtown Los Angeles. I planned to attend a movie while he applied. After dropping him off on the fifth floor, I went out to look for a movie but as things turned out I could not find a movie that I wanted to see. I returned to the fifth floor, deciding to read magazines and sleep in the waiting area until Rich was through. A sailor approached me and after talking for a while convinced me to at least take the preliminary examination just to see what my scores would be. Surprise, surprise, I passed and was then told that I had plenty of time to take a preliminary physical exam also. At the end of the day, I found that Rich and I had both passed the preliminaries. We headed for home for a couple of hours sleep before our graveyard shift at Vega began.

The next morning, after work, I again drove us downtown to the Federal Building for a more advanced written application and test along with a more comprehensive and complete physical examination. At the end of the testing, Rich had passed everything and I had also passed with the exception of my weight. I was ten pounds overweight. I was told to go home, lose ten pounds, and then come back and I could sign up. Unbelievable! I could not believe that I was qualified to become a "Naval Aviator!" I had not said a word to my mother and brother. My mother worked a normal day shift downtown; my brother worked swing shift at Vega and I worked graveyard shift. We seldom saw each other. I still said nothing to them or anyone else but gradually started to change my diet and started to lose pounds. After about a month I realized that I had lost the pounds and it was time to fish or cut bait. I decided that I really wanted to give this a try, told my mother and brother, got my high school transcripts and on August 5, 1942, enlisted as a Seaman Recruit, designated for Aviation Cadet training in the U.S. Navy.

As I put down these memories I look back on twenty-four years of Navy service followed by thirty-three years of civilian employment and now eleven years of retirement. I celebrate fifty-six years of happy marriage, four children, eight grandchildren and one great grandchild. All things considered, it has been a very happy story.

TALES OF THE GREAT DEPRESSION BY HOWARD KOSH

I was born in New York City on July 30, 1924, to Abraham and May Kusner Kosh. In late 1931, my father was sent to Los Angeles to represent his employer on the West Coast. Six months later he sent for my mother, my six-month-old brother, Ron, and myself. We traveled through the Panama Canal on the USS *President Lincoln* bringing all our belongings with us. I still have a vivid memory of the beautiful city of Havana, Cuba, with its stately almost blinding white government buildings.

Our neighborhood suffered severe hardships during the Great Depression. Many men were without jobs; many were forced to stand in line for food; children wore secondhand clothes--all signs of economic struggle. While my father was employed, at times his pay was delayed and we experienced a limited way of life. I have two distinct memories of the Great Depression.

When walking to school every day in 1932, I passed a tiny Japanese-owned fruit market. Sometimes, I would stop to talk with the storeowner; and he often gave me a piece of fruit to eat while I was walking. One day, on my way home, I came to his shop and saw him standing forlornly by his display of oranges. He said to me, "Here, little boy, take these home to your Mama. I can`t sell them and they will spoil." I staggered home carrying two shopping bags of oranges, which I could barely lift. My mother promptly shared them with our shocked neighbors. For all of us this gift was a blessing, while for him it was a loss of his livelihood.

On another occasion, my father, a commissioned salesman for an Eastern optical firm, had to make a sales trip to San Francisco. I don`t exactly remember why, but he decided to take my mother, my two-year-old brother and me, along on this trip. We drove in our 1930 Model-A Ford to San Francisco and went directly to the hotel that my father had reserved for us. His firm was rather negligent about paying his commissions, so he requested that his check be forwarded to the hotel. Alas, on arrival, there was no check. What few dollars he had in his pocket went for milk and some snacks for my brother and me. I really believe that my parents went hungry for those three or four days until we got home.

Gradually, our economic situation improved. Fortunately, because of my ability in playing basketball, I was able to obtain an athletic scholarship at the University of Southern California in 1941. After the attack on Pearl Harbor, December 7, 1941, I enrolled in the Naval Reserve V-5 Naval Aviation Cadet Program and became a pilot in the Marine Corps.

Following the War, I returned home to assist my ailing father with the management of his business. Afterwards, I pursued a career as a broker and partner in a New York Stock Exchange securities firm. I have two daughters, Susan and Jeri, from my first marriage. Later I married Ruth, who has two children. Together we have nine grandchildren and six great grandchildren.

While living in Santa Barbara, we decided to move to a retirement home and had actually made a deposit on one in our local community. Fortunately, through mutual friends of University Village Thousand Oaks residents, Lloyd and Grace Farwell, we learned of UVTO. Impressed by the Farwell's recommendations and our observations, we chose to move to University Village in February 2010. We're glad we did.

© 2012 Howard Kosh

RECALLING OLD MEMORIES OF THE GREAT DEPRESSION
BY KENNETH B. LARSON

I was born March 29, 1920, Cadillac, Michigan, where my brother Vernon joined me in 1922. At the time, Cadillac, a small city in the northern part of Michigan's Lower Peninsula, was experiencing a preliminary taste of the Depression the country and world would suffer ten years later. It was a pretty city located on a hill overlooking the eastern shore of Lake Cadillac. It had grown up around the lumber mills, which were closing because the forests had been depleted, creating economic suffering throughout the area.   When I was three, my parents, struggling financially, found relief in Michigan's capital city, Lansing. My father, who fought in France in World War I, got a job in the REO Motor Car Company not only because he was a good mechanic, but also because he was a clarinet player and REO needed one for their company band.

From that meager beginning, over the next nine years, my parents worked their way into the comfort of the local factory workers' middle class just in time to be hit by the onset of the Great Depression. REO (owned by Mr. Ransom E. Olds, the inventor of the Oldsmobile) produced good, sturdy trucks and passenger cars. But they couldn't compete with General Motors, Ford and Chrysler and quickly

faded as the Depression set in. My father, of course, soon lost his job at REO. Meanwhile, my two sisters, Norma and Geraldine, had joined the family.

The months which followed were rough. My father found a job in the nearby town of Owosso and commuted weekly until that job failed as well. Then, on hearing from Cadillac connections, my folks decided to sell the equity in their home and take on a small restaurant on Cadillac's main street in the four-blocks long retail business section. Their childhoods had provided them with the skills needed to operate a restaurant

My dad, the middle one of six brothers and two older sisters, lost his mother while he was still a boy. His father pretty much left those nine to fend for themselves, which they did even after the two older sisters left home at their earliest opportunity to become maids in the family mansions of the town's lumber barons who mostly lived up on "Bankers Hill" in Cadillac. As a result, my father had developed cooking skills during his childhood. Likewise, my mother and her eleven siblings grew up on a profitable farm near Cadillac, where she learned basic farm skills including cooking. Together, my parents did a commendable job in the restaurant and the little place was soon quite profitable.

By then, we were living in a comfortable rental home at the edge of Bankers Hill within easy walking distance to the "Club Café." My parents' success came partly because my dad kept his restaurant open until 10:30 p.m. at night to catch the truckers who had to drive up Cadillac's main street on their way to destinations farther north. He made excellent soup and sold good hamburgers for as low as 5 cents as an incentive. Then, upon closing, he would put the day's receipts in a bank deposit bag and drop it in the night-deposit slot at the bank before going home. Things were going well; he paid little attention to the financial problems building up in the nation's big cities.

Then, with the far-off financial situation worsening, my father woke up one morning, March 6, 1933, as I remember, to find that President Roosevelt had closed all the banks, including the two in Cadillac, never to open again. Shocked, my father found he only had the change in his pocket that morning; all his other cash was downtown in the closed bank.

Opening the restaurant that morning was a test of his determination. He borrowed meat from the meat market next door and groceries from the grocer a few doors away. But there was no business. The city was financially paralyzed. Those who had cash horded it, no one shopped or went to restaurants. My father gave up within two weeks, abandoned the restaurant and accepted an offer to try to keep one across the street running for its owner. That job lasted only a few days. Our family was completely broke. No cash to pay the rent. We quickly moved to a small frame house around the eastern side of the lake. The rent was $15 a month, and I know there were months we fell in arrears.

The house itself was a simple frame affair with a pot-bellied stove in the middle (dining) room and a wood-burning old-fashioned range in the kitchen, finagled from a friendly farmer who had it stored under his hay mow in a barn. The house had a small toilet partitioned off a storeroom in the back of the house. It was good for about seven months a year. When the first hard freeze came in the fall, the water pipes froze for the winter, and we had to use an outhouse behind the garage until the pipes thawed in the spring. In the summer I would convert the outhouse to my wood working shop, a "must" in my life even at the young age of thirteen.

If there was any consolation to our plight, it was that so many others were in the same fix or worse. The stories about the thousands of unemployed standing in bread lines around the county were scary. Would there be riots? Anarchy? No one knew, especially up in Cadillac, Michigan. So, beyond the few odd jobs my dad would find, we did what we could. We expanded our big vegetable garden; we had access to an ample supply of mostly free fruits and produce available from the local farms. My mother preserved dozens of cans of fruits and vegetables which lasted until the next harvest. Some of that supply came from helping at my grandfather's farm, but more came from the raspberries and huckleberries our family would find in day-long searches in the marshes near town. The whole family picked berries for an entire day and later sold most of the berries for 5 cents a basket, to the "wealthy" up on Bankers Hill. We kept the empty basket for another sale. What we didn't sell, we ate or my mother canned for the coming winter.

On rare occasions, the city received shipments of government beef, packed in olive green cans, for distribution to help feed the local citizens. Once after such a delivery, when we were selling berries on Bankers Hill, we found trash cans waiting to be picked up--they had trash pickup? Interestingly, inside some of those trash cans, in plain sight, we saw empty green cans. This observation proved to be an eye opener to the real financial situation in town.

Among our critical needs, fire wood topped the list. We solved this problem by scouring the woods for tree stumps and slashings left by lumber crews. We hauled the wood in my dad's old Chrysler with the back seat, removed to make space for the wood. At home we stacked the wood by the garage to use as cooking and heating fuel. We supplemented the wood with a little coal, compliments of the railroad. The railroad climbed out of Cadillac and passed the front of our house through a deep cut beyond the far side of the road. In the winter we could see the black coal in the white snow, where it had fallen off the railroad coal cars. In addition, in the winter, we and neighboring kids, on hearing a freight train coming, would stand in the snow on the top of the high bank and throw snow balls at the train's fireman as the train slowly worked its way through the cut. The fireman acted angry, but really understood the situation and would throw coal back at us; then wave when he got out of range. His kindness helped.

I was still in grade school at the time and on the first day after school let out in June, all the neighbor kids and I shucked our shoes and went barefoot for the rest of the summer--saving our shoes. After our morning chores were done, we usually spent our day at the lake and the nearby ruins of one of Cadillac's defunct lumber mills. There, at the lake, we fished or skinny dipped as we pleased. At the empty mill, a grand place for exploring, we scouted through huge stacks of hardwood lumber and played on the miniature rail trams that had carried the lumber to a then closed hardwood flooring mill nearby. It was a great time to grow up in that part of Cadillac.

But the winters, Ugh! Evenings, we kids spent huddled in the corner behind the pot bellied stove listening to the radio. Our bedroom windows were covered with ice on the inside. During the day, doors were kept closed to save heat. On week days, we four siblings walked to school like everyone else regardless of the weather. On weekends, my dad, brother and I scrounged firewood in the woods or went fishing through the ice on the lake. Any fish we caught were left on the ice, where they froze solid. Arriving home, we threw the fish in the bathtub filled with cold water. Amazingly, in a short time, they would be swimming around as alive as ever, waiting to be filleted for supper.

The worst period came early on at that house around the lake. Desperate, my dad one morning climbed the barb wire fence behind our house and walked across the frozen, snow covered fields to the highway far up the hill and hitch-hiked to Lansing to try to find a job. A week later, near dusk on a bitter cold day, we saw him trudging back across the same fields, arriving home cold, hungry, broke and very angry. My poor mother just about lost it then, but we survived.

Many months afterwards, my dad found some part-time work at the local table factory when it tried to restart production. Then he passed the civil service exam for the post office. He was not an educated man, perhaps not even completing the eighth grade, but he was smart and self-educated. I was in high school when he started part time at the post office. He delivered mail in Cadillac for another thirty-five years.

High school for me in the Depression was not a pleasant experience. I was small, skinny and younger than most. I had worked on my grandfather's farm for three summers in an attempt to help me grow, but to no avail. I was thirteen and weighed only sixty-nine pounds when I started high school and weighed one hundred twenty pounds when I graduated at seventeen. I believe my limited diet was partly responsible for my being so skinny, because I had been raised primarily on meat, potatoes and heavily sugared coffee. However, I was physically tough and could run forever. Since I was the runt of the class, our football coach, Lee Nelson, called me "Primo" after Primo Carnera, who became the heavy weight champ in 1933 only to lose the title to Joe Louis in 1934. He also appointed me to be the track and field team manager in the spring of my sophomore year. By tradition, I would have the honor of being the football manager the next fall. I was elated. but then, disaster.

My parents were both born into large families of first generation offspring whose parents, with one exception, came from Scandinavia. They believed that formal education beyond eighth grade or maybe high school was unnecessary and financially unthinkable. College was for the wealthy. Thus the future envisioned for me was a high school education and then a job in the local community. That plan was confirmed when the Great Depression smothered the country. As a result, I had to settle for the Commercial course, which included bookkeeping, drafting, shop and other related subjects. I passed most of them with ease.

My "disaster" came when my mother, a leader in the local PTA, asked the high school principal to help find an after school job for me. I wasn't aware of this until I found myself hired as a "gofer," serving as janitor, delivery boy, etc. for a local ladies dress shop run by a well-to-do, nice, mature Jewish lady, who drove a big red Buick covered with chrome plated gadgets. It was my duty to keep it clean and polished. This job killed my future as the football student manager. It also denied my participation in afternoon assemblies, plays and sports that occurred during or after school hours--not to mention the Saturday afternoon football games, a big local event. But worse yet, the store owner, without asking me, got my schedule changed so that I got out of school an hour early each day to work longer for her. This change denied me my daily hour in study hall, so I had to do all my lessons at home weekdays after 6:30, when my work day ended. My pay was $5 per week during the busy summers and $3.50 after the tourists left for the winter. With that income I bought most of my own clothes and put at least 25 cents in my piggy bank each week.

I graduated from high school in 1937--no prom or school dances to remember, but I did get a decent education. Bookkeeping came naturally to me and I earned straight A's and the same in mechanical drawing. Tests showed that my IQ was quite high, and I was encouraged to study architecture. This was impossible since I had no college prep courses and no cash outside of my piggy bank. However, one week after my graduation my life suddenly changed.

Unknown to me, one of my uncles had become aware of my bookkeeping marks and he offered me a job in his Goshen, Indiana office, where he managed a three-state regional telephone revenue accounting office. Within a week I had packed my graduation present, a fake-leather cardboard suitcase. I opened my little saving bank for the cash that I needed for my trip and was surprised to find less than $15, about half of what I expected. My mother told me she had needed to dip into my bank occasionally when she ran short of cash. So I hitch-hiked the hundred miles to Grand Rapids and then took the train to Elkhart, where my uncle met me. In Goshen, he took me to a rooming house, run by a friendly Mennonite lady. I rented a small upstairs corner room for $3.50 per week, laundry included. For my meals, he took me to a nearby restaurant, where I bought a five-day, two meals a day, meal ticket for $4.50. Our third stop was the local haberdashers, where he had an account set up for me. I purchased a suit, shirts, etc. and I was ready for work the next day. It was a good job in a nice office across the street from the county court house. My pay was a bit under $15. After paying my rent, buying my meal ticket and paying $5 a week to the haberdashers, I had enough left to eat on weekends plus 25 cents for a movie and a couple of quarters for pool at the pool hall or a milkshake at the ice cream parlor. I was free and solvent.

The job was interesting; I did well, became proficient on the comptometer and was eventually promoted to a better job "upstairs." But before long, I learned that the replacement for my original job, a nice guy sent from headquarters in Madison, Wisconsin, was getting paid considerably more than I was, even after my promotion. That fact, plus an ad in the newspaper offering civil service positions in Washington, D.C., prompted me to take a civil service exam. I applied for the exam, borrowed a car and drove on a stormy winter day to South Bend to take the exam. A long wait of several months passed before I was notified that I had passed the exam. Later I was offered a position in the U.S. Treasury Department next to the White House. I quickly accepted and in early March, 1941, I took the train to Washington, arriving on a Sunday morning. I quickly found lodging on 21st Street just off Pennsylvania Avenue and started work the next morning. I was one happy guy and totally unaware of the very eventful year that lay ahead.

Meanwhile, the Great Depression ground on, but there were glimmers of hope and some of the economy was beginning to sift through to the ordinary citizens around the country. Little did we realize, however, that it would take a great war to finally stomp the Depression out of our lives.

My youthful disappointment about not getting a college education did not, however, hamper my intention to succeed. Instead, I used the years that I would have spent in college to acquire valuable learning experiences which would help me achieve a successful career. Living through the Great Depression taught me that having a good family and living in financial security was a worthy goal. I did not aspire to great wealth.

After working three and one-half years in Goshen, I worked in Washington for one year, followed by another year in a Civil Service job in Panama. After World War II began, I returned to Washington, D.C., married my fiancée, Mary Knox, enlisted in the Navy as a Third Class Petty Officer and was stationed at the Naval Training Center in Bainbridge, Maryland. After two years, I was sent to Pearl Harbor and assigned to Admiral Nimitz' CincPac (Commander in Chief of the Pacific) headquarters and volunteered to serve at his new Advanced Headquarters in Guam. My duty was in the Admiral's top secret radio teletype communications room, where I attained the rank of Chief Petty Officer.

When the war ended, I returned to Cadillac to join my wife and our two-year-old son. We moved to Lansing, where I used the GI Bill to enroll in the state of Michigan's unique "On the Job" training for accountants. After almost seven years of study and work for a successful CPA, I passed all my exams and became a Michigan CPA on July 31, 1952. After many years in public accounting, I desired to work in the private sector. I joined a new manufacturing company, Demmer Corporation, as their accounting and financial advisor--a wise choice which set the course of my future career.

In 1972, after twenty years with Demmer Corporation, our children were grown and married and Michigan's long winters were taking a toll on Mary's health. So we decided to move to Carlsbad, California. There I became comptroller of a small manufacturing firm and later retired to the beautiful Rancho Bernardo community in July 1983. I had worked for forty-seven years, retiring with an unblemished reputation, which I believe is a more valuable legacy than any monetary inheritance I could leave. Our family includes two children, four grandchildren and three great grandchildren.

In 2010, our daughter, Kathryn, moved away from the San Diego area; and our son, Kenneth N., a longtime resident of Thousand Oaks, invited us to move to the area. We did and then lived in an apartment before moving to UVTO in April 2011. Here we are making new friends and living happily in the security and comfort of this our new home.

EXPERIENCES OF THE GREAT DEPRESSION BY GENE LORE

My dad, Elmer Eugene Lore, Sr., was born in Nebraska and my mother, Sarah Clay, was born in Pennsylvania. Both moved to Emporia, Kansas, where they were employed by the world-renowned editor of the *Emporia Gazette*, William Allen White. (White's famous eulogy, "Mary White" on the accidental death of his young daughter still appears in anthologies of American literature.) Mom was a typesetter; she took one letter at a time from a box of letters and handset the letters to form a line of type. Dad ran a machine called a linotype, which had a keyboard. When he typed out the words of an article, the linotype converted them into the columns, which formed a page of print. My parents married and had a son, my older brother, Francis. My mother suffered from recurring bouts of pneumonia.

The family moved to California following the doctor's advice that my mom needed a drier climate. I was born within a few months of the move on January 24, 1919, in Los Angeles at 16th and Burlington and named for my father. When I was two, we moved to Cottage Street off Slauson Ave. Because of Mom's health, in 1923 we moved to the San Fernando Valley, where it was drier. We settled in Lankershim (now called North Hollywood) and lived on Hamlin Street (near Victory and Lankershim) for thirteen years. Then we moved to Bradford Street across from the Victory Boulevard School, when I was about seventeen. (I lived there until my marriage to Patty Louise Watson, a friend of my sister.) I went to North Hollywood High School, graduating with the winter class of 1937.

My dad worked for the old *Los Angeles Record*, earning $40 a week as a union printer. The stock market crashed in 1929 when I was ten-years old. I had two brothers and two sisters. Our family was not destitute; we had the necessities, but no extras. We learned to save electricity and water. We never threw away anything. When our clothes became old and torn, Mom cut them up to make quilts. Dad didn't have a savings account or checking account, nor did he invest in the stock market. All his transactions were done with cash.

Many people had to move because they couldn't pay their rent during the Great Depression. Because of his steady employment, my dad was able to purchase a house and two lots (50 ft. by 165 ft.) for $750 on Hamlin Street. The house had two-bedrooms, a living room and back porch. My dad later added on two more rooms. I remember that my brother and I shared one bed as did our sisters. We had an extensive garden on the lot and were able to grow all our own vegetables. Our home was located in a subdivision, created from a former apricot and peach orchard. There were still some remaining trees, so Mom would can these fruits for use in the winter. We bought meat at the grocery store. We also had a flock of one hundred chickens. My dad sold the eggs to supplement his salary. We raised chinchilla rabbits, sold the skins and ate the meat. After five years, he gave up the poultry business and converted the chicken coop into a wash house.

During these years of the Great Depression, all the neighbors helped each other, sharing as they could. I sold the *Saturday Evening Post* for 5 cents and the *Ladies' Home Journal* for 10 cents to earn some money. I earned one-half cent for every Post sold and three-quarters of a cent for each Journal. I wasn't too successful; some months, I only made 15 to 20 cents. I was about twelve at the time.

After Franklin Roosevelt became President in 1932, people began having hope again. The hard times of the Great Depression eased. Roosevelt established bank solvency. He created relief programs to aid the destitute and established the WPA (Works Progress Administration) to provide work building roads, dams, parks and public buildings. I consider him our greatest President. When he died in 1945, I thought, "What do we do now?"

In 1935, Dad was elected to the California State Assembly. His district included the area from the Santa Monica Mountains east to San Bernardino County and north/west to Ventura County. Obviously, the population was sparse. He favored the EPIC (End Poverty In California) movement created by socialist Upton Sinclair. After graduation, I worked in the Legislative Bill Room in the Capitol from 1938 to 1940. My brother worked as a page and as an Assistant Sergeant of Arms in the State Assembly. Dad's income was only $100 a month in the Assembly; so he had to return to his printing job when the Assembly was not in session, not only to earn more, but also to keep his seniority. The newspaper put him on leave; however, he had to return one day a month to retain his job. We rented a room in Sacramento, while Mom stayed in North Hollywood.

Later I took advantage of the CPT (Civilian Pilot Training) program to learn to fly. President Roosevelt created this program because he sensed that war was coming, and he knew the United States would need many able pilots. I learned to fly in a fifty-horse power single-engine plane at Van Nuys Airport. After I earned my license, I enjoyed flying jaunts to nearby areas.

Beginning about 1940, I went to work at the Lockheed Burbank Aircraft Plant. I was in charge of the production tool crib, which provided support to the metal shop that made parts for airplanes.

After the December 7, 1941, attack on Pearl Harbor, I was exempted from the draft because I worked in the defense industry. My brother didn't qualify for the draft because he had a bad heart, so he was classified 4 F. After a time, I felt guilty that I had learned to fly for free in the CPT program, so I decided to join the Army Air Corps. However, two fellows from work mentioned they were going to join the Navy and become Aviation Cadets. I decided to join them. Ironically, I was the only one to qualify, as the other two were rejected. Soon I was on my way to the University of Georgia at Athens for pre-flight school for a three to four-month pre-flight training course.

I had survived the Great Depression, but had no idea of how my life would be changed by my World War II experiences.

GREAT DEPRESSION DAYS BY MEL LOWRY

I suddenly find myself experiencing another economic depression.

I was born August 28, 1928, to August Edward Hill and Catherine Powers in Butte, Montana, the home of William Andrews Clark, one of Montana's three famous "Copper Kings." His mine was part of the famous Anaconda Copper Mine. We were a mile high and had mines a mile deep. I was born during the Great Depression and hope not to die in this one. However, I am not certain which fate is more to be feared. My recollections of the first are not very scary. It just seemed as if this was the way all things had always been. But now, our immediate future in 2011 seems to get worse day by day, not so much for me but especially for our children and grandchildren.

When I was still a baby, our family moved to Port Angeles, Washington. Sadly, my mother died and my father was overwhelmed by the care of three youngsters and a baby. He asked my Aunt May, my mother's half-sister, to care for me. She agreed on the condition that she and her husband, Jay Lowry, be permitted to adopt me. My father consented and so Aunt May (Mary Ellen Powers Lowry) along with my Aunt Jose (Josephine) took me back to Butte on the train. As I research my genealogy, I am Lowry, born Hill.

In Butte, I attended Emerson Grade School for all eight years and went one-half a year to Butte High before we moved. Neighborhood friends including Helen Mullin, Joe Mullin, Tootsie Schoenberg and Jackie Powers plus many more joined in all games from kick-the-can and hide-and-seek to baseball on a dirt open area. We had one ball and maybe two gloves. But who needed gloves?

In the wintertime the favorite pastime was sledding. We lived on the Flat; and when it snowed, the street would get packed down, so we could glide on it. Few cars traveled the streets, so our sledding out of a blind alley into the street was fun and generally not dangerous. Occasionally, after dark, when we would come shooting out of a blind alley, we would terrify some unsuspecting driver.

I remember one time, when I was riding my bicycle at dusk approaching a cross street. It was my practice to ride without ever holding on to the handle bars or more often to sit on the crossbar like a passenger. On one occasion my timing was bad. A car and I both arrived in the intersection at the same time. The visibility was bad and the sight lines were short. The result was that I got caught on the front metal bumpers and was carried through the intersection. As the car stopped, I fell forward impacting the street, receiving a good deal of bruising.

I was the youngest of two older brothers and an older sister. My father and my older siblings were often on the move. As I was told, my father, Ed Hill, moved all the way around

California through the state of Washington, picking fruit and vegetables during the Depression. My oldest brother was in the CCC, the Civilian Conservation Corps. He recalled this experience as his best opportunity as a young man. He helped build parks and bridges and worked on other projects. My six-year older brother, Hal Hill, told me he went to perhaps twelve or fourteen different high schools. My sister, Audrey, spent a good deal of time living with my mother, Aunt May to her and me. My brothers and my sister said that I was the lucky one. I actually had a home and mother to take care of me. Mother May's husband, Jay Lowry, had a twin brother, George; and I was led to believe that along with my Aunt Jose, they were actually triplets. One birthday party, the cake had a tiny bed on top with three babies in it. Later in life, Aunt Jose's daughter, my cousin, Marion, told me otherwise. I never confirmed it one way or the other.

I never really understood how my adopted mother, May Lowry, managed to survive. In addition to me and her husband, her brother Mike Powers and her husband's brother, George, lived with her. Her husband, Jay, was very crippled for as long as I knew him. I never saw him other than sitting in a wheelchair. I'm not certain what the problem was, but he had his legs firmly fused or fixed in a bent position, so he could sit on the wheelchair. The wheelchair was actually a piano stool that his brother, George, had modified by adding a wire back. It was necessary for my mother to help him into and out of bed; and judging by his brother, George, he was well over six feet tall. He had been a very active person before being handicapped. I don't know where the money came from, perhaps from George. My father Jay died when I was about ten or eleven. After Daddy Jay died, my mother had a variety of jobs. At one time she worked as a dish washer at a number of places in uptown Butte, including a Chinese restaurant. About 1940, she also set up a penny candy store in our front room. I was often caught crawling into the display cabinet trying to reach the chocolates.

As a young boy, I became a paperboy delivering the *Montana Standard* in winter and summer. My last stop on my delivery route was always at Aunt Jose's. She would sit me down in front of the stove, put my feet and boots into the oven to warm me and feed me a piece of apple pie. She often related newspaper information about the atrocities the Russians committed in attacks on their own people since the Revolution. At home we never seemed to lack anything. All the money I received for delivering papers was mine to use as I chose. When I left Butte, I forgot to get back the $5 deposit from the paper.

Butte's copper mines provided the chief source of employment. Other sources of income included prostitution, bars and gambling. I had many opportunities to visit the mine. I saw the miners riding down in cages holding twenty or more. When the cages were full, the operator released the brake and allowed it to go essentially into free-fall. He knew when to start slowing the cage so it would stop at the right level. I never heard any complaints or even any discussion about the whole operation.

I have seen many, many men, particularly my uncle Mike Powers, come home with their helmets bashed in from rock falls in the mine. It was not unusual to go down one mineshaft and then have to walk miles through the mine tunnels to another shaft in order to take a different cage to the surface. None of this ever made me interested in taking a ride down into the mine. I was invited many times, but always shied away.

Most of my recollections of Butte are of a small house at 1701 Marcia Street in the part of town referred to as "The Flat." Our house was as simple and meager as one can imagine. The general appearance contrasted sharply to all the other houses around. Interestingly enough, we lived catty-corner to one of the richest persons in Butte and perhaps in Montana. The Hagensons owned gambling houses in both Butte and Reno. Directly across the street was another gambler who worked nights. I never saw him. Two doors up was another gambler. Nearby on Harrison, the main road, the Mullins lived across from the fire station. The father, a gambler in Butte, died very young. I remember that the Mullins bought a brand-new, black Packard automobile every year. From all appearances, I lived in a very wealthy neighborhood. Certainly, our house and yard didn't match the neighborhood. We, obviously, didn't have much money, but the contrast to the neighbors didn't seem to matter. Although we were poor, we survived.

I've always remembered that Daddy Jay's brother, my uncle George, was an electrician. He wired our house so that the electricity coming into the house could bypass the meter to save us money. On the day that the meter reader was coming, it was generally my job to remove or unscrew the shorting fuse so the meter would operate. Consequently, we always had a very low electric bill.

During this time period, I was well aware of the WPA, Works Progress Administration. Without the WPA, Butte would have just mushed, on (kept going).   Some of my relatives and others benefitted from the WPA. My aunt Josephine became a sometime artist. Many others were on the "pick and shovel brigade." A complaint then and probably still today in our modern Depression is: "They don't do anything, but sponge off the government. All they do is stand around leaning on their shovels and get paid to do nothing." Nobody I knew ever suggested, "Why don't they get a job?"

What really happened was they built roads, bridges and infrastructure and they received cash or pay at week's end. What did they do with that pay? They went to the baker and bought bread and milk. And what did the baker and dairyman do? The baker went to the farmer and bought wheat to grind into flour to make bread, while the dairyman bought feed for his cows and milk bottles for delivery to his customers. The farmer bought seed and paid his help as did the dairyman. This "cash flow" went on and on and made our economy work, building a strong sense of community. (Camarillo State Hospital, now the site of California State University at Channel Islands, was the first WPA project in the United States. Built in 1933, the structures are as sound today as they were then, an exemplary tribute to the Save America purpose of the WPA.)

Just before starting Butte High School, my sister, Audrey, who had been living with us, married a local boy and moved to Bremerton, Washington, when he joined the Navy. At this time, I was at Butte High School, and we had moved to a one-room apartment on Main Street. I continued to sell newspapers, but I was very upset not having my sister with me. My only excitement was selling all the newspaper extras covering the attack on Pearl Harbor, December 7, 1941. I went from bar to bar at 5 a.m., selling all the papers I could carry at 5 cents each.

Butte's center of higher education was the Montana School of Mines. Graduates worked in the mines. I suppose it was possible to find a surface job, but that never occurred to me. To avoid the mines and to leave Butte resulted in my saying to my mother, "I am leaving. Do you want to go with me?" Neither Mother nor I ever regretted our decision. (Butte to this day has never recovered from the 1929 Great Depression.)

Subsequently and shortly thereafter, we abandoned everything we had and took the train to Bremerton. I had come back to Butte on a train and I left on a train. We only stayed there a month because it was too much of an imposition on my sister. We traveled by train to Oakland, California, where we had some relatives who had also recently moved from Butte to Oakland.

We found an apartment near 21st Street and Telegraph. I graduated from junior high school and next went to Oakland High School. Soon after our move, I got a job in the mailroom at the Moore Drydock Company. This was an ideal job for a young man, for I was the only guy in the mailroom. Most of the young women were busy making mimeograph copies of all the endless paperwork needed to run a shipyard. I kept busy delivering mail around the whole shipyard. Using a motor scooter, I rode everywhere going from wood shop to the metal shop. I learned how a ship was built and witnessed many launchings from dry dock. One unusual event occurred when I delivered a notice to a man working on repairs to a small carrier. As I climbed on board, I saw some welders directly in front of me. All of a sudden one of the welders lifted her safety helmet, and all her hair fell down. I was looking at and almost touching Rosie the welder. This reminded me of the popular wartime song, "Rosie the Riveter."

After a time, we moved to Los Angeles, where we lived in an apartment above the garage of my birth father, Ed Hill. I got acquainted with my father's new family. We moved shortly thereafter. By a strange coincidence, my older brother, Hal, and I both graduated from Los Angeles High School in the same year, 1947. His education had been interrupted by his service in the Air Corps.

My dear Mother May remarried and eventually moved to Hemet. I am indebted to her for providing me a home and for nurturing my spirit. I will always remember her with deep love not only for her personal care and devotion to me and my family, but also for her service to our entire Butte community. Sadly, I was unable to be with her when she died in the 1970's, for by then I had moved to Boston.

After high school, I worked for SoCal Gas Company. During this time, I attended Los Angeles City College, taking a variety of science courses, but never finding the one that I wanted to pursue as a career. I was drafted into the army and by test qualified to attend the Fort Bliss Anti-Aircraft School. There I studied electronics and radar mechanics, finding a field that engaged my interest.

After my service in the army from 1952-1954, I attended UCLA on the Korean Education Bill of Rights, graduating in 1957 with at B.S. in physics. During my two years at UCLA, I was employed as a test engineer by Honeywell, beginning my twenty-plus year career in aerospace. Graduation was the start of a series of serendipitous happenings that continued throughout my whole life.

My first day on the job as a new titled engineer, I was given an airplane ticket and sent to Dallas, Texas, to monitor Texas Instruments' project for Honeywell's missile program. Coincidentally, I had my very first airplane ride and my first engineering assignment at the same time. I had no idea what was expected of an engineer reviewing the work of a company like Texas Instruments. Fortunately, I didn't embarrass either Honeywell or myself and thus began my career as a Project Engineer or as I say a System Engineer. From that day forward when anyone asked me what I did as an engineer, especially my daughters, I would always say, "All I do is talk and write."

I worked for Honeywell for ten years in Boston. I also worked briefly for Raytheon. I was next recruited and employed as chief of the engineering group by Electrico Optics for Owens Illinois in Pittsburgh, which produced commercial and military telescopes.

Another fortuitous moment occurred when I returned to California and bought a franchise for professional recruiting. I discovered that the city of Thousand Oaks provided an excellent commercial location near the Los Angeles metropolitan area, and it was a great community for my family as well. I operated my business, Management Recruiters of Thousand Oaks, for nine years in the 1960's. When the Ronald Reagan recession depressed the economy, I sold the business to Steve Ferry, one of my recruiters, who to this day is a successful international headhunter.

In October, 1984, I invested in Sealing Corporation, a North Hollywood company that manufactures high performance gadgets. I am still actively involved with this company, continuing under a long term buyout agreement. My role now is to provide technical and sales support.

The habits and work discipline I learned as a paperboy and as a mail courier during my youth during the Great Depression have guided me throughout my life. I attribute my successful engineering career and my business achievements to the insights gained from my early work experiences. These traits have enabled me to continue actively working to the present. Whenever I am asked, "When are you going to retire?" my answer is an unequivocal, "I'll be the last to know."

On a personal note, I have been married to Joan Martin Lowry for sixty years. She is a native-born Californian from Alhambra and also a UCLA graduate in bacteriology. She had her own career as a lab technician. As I traveled a great deal on business, she almost single-handedly raised our two daughters--Catherine, a psychologist, of Silver Spring, MD, and Susan Diana Lowry Ball, CPA, of Camarillo, CA. Susan is the mother of our two grandchildren--Michelle, a January 2011 graduate of Cal State University Channel Islands, and Nathan a sophomore at Camarillo High School.

After living in Thousand Oaks for thirty-five years, we decided it was time to downsize. We investigated a local retirement community and then fortunately received an invitation to dine at University Village. After further visits, we moved here on June 12, 2009. I currently lead the Autobiography Club and the cribbage game, and I became a member of the Activities Committee in January, 2012. We are pleased with our decision, and Joan says, "This is the best place we've ever lived."

MY LIFE IN AN ORPHANAGE BY BILL MARSHALL

I, William Edward Marshall, was born July 24, 1925, in South Amboy, New Jersey, the second of four children and first son born to Mary and William Marshall. My sister, Hilda, was two-and-a-half years older. A second son, Elson, was born one-and-a-half years after me, and a third son, Leonard, was born another one-and-a-half years later. My mother, Mary Irene Hyer, born in Matawan, NJ, had an older brother, Edward, from whom I was given my middle name. My father, born in Lincoln, Nebraska, was one of eleven children--ten boys and one girl. My father met my mother when he relocated in New Jersey after returning from World War I.

I don't remember very much from those early years when we were living in Rahway, NJ. Some grape vines grew in the backyard. We picked the grapes and ate them. I remember the large back porch and people stirring a round wooden bucket making ice cream. They let us try stirring and gave us samples of the ice cream. My Christmas memory includes my mother and all us children eating dinner. Out of the darkened living room came my father in a Santa Claus outfit saying, "Ho Ho Ho." I along with my two younger brothers started screaming and running to our mother. It wasn't until after he took off the fake beard and Santa's hat that we recognized him and things returned to normal. Another event I remember is having a tug-of-war with my sister on the living room couch. I had the towel in my mouth. When she pulled it out, one of my baby teeth came out too.

When I turned five, my sister walked me to school on my first day and dropped me off in the kindergarten class room. It wasn't long before I started crying and saying I wanted to go home. The teacher called for my sister and she took me home. My sister sat with me in class for the next several days before I felt okay being by myself. Shortly thereafter, we moved to an apartment above some stores. In the back was a parking area with some trees that my brother Elson and I used to climb. I remember the two of us being punished and sent inside because we were making too much noise early one Sunday morning, disturbing the neighbors. We were bathed in a large metal drum on top of the kitchen table. The water was heated on the stove. I don't remember if we had a bath tub, nor do I remember who gave us the bath other than it was a woman. My mother had already developed tuberculosis and had been placed in Bonnie Brae Sanitarium, located in Scotch Plains, NJ.

Unfortunately, the only memory I have of my mother is of seeing some woman in a hospital bed that we children visited with my father. Shortly thereafter, at age six, I along with my sister and two brothers was placed in an orphanage in Elizabeth, NJ, called the Janet Memorial Home. I never did find out for whom it was named. Although I don't remember it ever happening, years later my sister told me that our mother had left the TB sanitarium for a brief period and did visit us at the orphanage. My sister gave me a copy of a picture of all of us together taken in the backyard of the orphanage. I do not remember this happening and to my knowledge, it is the only picture taken of my entire family. A 5 by 7 copy of that picture hangs on the wall in my den at UVTO (University Village Thousand Oaks) along with some other family pictures given to me by my sister.

I turned seven in July 1932. A few months later that fall, my father came to visit us at the orphanage and took us to a small room where he told us our mother had died. She was only thirty-nine years old. Leonard ran out of the room crying, out of the building and down the street before I had a chance to reach him. I don't remember too much about the memorial service, but I do remember walking in the cemetery behind the hearse carrying my mother's casket. Many years later when I was much older, married with children of my own and living in Southern California, I learned from my sister, who lived in New Jersey and whom I would try to visit on business trips to New York City, that our mother was actually cremated and her remains were interned at the cemetery where we had the funeral   This particular trip East was brought about because my father had died a few days earlier and we were discussing his funeral and his burial. My sister had made her own arrangements to be buried near her home and had planned to have our father buried in the same cemetery. Our younger brother, Leonard, was already buried there, having died several years earlier at age thirty-seven of double pneumonia. At my request, our mother's remains were then removed and placed alongside our father.

The orphanage was a multi-storied building with a large dining room and living room on the first floor along with some small offices. The boys all resided on the second floor, which had a very large balcony overlooking a very large backyard. Boys eleven-years old and younger were located on one side in a large room. We each had our own bed and locker. I think there were about twelve of us. When a boy entered junior high school, he moved to the Big Boys side, where there was about the same number of boys each with his own bed and locker. On the wall behind each bed, there was a large framed painting of a sports star.   Behind my bed was a painting of tennis great Don Budge. Later on I moved to another bed and had a picture of Joe DiMaggio of the New York Yankees.

We all learned how to make our own beds and box the corners. Knowing these techniques came in very handy later on when I was going through the Army Air Corps aviation cadet program during World War II. There our instructors were mostly West Point graduates and that is how they had to make their beds. All of us had extra jobs. Another boy and I were in charge of cleaning the entire bathroom, consisting of about twelve sinks, half-dozen toilets and two very large shower stalls. I learned to sew, darn socks and iron my own clothes. The last chore came in very handy when I was in the Army Air Corps. I made extra spending money by ironing other cadets' uniforms. Many of the clothes we wore in the orphanage were handed down from the older boys.

Lights went out at 9 p.m. during the week and 10 p.m. on weekends. We had to remain very quiet. No talking, etc. otherwise, Ms. McCauley, whom we called the night nurse, would come to a boy's bed, pinch and twist his ear until he cried. On the bright side, if we were all good little boys during the previous week, she would turn on the radio on Monday nights so we could listen to *Lux Radio Theater,* narrated by Cecil B. DeMille. Remember, there was no television in the early 1930s.

I don't remember very much about the third floor, where my sister and the girls lived. I do remember that they also had a very large balcony with stairs down to the ground floor. Older boys on the second floor would go up the stairs to see if they could see some older girl taking a shower, etc. Not me! A boy could get into a lot of trouble, if caught.

At Christmas time, we would be taken in a bus to some large hall, where we formed two lines--girls in one and boys in another. Then we walked to the front of the stage. Once we reached the stage, someone gave each of us a present. Usually, there was a puzzle or model airplane kit for the older boys, while the girls mostly received dolls. I don't remember what we received when we were younger. There was a large play room on both floors in each living area with a long table where we could work on the puzzles and build our model airplanes. Months later when the airplanes had survived many a crash, we would go out on the second or third floor back balcony, apply glue to the model, light a match to it, and send it on its last flaming flight. There were many crabapple trees growing in the front of the orphanage; and when the apples ripened, we would climb the trees and eat them. In the fall when the leaves fell and were raked into a big pile, we would jump on them.

Years later after there was a change in management at the orphanage, we were able to dramatize the Christmas nativity pageant in our large living room. We wore homemade costumes, and later sang Christmas carols. Those who were interested were even given dance lessons, but I'm getting ahead of my story.

The early years in the orphanage were not always happy times, especially if a child misbehaved or didn't follow the rules and regulations. Often the offender got no meals and might be placed in a dark closet for hours. Others were confined to the attic room for days with no visitors. There were some beds and they did provide three meals daily.

The boys' adult advisor was a man named Jack Banks. I'll never forget his name. All the boys would stand in line in the basement room, which was mostly used as a play room during the cold winter months and in bad weather throughout the year. We repeated this ritual every day before dinner. We were then ordered to show our hands, palm side up and if he didn't think they were clean, he'd hit them with a heavy razor strap, the kind used in barber shops to sharpen the razor when men wanted a shave. One day he started hitting my brother Elson with the strap. Elson tried to get away, but Mr. Banks went after him hitting him repeatedly. My brother then climbed up on top of a small cabinet where we stored sports equipment. Mr. Banks continued to hit my brother until he fell off breaking both bones in his right arm. I went to help my brother only to be hit with the strap.

Years later I learned that early on during my stay in the orphanage, my uncle Edward Hyer, my mother's brother and source of my middle name, wanted to adopt me. Fortunately for me, my father said, "No," but told my uncle he could adopt my youngest brother Leonard, who was probably three-years old at the time. Neither my Uncle Ed nor his wife, my Aunt Mae, who lived only a little more than an hour away, ever visited us at the orphanage. They never had any children of their own.

Our father's visits were infrequent. He did not have full-time work and had very little money--not uncommon in those Depression days. I don't know how or where he lived. He was not an educated man only going as far as the eighth grade in school. I do know for a fact that he siphoned gasoline from other cars so he would be able to visit us on the very rare visiting days. He used what money he could save to buy candy, which he put in four small white bags and gave to us. I found out much later that many a night he went to bed hungry.

I don't remember exactly when or why new management took over the orphanage, but with the change happier times prevailed for all the children. We formed Boy Scout Troop No.13 with Mr. Richard Norton as Scout Master. We all called him Dick. We went on overnight camping trips; we also went fishing and to baseball games in Newark, NJ, to see the Newark Bears play. They were a minor league team owned by the New York Yankees. We saw many future Yankee greats such as Bill Dickey, catcher, and Joe Gordon, second baseman, before they moved up to the big leagues. We had to be on our best behavior the week before the game to be selected to go. I don't know what it cost to go to the games or if there even was a charge, paid by Dick. Although we had our seats, we were still known as the "Knothole Gang." This term was first used early on when baseball was in its infancy to describe young children who could not afford the price of admission. They stood outside the field and watched the game by looking through a knothole in the wooden fence.

We marched in parades. I'll always remember one particular parade, the opening of the 1939 World's Fair. We wore short pants and led the parade. We started going to Sunday School at the First Presbyterian Church in Elizabeth, NJ, where many from Revolutionary War days were buried. Dick was our teacher. We would go through that week's Bible lesson very fast so we could talk about our next camping trip. We also had Bible studies on Saturday night at the orphanage.

We started going to the local YMCA to swim. Most of us had never seen a pool before let alone knew how to swim. I learned how in a hurry when some of the older boys threw me into the pool because it was my birthday. I remember getting the mumps and poison ivy, which itched, and suffering from very bad sun burn, which blistered and peeled. Some of the bigger boys loved to pick on the smaller ones including my younger brother, Leonard, who was very small for his age. Needless to say, as the older brother I usually ended up in many fights trying to protect him.

I don't remember the year, but Leonard was probably about six-years old and was very anemic. I never did know who authorized the move, but Leonard was sent to the same tuberculosis sanitarium, where our mother had died, and I was sent there to look after him. I don't remember how long we were there, but it was during the cold winter months. Being one of the older boys, I was assigned a bed on the sleeping porch on the second floor. The porch was open with screens, but no windows. Many mornings I would wake up with snow on my bed. Nighttime, before going to bed, we would place a jug, called a "pig", filled with hot water in our beds to help keep us warm. I got in many snow fights during our short stay and have a scar above my upper lip as a daily reminder. I also have a similar scar below my lower lip as a reminder of another event that happened years later at the orphanage.

The backyard at the orphanage was very big, almost as long and wide as a regular football field. I don't remember how we obtained our uniforms and other football equipment, but most of it was very old.

I painted a white stripe on my helmet and played halfback and end because I could run very fast. I don't remember the details, but one year our football team went on to an undefeated season winning ten games and playing a championship game, named the Oatmeal Bowl. We won that game too. During the summer months we used the field for soft ball. We played volleyball, basketball, horse shoes and went roller skating. Sometimes we climbed the trees growing in the front lawn and ate crabapples.

During the cold winter months, I remember it snowed a lot and we would have snowball fights and build igloos. I had my first kiss with a girl in one of those igloos because I lost a bet with some boys. We made our own costumes for Halloween and went bobbing for apples. Someone gave us dance lessons on Saturday afternoons, and I've been enjoying dancing ever since.

Life in the orphanage got much better. A child who had money kept it in a small box with his name on it, locked away in a safe in one of the offices. He could spend it to go to movies on Saturday afternoons if he hadn't been in any trouble during the week. The movie cost 10 cents and candy was 1 cent. About that time, I built my own bicycle out of spare parts and my own '"Soap Box Derby" made from orange crates and broken roller skates. I used the bicycle to get a job delivering groceries. Now I had some money and could go to the movies on Saturdays if I had behaved during the week.

We went to Robert Morris Elementary School, walking two-by-two in a straight line. All the other children knew we were from the JMH orphanage. Before leaving for school, we would all go to the dining room and pick up a brown paper bag which contained our lunch--a peanut butter and jelly sandwich or a bologna sandwich and some fruit. Many times we traded half our peanut butter sandwiches with those who had a jelly sandwich. By now, it was easier for me and I enjoyed school. Then it was on to Alexander Hamilton Junior High School. I liked math and usually received the highest grade and would try harder if someone else received a higher grade.

My liking for classical music started when I enrolled in a music appreciation class in the seventh grade directed by Ms. Scott. I joined a choral group. We put on a Christmas show singing all the favorite songs. Then I joined a school theatrical group. I never did get the male lead. I still remember several of us from the orphanage going to what turned out to be my very first concert. We heard the famous Polish pianist and former Prime Minister, Ignacy Jan Paderewski. In school we would go to the auditorium and listen to the broadcast of the New York Symphony orchestra conducted by Walter Damrosh.

I liked art too. During the seventh grade, I did a black ink and white scratch board sketch of Mt. Rushmore National Memorial with the carved faces of Washington, Jefferson, Theodore Roosevelt and Lincoln by the sculptor Gutzon Borglum and his son Lincoln. The sketch was printed in our year book.

A self-portrait pencil sketch drawn when I was twelve-years old and in the seventh grade was also printed in that year's yearbook. (Unfortunately, I lost all my junior and senior high school yearbooks plus all my college yearbooks when the basement of our home in Mill Valley, California, was flooded.) I learned later that the elder Borglum was a friend of President Theodore Roosevelt. My art teacher, Ms. Hammond, liked the sketch so much that she sent it to the Borglums. Shortly thereafter, we received a letter from Lincoln Borglum thanking us for the drawing and saying that his father had died and that they had framed the sketch and had hung it in their home. I've been trying ever since to make a trip to Mt. Rushmore to see if my sketch is still hanging in their home, which I understand is now a museum.

I became very active in junior high school, not surprising to anyone who knows me now. I ran for ninth grade class president and lost. However, I was the one who ended up taking the prettiest girl in our class to the Prom. I remember trying out for the male lead in a school play called *Sunbonnet Sue.* I did not get the part and ended up playing Sue's father.

Sunday was always visiting day for those of us who had any family. Most of the children were true orphans with no immediate family. Our dad began coming to see us more frequently, a good sign although we didn't know it at the time. Dad was now working full time as the maintenance/engineering supervisor at the tuberculosis sanitarium where our mother had died. Upon my graduation from junior high school, Dad told us he had bought a small house in North Plainfield, NJ, and soon we would all be together again. That was the summer of 1940 and I was fifteen. (On our family trip east in 1976, I drove by this house so my family could see where I lived for a few years after leaving the orphanage and before departing for military service in WWII.)

I graduated early from high school in an accelerated program created for students who were entering the military. I left home in December 1943 for Miami, FL, to begin my Army Air Corp aviation cadet military service program and was honorably discharged in spring 1946. In the fall of that year and not knowing anyone in California, I left home to attend the University of California at Berkeley, where I studied architecture. I became very involved in campus activities and joined Alpha Tau Omega fraternity. In my junior year, I changed my major to business with an emphasis in advertising. I was the first member of my family to go to college. My education was financed by the GI Bill for veterans, with money I saved while in the service and from wages I earned as a waiter in a sorority and from odd jobs. I graduated in spring 1950.

I met my future wife Barbara Jean Towne, a native Californian, at a Christmas party in 1954 in San Francisco. We became engaged three months later and were married at the Grace Cathedral on Nob Hill the next summer. (In jest some of her friends liked to call Barbara "the town marshal.") We moved across the Golden Gate Bridge to our new home in the hills of Mill Valley.

Years later in 1976, I decided to take our family on a combined business/vacation trip to celebrate our country's bi-centennial. After starting in New York City, with a trip to the top of the Statue of Liberty and a boat ride around Staten Island, we headed south with stops in Philadelphia, where I had a business client and Gettysburg before reaching our final destination, Washington, D.C., where my wife Barbara had relatives living in nearby Georgetown. On the way, we stopped in Elizabeth, NJ, and visited the orphanage. I wanted my family to see where I grew up as they had heard the stories for years. It was now a home for girls. On one of the hall walls on the first floor was a plaque listing all the names of former residents who had served in World War II. My name was among those listed. How they knew is still a mystery to me. However, a name that caught my attention was Dick Norton, my former Boy Scout leader and Sunday School teacher. It had a gold star after it, meaning he had died in the service of his country.

I spent forty-seven years in advertising working for an advertising agency, newspaper, television station, and magazine--all in San Francisco before transferring to Southern California in fall 1963. I took charge of the reorganized Los Angeles office of the publishers advertising representative firm Scott, Marshall, McGinley and Doyle, established in 1931. My specialty was representing international publications which started my fondness for traveling the world. Barbara and I with our two daughters moved to our new home overlooking the Pacific Ocean in Palos Verdes Estates. Our older daughter, Beth Ellen, is married to Thomas Lee Jack and they have one daughter, Shelby Leigh, age seventeen. Our younger daughter, Gayle Irene, is married to Charles Randall Barnes, Jr. and they have three children: Katrina, age twenty-one; Brandon, age thirteen; and Brianna, age nine, as of this writing 2011.

Barbara and I lived in Palos Verdes Estates until we moved to University Village in Thousand Oaks, CA, in July 2007. I was selected to become a member of the first University Village Resident Council that fall and privileged to be elected its chairman. In December 2008 Barbara, the love of my life for over fifty-three years, died from cancer two days shy of her birthday, New Year's Day. My family and the many new friends we both had made at University Village helped me through some very difficult days. When my Resident Council term ended in December 2009, I continued to be active as a member of the Activities Committee, serving as the contact with our neighbor California Lutheran University. I also served on the Board of Directors for our Men's Club and as a resident member of the Marketing Department. Daily contact with my many new friends and participating in UVTO events have truly enriched my life.

THE DEPRESSION IS UPON US BY THOMAS MAXWELL

At the time of my birth on June 22, 1924, my father was out summoning the family physician to our home, the Methodist parsonage in Bryantville, Massachusetts. He also had to get to church on time that Sunday for the morning worship service. When he finished seminary the next June, the family moved back to Ohio.

On September 15, 1931, my family moved to Vickory, Ohio, just a few miles from the shores of Lake Erie. I, Thomas J. Maxwell, Jr., had already completed the first grade in Kirkpatrick, Ohio, and had begun my studies in second grade two weeks before the move was announced. At our new home in Western Ohio, both Miriam, my sister, and I continued our learning exercises. The school bus stopped catty-cornered from our home on an unpaved street. The ride was three miles to Township Unified School way out in the country. Usually the bus was full. My seat was sometimes unoccupied because I was so susceptible to colds and earache. It wasn't until after I was married and went to the Cleveland Clinic for a full round of allergy tests, that I understood my morning sickness was the result of post nasal drip brought on by an allergy to house dust, mites, smoke and any kind of smoke including that which came from the furnace. Cold germs breed in mucous that the allergy produces; and coughing, now suspected to arise from acid reflux, forced the infectious germs into my Eustachian tubes leading to inflammation and the proverbial earache.

Now, back to the school bus and the ride to and from school. I remember two specific days. One of those days, my sister and I were not ready when the bus came and it was waved on without us. Finally, fully breakfasted and loaded in Dad's car, we started off. About two miles into the trip, the driver of a utility repair truck, while watching for a break in the electric line, approached us on the wrong side of the road. Dad, Rev. Thomas J. Maxwell, Sr., applied his brakes and we slid on the ice-coated roadbed sideways into the truck. Our car was badly damaged and we three passengers were injured.

As I remember it, the school janitor's house was just down the road and we were helped there and comfortably seated in chairs hastily moved into the front room. The country doctor was summoned. Dad was injured and unable to rotate his head. My sister, Miriam, could not move her right arm. I seemed fine and was asked if I would like to go on to school. Dad and Miriam returned home to recuperate.

"Fine" was not the right word. I was severely shaken and most likely also in emotional shock. I declined the offer to be chauffeured the remaining half-mile to school and removed my hat to settle in to wait for the doctor's arrival. When I removed my hat, I discovered that it was full of blood. That certainly cancelled school for the day. There was a gash on the top of my head on the right side; the bleeding had stopped, but my hair was clotted with a bright red substance known thereabouts as blood. Blood indicated that I was not all right. The only treatment I received was a splash of alcohol on the wound.

Nearly a week later, perhaps two weeks, the doctor was summoned again; but this time a different, more discerning physician came. Dad's neck was giving him trouble. He was put to bed with a strap around his forehead. The strap was tied to a brick, which hung over the head of the bed. It was to keep his neck stretched and immobile while the two injured vertebras healed.

Miriam's arm was now strapped to her body to keep her from moving her shoulder until her clavicle healed. Its being broken disabled her use of the arm entirely. She wore that strap for several weeks.

My head wound had become infected. The doctor diagnosed the problem as "proud" flesh. I was stretched out on the bed and a portion of my hair was shaved. So far, the treatment had not been painful. The family gathered around while the good doctor poured nitric acid into the wound. It sizzled and steamed. I made not a murmur. The infected flesh dissolved away. The wound bled and was bandaged. The next morning I was sent off to school with my quite visible head wrapping. It took a while but the infection had been defeated and I lived to tell the tale.

Another trip to school that I also remember was the day when I was not on the bus when it returned to Vickory. Needless to say, my mother, Margaret, was quite concerned. "What had happened and where was Thomas?" she asked. It was simple: I had remained at school to watch a high school soccer game on the field behind the school. The suggestion to attend the event had been made by one of the fellows in my class, but it meant that we would not be on the bus going home. I had not foreseen that problem. Eventually, the game ended and the problem was solved. We simply walked home. It wasn't far. The railroad tracks were easy to follow.

What! We walked the railroad tracks? What did we do when a train passed by? Did we encounter any Knights of the Road--hobos along the way? Who was with us? None of these questions had ever entered our heads. We watched for trains and handcars and if and when needed, we simply intended to move off the tracks and wait for the freight train to pass by. Bums didn't walk the tracks late in the afternoon. We didn't even imagine a problem and certainly expected to arrive home safe and sound. Why should anyone be worried about two little boys hiking through the fields? I try not to remember missing the bus, nor the day the teacher would not allow me to leave the room when I held up the two fingers of desperation. I'm not even certain I have told the story right when I wrote it seventy-five years later.

I also have almost forgotten my first platform experience. I narrated a poem and ended with an audible bow from the waist, like any professional performer might do silently. Clearly and audibly, I spoke, "Bow!"

Missing the bus was not the only excitement that occurred during our stay in Vickory. The house next door to the parsonage stood empty for a spell; but towards spring, it became filled with young Filipino men, who had come to work in the beet fields. As I remember there were fourteen of them when they moved into the house. That spring and summer, I often played tennis with them on the court at the Methodist church in the next block. It might have been that I was invited to join them because I had an in with the pastor of the church, my father, and their being on the courts would thus not be questioned as long as my presence was recognized.

The Filipinos, I believe, had found a real bargain. It was in the early years of the Great Depression. That rental house cost them 50 cents apiece each month; I do not know how much they earned weeding sugar beets but certainly, it was at least 50 cents per day.

One fine day the fellows brought home a baby Barred Owl also known as a Hoot Owl, which they had found in a nest in a hollow tree they had come upon while frolicking at the beach. It was just a few miles from Vickory to Lake Erie. They asked me to take care of the bird because they knew I was interested in pets. I didn't even know that owls ate mice, but I tried my best. We took a photo of the baby owl perched on the back of a toy chair not much bigger than the owl. It lived a month or so before expiring from starvation or from the effects of the diet I thought would sustain it.

The next year, after the beet field hands moved on, a family occupied the

house next door. My thoughts go back to the day one of my rabbits escaped and was spotted under the front porch of that house. I was trying to entice it out into the open when the neighbor man, attempting to help, threw an unripe pear at the rabbit hoping to frighten it into running out from under the crawl space. The pear hit the rabbit on the head and it dropped dead. Rabbits are like that; sometimes when a dog frightens a rabbit, it will jump up and do a sharp spin in the air breaking its own neck. All of this I tearfully reported to my parents that same afternoon. Later on, I was somewhat appeased by the fact that my warren of bunnies multiplied during the year from two to one hundred. During one cold spate that winter, many of them froze to death. Their only protection from the cold was the heat generated by a bin of corncobs in the other half of the shed. If the cobs had been accessible, the rabbits might have bored into the pile and been protected. Actually the ones, that did survive, did so by burrowing into a pile of corncobs which had spilled over from the other half of the shed.

We lived but one block from the grain mill. Along the tracks, trucks brought in the grain to be milled during the summer and stacks of coal lined the railroad right-of-way during the winter. I was paid one cent for each bucket and a nickel for a wagonload of corncobs that I brought home and deposited in the rabbit shed. We used the cobs to start the fire in the Heatarola each winter day.

Usually, I was first up in the morning. That partly resulted from the fact that I was sent to bed each evening soon after the daylight subsided. There was no television. There was not even a radio to listen to and we could not afford a Victrola to play the latest musical hits. The folks used the lantern to read by and the children were tucked into bed with a hot brick to warm their feet soon after supper was eaten. We called it supper, not dinner, in those days and in that place.

As a result of my early rising, I often started the fire in the stove as soon as I was dressed. We placed a bucketful of corncobs in the body of the stove, added a little kerosene and threw in a match. One evening, my mother, fearing my handling of kerosene, decided to pour the liquid fuel on the cobs in the bucket ready for the morning fire lighting. I lit the match, the way my father usually did and placed it on the cobs, then proceeded to throw the entire bucketful into the belly of the stove as he always did. Having been wet with kerosene the night before, the cobs stuck to the bucket and did not fly in a wad into the stove, but fell out as the bucket swung back in an arc. I scattered burning cobs all over the floor of the room. Needless to say, the entire household was up and at-em that morning. The flaming cobs were swept up and scooped into the stove on a dustpan and the house didn't burn.

My dad was a champion horseshoe player and had a court where he played the neighborhood men on occasion. I constructed a miniature horseshoe court alongside his, and the neighborhood boys tested their skills against mine many an afternoon after school or during the summer evenings. There was that notable day when I was being punished for having wandered off on some adventure without having apprised my mother of my doings. The punishment was for me to remain in my room until suppertime. I stood at the second story window and watched my friends play horseshoes without me, using my court and my dad's shoes. What pain! In retrospect, it seems the worst punishment I ever endured. I begged for a paddling so that I could return to the court and be with my friends.

How could a parent be so mean? Nevertheless, I survived the ordeal and the next year gave up horseshoes for archery.

Water seemed to stand out in my mind at every home we inhabited. Our source in Vickory was an artesian well located just outside the grain mill. We had no well. We used water collected from the roof by metal spouting and stored in the cistern under the back of the house. The pump had to be primed. We kept a pitcher of water close by the kitchen sink to pour into the pump each time we wanted to raise a pan full or a tub full from the cistern. Cistern water was used for bathing and for cooking. Drinking water had to come from a germ-free source. An Artesian spring poured sulfur-flavored water continuously just across the tracks at the grain mill. It was my job to keep the house supplied with water. Have you ever tasted sulfur water? It often accompanies an oil well. Ours had no hydrocarbon, but it was well-flavored with sulfur. A few years ago on a caravan to Baja del Sur, I discovered that I had developed a strong allergy to sulfur-cured dried fruit. How do you suppose that happened? Three blocks the other direction, one of the Methodist parishioners had a sweet-water well, which had been made available to us. Once or twice a week. Dad walked over there and brought back a pail full.

It was at Vickory that I returned home one evening with what must have seemed like a slit throat. I had been flying my homemade kite in an open field nearby. Sometimes, I could get it so high it used up two balls of string. This particular day I fell while crossing the barb wire fence and received a deep gash just below my jugular, or was it the carotid? I was bleeding so profusely that my mother, upon seeing me when I reached the back door, declared that I had been punished enough for running away that day and that I would not be confined to my room a second time.

The street was not paved, but there was a cement sidewalk on our side. A favorite entertainment was watching baby buggies, wagons, scooters, and velocipedes parade along that sidewalk. Because I owned the only wagon, I often led the parade by pulling the wagon with a couple of smaller children in it. I was also able to pull a tricycle by attaching a rope to the back of the wagon. Sometimes there were ten or more playmates in the lineup.

At the far end of the street that ran by our house was a swamp, where we wee lads occasionally went exploring, without parental permission. I remember spending several hours one day trying to start a fire by friction as we huddled in a circle at the edge of the swamp learning outdoor skills. We made smoke but never an open flame.

The boy up the street missed many days of school one year; it set him back a year. He had cut his foot on a nail in that swamp and contracted lock jaw. He was at death's door for weeks, it seemed. I never returned to the swamp after his unfortunate experience.

I broke my nose while living in Vickory. My dad tried to pick me up by the ankles as he would do with Miriam. I did not keep my knees stiff and fell forward onto a red-hot register above the furnace nine feet below.

Santa found us in Vickory at Christmas of 1932. My grandmother, Martha Arnold, and her other daughter, Aunt Grace, came to visit. The tree stood in the parlor, which during the winter was normally shut off from the rest of the house to save heating costs. Dad left the room. Suddenly, there was a noise outside the front door and then a knock although it was still early in the morning. Mr. Claus, Kris Kringle, was invited in pulling a brand new wagon behind. Without a word, he unloaded the wagon and placed a pile of presents under the tree; then still silent, he left the room. Dad was there when I claimed the wagon and Miriam unwrapped whatever it was that she had received. My brother, Paul, was still too young to understand, but he surely was present for this one and only real live visit by Santa, the idol of childhood dreams. I didn't believe the visitor was from the North Pole, but I assumed that the folks had made arrangements for an impersonator to make a costumed appearance. I appreciated the effort taken to make Christmas so exciting.

When it rained anytime after Memorial Day, the ditch around the front and side yard would fill with water. That ditch was our own private swimming hole, and both Miriam and I loved to roll in it whatever the temperature. We did, however, observe that rule: no swimming or going barefoot until after May 30.

I was visiting the home of a friend my own age one afternoon. His father showed me their new batch of puppies and asked if I would like one. It would cost $1.50. Surely, I wanted the pup but I had no money. Two or three weeks later, I visited the family again and the man asked why I had not come to claim my dog. I explained the money problem, and he gave me the pup for nothing. My mother was not pleased but acquiesced to my having a pet. I trained that dog to play dead, to jump through a hoop, to roll over, and to fetch. I had my bosom buddy for more than a year into the next move.

The Chicago World's Fair occurred during the time we lived in Vickory. I remember learning, just the day before my father was to leave for Chicago, of his impending trip. A young man from the church was to go with him to share expenses. I had not been included! Learning this set me off on the finest presentation of self-assertiveness I ever made. I pled and argued like an experienced debater. The next morning I was packed and in the back seat of Dad's car when he began his journey. This story deserves a document of its own, and someday it too will be put on paper.

I have a faint memory of a time when Miriam, Paul, Mother, and I stayed in Warren for a week while Dad drove home to preach the Sunday sermon. When we returned home later that week by train, we learned that our car was in the repair shop. Dad had turned the car over, by dropping off the pavement and turning too sharply to recover. He had not been hurt but the car rolled over. The wound he sported when we saw him on our return had been inflicted by the family cat, which had scratched him on the wrist.

In mid-September 1933 we left Vickory and moved east nearly to the Ohio River. Our new home was Rogers and that is where my most glorious years of childhood were celebrated. I was twelve-years-old and mature enough to enjoy a wide range of activities. I hiked and fished in summer, made my own small golf course and challenged my friends with swords made from black mustard stalks. From Rogers, we moved to Brilliant and then to Akron. I graduated from high school and entered Mount Union College. After eight months I was drafted for three years in the Army Air Corps. I became an airplane mechanic, a navigator, and finally a flight engineer on the largest plane then in service, the B-29.

After the army, I completed my undergraduate studies at Wooster College in Ohio. There I met Ruth Lautzenheiser, and we were married on June 25, 1950. I earned graduate degrees in anthropology including a PhD from Indiana University. We spent nine years in San German, Puerto Rico, where I taught at the Inter American University.

Our next assignment was at California Lutheran University in Thousand Oaks, California, where we remained for twenty-one years. During this time I accepted visiting professorships in the United States, Europe, and South America. I also led or participated in archaeological expeditions in Puerto Rico, Peru, Honduras, India, Spain, France, and Israel to name a few. I retired from CLU in 1986, but I continued to accept part time positions and join archaeological expeditions.

In Thousand Oaks, I served as a naturalist for the Conejo Recreation and Park District. I was a founding member and first president of the Conejo Audubon Society. I was a founding member of the Conejo Nature Preserve and served on the Conejo Future Canyons' Study, which led to the creation of Conejo Open Space Cooperative Agreement. In addition I completed one hundred archaeological surveys for developers as part of required environmental reports to protect historical relics before they could break ground on their projects.

In September 2007 we planned to move to University Village, but Ruth was denied entrance when the facility was finally completed. She moved to Thousand Oaks Royal to await the opening of Oak View's assisted living units. A year later, she was again denied entrance. She died of Parkinson's Disease in January 2009.

Our three children remain: Linda Maxwell Case of Sun Valley, NV; Susan Maxwell Smith of FL, and David Maxwell of Westby, WI. Our four grandchildren are: Rachel and Rebecca Maxwell and Austin and Cody Smith. Our great-granddaughter is Sara Smith.

GROWING UP IN THE 1930'S BY CHARLES R. MORTENSEN

My first nine-and-one-half years up to March 1933 introduced me to life as a city kid in Los Angeles on Sycamore Avenue between Beverly Boulevard and First Street. We lived in a two story, four-flat apartment building my father built, one of several he constructed on Sycamore.   My birth certificate from the Hollywood Hospital, where I, Charles Richard Mortensen, was born   October 18, 1924, indicates that my mother, Alma Elizabeth Mortensen (nee Anderson), a housewife, was born in Sweden, and that my father's trade was that of a cement worker.   How he, Charles Adolph Mortensen, advanced from that occupation to that of a contractor I do not know. He had been born and raised with a sister in Chicago, Illinois, went to Hyde Park High School, and had worked as a shoe salesman in the family store, "Mortensen and Son."   He served in the army Quartermaster Corps during World War I and while he never went to France, he did contract influenza, a disease, which required a convalescent period of some duration.

Mother's father had come to Illinois initially attracted by railroad job opportunities, but soon after his marriage he became a dairy farmer.   My grandparents returned to Sweden, where they resumed farming; but after mother was born, they determined that farming offered more opportunities back in the United States. They returned to the Geneva/Batavia area of Illinois, where other relatives lived, and began the demanding dairy farming life. That farm is no longer in the family, but two of my cousins who were born and raised there, live just across the street. Visiting family members are still welcome to tour the old Italianate farm home, barn, and other outbuildings.

Mother attended the nearby one-room school house with her younger brother and sister, learned how to be a telephone operator, and before too long made her way to business school in Chicago, where she lived with a cousin, and soon was employed as a bookkeeper for a small coal company. It was during this time that she met my father, and they were married in 1922. The lure of the West and the attraction of a milder climate than the Chicago winters soon brought them to Los Angeles.

Apparently, my father earned a profitable living as a contractor; he could take the time to enjoy golf--his high school sport--hunt deer and ducks, trout fish with creel and fly-rod, become a Shriner, buy into a ten-acre orange grove, own a four-door Studebaker, and later a Packard motor car. Family car trips taken to the Sierras and June Lake introduced us to camping, fishing, and the out-of-doors. Mother was the homemaker, and in 1929 my brother, Norman Lee, was born.   I entered Third Street Elementary. There in kindergarten I learned I was left-handed when I could not get the "dumb" scissors to cut a piece of paper.

When I complained, the teacher observing me said simply, "Try using your other hand." Well, that was a simple solution that did not always help with other left–handed tasks, especially when it came to learning handwriting with pen and ink. This pleasant time of roller-skating around the block, learning to ride a bicycle, walking even skating by myself to

Happy Days

the Saturday matinee at the Ritz Theater on Wilshire and La Brea, obtaining a library card, playing "kick the can" of a summer's evening with the other kids on the block, and soaping window screens on Halloween evening ended in March of 1933 at the time of the Long Beach earthquake, one readily felt on Sycamore that afternoon.

By then financial fortunes for my father reversed. He managed, however, with some financial assistance from my maternal grandfather to move our family to the new house he built on an acre-and-a-quarter on Sherman Way, just east of Sepulveda Boulevard in Van Nuys, a semi-rural farming community in the San Fernando Valley.

What a change for me and my little brother, from city kids to rural kids, but we certainly were not alone. Like many other families, as soon as possible my folks started a vegetable garden, planted fruit trees, and began raising white leghorns chickens for egg production.

My father erected two long chicken pens, each comprising four separate pens, with a total capacity for 2,000 chickens.

We even added a small enclosure for mother's Bantam chicks. I soon learned the farm chores, sometimes not so willingly, of weeding and irrigating the garden, gathering eggs, raising baby chicks, culling the runts, and helping where I could. With no fences separating houses, I easily became acquainted with neighbors who seemed not to object to my trek through the backyards plinking away at times with my BB gun.

My mother's skills learned as farm girl enabled her to cook, sew, mend, preserve fruit, bottle grape juice from the Concord grape arbor, and candle eggs for brooding. A small cellar accessed from outside the back porch provided extra storage for preserves, and a utility room off the kitchen held our icebox. How we kids in the neighborhood looked forward to the arrival of the Union Ice truck and those slivers of ice that fell from the block when the iceman chipped out the delivery for the homes. One summer my father fermented enough Concord grape juice to produce a small oak keg of wine. Drinking a small glass of this wine with him was a special treat after working with him to clean the chicken roosting and nesting areas. During these years we always had pet dogs and cats on our chicken ranch; we had never before owned pets until we moved here.

Van Nuys was rural enough and the Depression deep enough that many children, boys especially, went barefoot in elementary school. I cannot recall that the girls did. I wore Keds (tennis shoes) to school, but to be one of the boys, I would take them off once I arrived and put them on again for my homeward journey. Teachers had to be tolerant of dirty smelly feet. The Long Beach earthquake damaged some of the school buildings in Van Nuys, and during the reconstruction time we attended class in wooden-sided canvas-covered tents. Double sessions were required for a time; and early morning class time could be cold, while in spring and fall, warmer days called for rolling up the side panels to circulate air.

By the time I reached Van Nuys High in 1936, a six-year school, grades 7-12, the boys knew enough, no matter how poor, to wear shoes, and gratefully, for many, the showers and foot baths required at the conclusion of physical education brought us a sense of cleanliness as we went to the next class. We wore what we had, but many of us proudly came to school attired in corduroy or colorfully patterned shirts sewn by our mothers.

During those depression years for me and perhaps for many others, school provided a refuge. At our schools, in both elementary and high, few of us had more in the way of possessions than anyone else. To one degree or another we all came from homes troubled by difficult economic circumstances; we shared in a social milieu where no one was too much better off than the next classmate, and for many we were still very much a part of the American melting pot.

My 25 cent weekly allowance provided me ice cream money at the school cafeteria. Like most of my friends, I brown-bagged my lunch with my sandwiches snug in Weber's brown or blue gingham bread wrappers. I do recall one of my friends frequently eating his daily lunch of mustard and onion sandwiches. My family never went hungry during this time, for food was always on the table. However, I clearly recall the odor of stewed chicken and chicken soup wafting from the kitchen stove, neither one a favorite, but dishes that helped stretch the food pantry. Potato soup never excited my palate either, and today these dishes still do not whet my appetite.

Life was simple for me on Sherman Way. We were several miles from downtown Van Nuys, which was easily accessed by riding the Pacific Electric Red Car. The tracks stretched from Canoga Park to Van Nuys down the middle of Sherman Way. On rare occasions we could look forward to the big adventure of riding the Red Car all the way to downtown Los Angeles. I could walk or ride my bicycle to high school, and for one year I was eligible to ride the school bus to the elementary school.

Summertime wear during the day called for a shirt, shorts, and Keds, and not always the shirt or the Keds. I learned how to swim at the Crystal Plunge, a privately owned pool on Kester Avenue about a mile from home. The 25 cents earned cutting our lawn provided my entrance fee. The admission to the theater in Van Nuys cost all of 10 cents for those of us under twelve, a price I paid well into my thirteenth year since my adolescent growth spurt came late.

Soon I learned to assuage the warm summer nights in the San Fernando Valley by sleeping outside. My first summer had me placing my camp cot and army blanket next to the dining room French doors, for I did not want to be too far from the safety of the house. Summers that followed found me behind the family garage sleeping on the cot in our camping tent and later on that same camp cot with a sleeping bag in the grape arbor, where on occasion in late summer I could reach out to gather a cluster of grapes. To add to my comfort I set my crystal set on a box next to the cot so I could listen to the Pacific Coast Angels play night baseball and hear the Friday night fights at Legion Stadium.

While my father worked our chicken ranch--ours was one of many in the San Fernando Valley, he searched for construction jobs to add to the family income. On one occasion he contracted to build a home for a friend in the Hollywood Hills. Finally, through the Works Progress Administration (WPA) during the mid 1930's and later with the United States Engineering Department (USED) he secured permanent work. Initially, these jobs related to building check dams and flood control channels. In 1933-34 and in 1936 severe flooding occurred in the San Fernando Valley with the loss of homes and life. My father was a part of this government effort to prevent a recurrence of this tragedy.

The family still took vacation time even driving in the Packard during the month of January 1937 to visit relatives in Illinois, the first introduction for my young brother and me to snow and ice as we made our way through Oklahoma and Missouri. Even though I was visiting my grandparents, Chicago proved to be a disappointment for there was no snow to play in. However, at the dairy farm I did slide down the iced barn ramp from the hayloft on a big corn scoop shovel. Farm kids did have some fun.

For several summers my father took us to the Carpenteria beach campgrounds for a week at a time. He would commute on weekends. Enjoying the sun, body surfing, swimming, and surf fishing, with the added bonus of sharing these good times with a friend, ensured endless days of fun for me. When he could take a vacation, Dad would drive to deer country, and frequently I could go with him. More than once venison added to our larder. Years later my brother and I joined him in what turned out to be his last hunt, but a fond memory nevertheless.

Church life figured in our family as well. Not only did I become acquainted with the girl who became my first big date on my eighteenth birthday and my only true girlfriend there, but membership in the Van Nuys Methodist Church provided me the opportunity to join with several of my chums the church sponsored Troop 1, Boy Scouts of America.

Several of us reached the rank of Eagle, and I believe my camping experience with family, the scout training, and my church membership prepared me far more than I might have anticipated for my thirty-five months in the army. I served a major portion of that time in the 42nd "Rainbow" Infantry Division with five of those months in combat duty during the final combat stages of the war in Europe through France, Germany and Austria.

By the late 1930's and very early 1940's the economy had improved. No longer were hoboes coming to the door at Sherman Way to exchange several hours of work around the yard or chicken pens for a meal. Our poultry enterprise in any case had ended by then. Employment of many sorts became available, from CCC camps to the beginning of military draft service, to manufacturing, and to the awareness that the United States might soon become the arsenal for the allies. Lockheed in Burbank began the construction of the P-38, and on many days flew test planes over Van Nuys. Uniformed military were to be seen everywhere. The December 7, 1941, attack on Pearl Harbor suddenly became that seminal event that changed the course of events for all of us. Blackouts were enforced over the city of Los Angeles. I enrolled in UCLA in July of 1942, and by April of 1943, I was in the U. S. Army. The Great Depression years faded, people focused on confronting the tyranny of the war, and our country took on a mantle of world leadership that had not been ours before.

After the war in 1946, I married my high school sweetheart, Martha Ellen Mollett and completed my degree at U.C.L.A. I began a thirty-five year career with the Los Angeles City School District, from teacher to counselor, vice-principal, culminating as a junior high principal. Blessed with a son and a daughter, Martha and I were fortunate to live in our first Canoga Park G.I. home on a half an acre with seven walnut trees. We harvested the walnuts and sold the extra to family and friends.

With our family we visited our National Parks enjoying camping, fishing, and skiing. We are the proud grandparents of seven grandchildren and twelve great-grandchildren. We later moved to Northridge and after forty-two years there, we learned of University Village and moved there in August of 2007. We enjoy our new friends and easily keep busy with the wide variety of activities here at UVTO. Our move has been a no regret transition.

FROM THE BARN TO THE BOARDROOM BY JOHN O'DONOGHUE

I was born June 28, 1929, in Emmitsburg, Maryland, at home in a farm house, eighty-three days before the great stock market crash. At that time, our home was a big two-story fieldstone house with walls two-feet-thick and a metal roof. The house had two staircases, a central heating furnace, a telephone with a party line, hot and cold running water and a bathroom with a tub. We had a Chrysler Touring car, a refrigerator and a pony. My mother, Dorothy Mary Gloninger O'Donoghue, had a cook and a maid; and my father, David Allen O'Donoghue, had "farm hands" to operate the dairy farm, one of the best in the county. My father was a "gentleman farmer." This all ended, and in 1935 the farm and house were sold at public auction. The pony, touring car and just about everything else were gone-- even my father's shotgun. After the sale, we should have moved out, but we stayed in the house for about a year. The electricity was shut off, and I clearly remember my oldest sister cooking and using a coal oil lamp for lighting.

In 1936, the family was split up. All my older brothers and sisters went to live with grandparents and/or aunts and uncles. I am the seventh of thirteen, but at that time there were only twelve. The rest of us moved into a very small one-bedroom house on the side

of a mountain in the village of Sabillasville with a population of about two hundred people. The rent was $10 a month. It had electricity but no running water or bathroom. The outhouse was in the backyard. The well was usually "dry" or contaminated and I had to get water by the bucket from the neighbors. Our closest neighbor had a well about thirty feet from our back porch, but refused to let us have any. Sometimes others also refused, and I had to walk farther to find water. It wasn't until years later that I figured out why some neighbors refused us water. Our former home town, Emmitsburg, was predominately a Catholic place. The population was only about five hundred, but it had two Catholic colleges plus two Catholic churches. We were the only Catholic family in our new village.

About a year after our move, one day I went to play at a nearby classmate's house. Shortly thereafter, another neighborhood boy joined us in the barn where we were playing. (Barns were very important as they sheltered horses which many people used for transportation. There were only five cars in town.) Very shortly, I realized that I was in a bad spot--there were two of them, both bigger than I. The guys started whispering to themselves, excluding and ignoring me. Sensing trouble, without delay, I decided it was better to run than fight. As I was jumping over a wall, I felt a sharp pain in my butt. I had been stabbed! The father of the second boy was allegedly a member of the KKK. Some years later I heard the man bragging to others, in my presence, about keeping "undesirables" out of town. I now believe we were refused water because we were Catholics. I do not believe it was the individual neighbor's idea to refuse us water, but each acted out of fear and pressure from a few very prejudiced people. Anyway, I ran home bleeding and crying to tell my father. He looked down the road and seeing no one coming, did nothing. There were no telephones or police to call to report the incident. I did not go to a doctor. Thank God I decided to run rather than fight or my life might have been very short. From that day forward, our family stayed home all the time except when I went to the store for food, or to a neighbor's place for water, or to get milk from a dairy. We children did attend the local four-room school. My father went to work, and he and I walked two miles each way to Sunday Mass. For about four years my mother almost never went beyond the front porch.

Our living conditions were primitive. There was no central heating; we used a "chunk" stove--kind of like a wood-burning pot belly stove that only slightly heated the living room. We no longer had a telephone or a car. When I mentioned *electricity* earlier, I meant that there was one electric outlet in the entire house and one light bulb in each room. We had an icebox on the back porch but no way to get any ice. By the way, we never had any leftovers to keep anyway. My mother and father slept in a bed at one end of the bedroom. Then there was a crib for the baby and all the rest of us slept in the second bed. The room was like a loft about 8 by 20 feet and with virtually no heat.

My father got a job as a timekeeper with the WPA that paid $56 a month. The project where he worked is now known as Camp David, the country retreat of the President of the United States, located in Maryland about sixty miles northwest of Washington, D.C. WPA stands for Works Project Administration, one of President Franklin Roosevelt's attempts to pull the country out of the Great Depression. For us, 1937 was the worst year of the Depression. The WPA job ran out; and my father, a college graduate, was out of work for a time until he got a job at a "Grit Mill," handling 100-pound bags of ground rock.

My mother had been raised to be a rich man's wife and did not cope well with the situation. At the age of seven, with all the maids and older children gone, all the chores fell to me. I not only got the water but emptied the commode, did most of the *cooking* and almost all the other house work that was done--very little!! I also chopped most of the wood for the stoves and kept the fire going. My mother did do the laundry and some ironing.   There was no "wash and wear."   I had to bring in the water and empty the wringer-type washing machine.   Since there was no dryer, I usually hung the laundry outside on the clothesline to dry, and in winter the clothes often froze.

The *cooking* mentioned above was very limited.   The very small local store did not have a refrigerator and did not sell fresh meat or anything that needed refrigeration.   The stock consisted mostly of canned vegetables, Campbell's soups, potatoes, hominy and rice.   With no meat, *cooking* was boiling rice and potatoes and heating canned vegetables and soup.

Four evenings a week, I would walk about a quarter-of-a-mile to a local farm to get two quarts of raw milk at 7 cents a quart; neither pasteurized nor refrigerated, a total of eight quarts a week for all of us.   For breakfast, after I started a wood fire, I usually cooked old-fashioned oatmeal, not the instant or one-minute kind Monday through Saturday.   On Sunday we had bacon and eggs--one pound of bacon and one dozen eggs at 15 cents a dozen--neither was refrigerated.

By the way, at age seven, I also bought the groceries six days a week.   I was only allowed to spend $1 each week day, but $3 on Saturday, which included purchases for Sunday.   Included in that dollar was 10 cents for a pack of cigarettes for my father.   I guess this was my first exposure to accounting!   I was too young to question why 10 per cent of our meager food budget was being spent on cigarettes--"drugs." Virtually, all men smoked in those years and I never questioned why.

Life for my father and mother had been and was very hard.   In today's world, I believe that they would have been diagnosed with clinical depression.   They just kind of gave up on life and accepted things, as they believed they could not do anything to improve their situation.   Although I did hear my father sing two or three times, I never heard my mother sing.   During my childhood, my father only once played sports with me for about twenty minutes when I insisted.   Most of the time from 1940 to 1947, my father worked in Baltimore and only came home on weekends.   Sometimes, when there was overtime, he would not be home for two or more weeks; and I was the "man of the house."

Two childhood experiences profoundly affected me. During the summertime, we went barefooted except for church on Sunday mornings.   In 1939, when I was to begin fourth grade, I did not have any shoes for school, so I was given a pair of my older sister's shoes to wear.   I was able to get the small bows off the toes but could not cut down the heels, which were about an inch high. It was a pretty tough time for a fourth grader, classmates can be very cruel.

I was born with about 20/80 eyesight. In school I sat in the front row but still had to walk up to read the blackboard. Our four-room school had no health facilities and the few notes I took home went unanswered. This made school very hard. Since I had such an eye problem, I was very poor in sports that used a ball. I could not see it until it almost hit me. Although I was quite quick (to some extent because of my eye problem), the only sports I did OK in were track and dodge ball--where good eyesight was not so important.

Some five years later, I returned to visit the neighbor boy whose friend had stabbed me years before. We played out in the yard for about an hour and then his mother came out and called us in for dinner. I was shocked--*his* mother fixed dinner and cleaned up afterwards! I went home and told my mother she had to prepare the meals because I was not going to cook anymore. This was met with great resistance from both my mother and father.

I rebelled; and having lived in a family in disarray for the past five years, I ran away from home. My parents had been talking about sending me to "reform" school. I first went to my Grandmother's. She had a lovely home. After two weeks, my aunt, a wonderful lady, and also my godmother told me I had to go back because my mother needed me to care for my younger brothers and sisters. Reluctantly, I returned to experience another very stormy year.

That summer when I was twelve, I ran away again to work on a dairy farm about four miles from home. We worked seven days a week, for the cows had to be milked and the manure cleaned out every day. I usually was delegated manure chores. The farmer, his son and I worked about twelve hours Monday to Friday, ten on Saturday and six to seven on Sunday. I had my own room and ate well, but did not know what my pay was to be. After six weeks, the farmer finally told me I would be paid $2 a week (a total of $12 for the six weeks); but he only gave me 50 cents, owing me the rest. I now think he thought that because the pay was so low, I would have just quit and walked away if he had paid me the whole $12.

He finally did pay me and that enabled me to buy my first pair of glasses. The exam and the glasses together cost $15--seven and a half weeks pay for me. I will never forget the first time I saw clouds! I stared at them for hours. With my glasses I suddenly became pretty good at sports, which I have continued throughout my life. (I ran 20 miles in under 4 hours at sixty-five and carried a bowling average of over 200 in my seventies.) Remember that 10 cents a day we spent for my father's cigarettes? It would have paid for my glasses in about five months.

Since I was such a hard worker, the farmer continued to pay me $2 a week during the school year. I worked before and after school and on weekends, about 45 hours a week. In the morning, I caught a four-mile ride to the school bus stop on the milk delivery truck, then a seven-mile ride by bus to the school. In the afternoon I had to walk the four miles back to the farm. In my second year of high school, I missed thirty-four days. I got paid $1 for each day I took off to work. I nearly flunked out. For the first two years of high school, I was the "anchor" man in my class since I had the lowest passing grades of any one that passed. Only one boy was below me and he flunked. The last week of school the farmer bought automatic milking machines. Since I had fewer cows to milk, he cut my pay for that one week to $1. That was the second low point in my working career. After school was out, he resumed paying me $2 because I worked fulltime, about 75 hours a week.

I remember after work one evening standing with the farmer on the edge of a fifteen-acre field that was to be harvested the next day, when the community combine was scheduled to come to cut and harvest the grain. It was the major crop of the year. Looking to the distance, we noticed some small clouds on the horizon. Within one hour, a thunder storm with high winds blew in and the entire field of wheat was flat on the ground--a total loss. Farm life can be very hard.

About 1945 I returned to live at home with my family. I continued to work on the farm on weekends. In 1947 when I was seventeen, I graduated from high school. I was able to buy my first suit from Montgomery Ward's catalog for $15 of my savings. And I proudly wore it to graduation.

I was pretty much a mountain "bumpkin." I must have been pretty smart, and I'm sure I was very aggressive; but with no social or people skills, life was a big challenge for me. During my teens, I never went to a party, I never had a date, danced or kissed a girl. Through all this time, I never thought that we were poor. I knew that my grandmothers were rich. They never came to our house, and we rarely went to their homes. We did not have a car and they lived about eleven miles away. I never knew either of my grandfathers as they had died earlier. My father and mother never visited my mother's mother's home and only visited my father's mother's home about five times during the eleven years we lived in Sabillasville

On a positive note, my father and mother did teach us some very valuable skills. First, they taught us proper English. In a very small mountain town saying *ain't,* and misusing *I* and *me* and *teach and learn,* etc. were common in everyday language. They also instilled in me a very strong respect for being honest and the importance of doing what is right. These values have been very helpful and important to me in both my professional life and private life.

By the way, nobody ever moved into our Emmitsburg home after we were evicted. The last time I saw it only the 18-inch-stone portion of the walls were left. Most of the

doors and windows were rotted and the metal roof had collapsed into the basement.

After my graduation from high school in 1947, the family moved to Baltimore and I went with them. Now, after about seven years, my father was home for dinner each day; so our family life was much improved. My father was working as a carpenter, and he and my mother, thankfully, were in a much better state of mind.

I had various jobs including working in a tomato canning factory, as a soda jerk and as a gas station attendant--usually for about $20 a week. About this time I went to live with my older brother, David Allen, Jr., and his wife, Gloria Dulom, to whom I am eternally grateful. Gradually, our family life and my relationship with my parents vastly improved and our family bond remained throughout the rest of their lives.One day while riding on a trolley car in Baltimore, I picked up a book of matches and opened it up; it read: "Be an accountant, go to Eastern College." Eastern College was a very small business school with absolutely no social activities--it was purely business. I had never had any kind of career counseling and my attempts to talk with my father were quickly rejected and he discouraged anything I suggested doing. When I told him that I had quit my gas station job and was working as a junior accounting clerk and studying accounting a night, he warned me about "putting all my eggs in one basket." He did not encourage me at all.

From 1952 to 1954, my studies were interrupted by my service in the Marine Corps during the Korean "Police Action." I was stationed at the Opa-locka Air Station, an old Navy base about ten miles north of Miami, Florida. Somehow the officer in charge of the Officers Club, learned that I had some accounting training and so he put me, an NCO, in charge of running the bookkeeping department of five employees for the Officers Club. This was a lucky break for me; I was handling a complete set of books. During this time I met Mary Taylor of Miami, and we were married in the USMC chapel in July 1954.

After my tour of duty ended, we returned to Baltimore, where I again enrolled in Eastern College. When I graduated in 1959, I was the father of four children. I was the only one from my family of thirteen to finish college. Only my wife came to my graduation. There were about ninety students in the class that had started in 1949, but I was the only one to get a CPA. Happily, this time I finished first in my class contrasted to being the "anchor man" in my first two years of high school. All my classes were at night; I worked to support my family and paid most of the costs. I did receive some veteran's benefits during the last few years. Paying my own way was a big incentive to studying hard.

I still wonder what would have happened if that book of matches had said, "Be a barber or a mechanic or a doctor or an engineer?" But I am very thankful for how things worked out. My career was long in both time and distance, lasting fifty-two years and went from cleaning out cow stalls to the boardrooms of NYSE companies in Manhattan.

My first accounting job was as a junior clerk in 1949; I had several jobs and in 1956 I went to work for Westinghouse as an auditor. Eleven years later in 1967, I was controller of two Westinghouse divisions near Pittsburgh, Pennsylvania.

Within ten years of getting my CPA, at age thirty-nine, having moved to Pittsburgh in 1963 and to California in 1967, I was a Vice President of the New York Stock Exchange company, Menasco Manufacturing in Burbank, CA.

Along the way I worked for Westinghouse, Bendix, Menasco, EM&M and others. Thirty-six of my fifty-two years were in the aerospace industry. I traveled over most of the United States and made some trips to Europe and China. I was the principal negotiator on many government contracts and had a major role in many computer/systems conversions from mainframes to super minis. All of mine were successful while about 85 per cent of such conversions failed. I also had a major role in three successful "turnarounds" of companies or divisions that were in serious trouble.

Sadly, my wife Mary died in 1973. I was then left with the sole responsibility of caring for my eight children including parent/teacher conferences. At one of those conferences on January 10, 1975, I met Ida Quatro, my son's Spanish teacher; and we were married August 30, 1975.

My family life was filled with many wonderful times. While the children were growing, our lives were very family oriented. Unlike my childhood, my family always did things together: playing games, participating in sports and traveling.

My life was not without deep sorrow. Besides my first wife, I have lost a daughter, a grandson, and a great-grandson and I have one son now fifty-two, who still seems to act like a teenager. I have been truly blessed by having two wonderful wives and I am so thankful for my eight children, my fourteen grandchildren, and my three great-grandchildren. While I have worked very hard and long, I am grateful for my good fortune and many joys, especially for being born in the USA.

© 2012 John O'Donoghue

GREAT DEPRESSION YEARS IN CHINA BY HELEN PAO

The Great Depression in the Western Hemisphere, 1929-1941, was a relatively prosperous time in China simply because the merchandise we relied on from the West stopped coming into the country. During this time small factories sprouted up in China creating work for the local people and providing consumers an opportunity to buy Chinese products.

In 1929, my family consisted of my father, T.Z. Koo, my mother, Ge-Tsung, and four children: Lucy, Robert, Helen (me), and Alice. I was born in Shanghai on May 18, 1923, in the house my father built for us. Both my grandparents and my parents were educated in missionary schools. My grandfathers were Anglican priests.

My father was good in English. He became an accomplished speaker of English, carefully choosing appropriate words and giving a superb quiet presentation. At that time, there was no radio and the Western world wanted to know about China. Imperial China was losing popularity and Sun Yat-Sen's Chinese Republic was on the rise. He also visited Mohandas Gandhi once in awhile during this time. Gandhi, however, was often jailed in England because of his opposition to British rule in India.

After World War I, Father was sent as a Chinese delegate to the League of Nations meeting in Geneva, Switzerland. After Father spoke, United States President Woodrow Wilson went over to Father, shook his hand and told him he had spoken very well. (Before World War II, Father gave the Easter service sermon at Radio City Music Hall in New York City. The auditorium was full.)

Father usually traveled alone, but in 1929, our entire family traveled around the world. We started from Shanghai and traveled to India, England, U.S.A, Hawaii, and

Yokohama, Japan, and finally back to Shanghai. When my father was busy, Mother took us to see places of interest. In Hawaii there were no skyscrapers and many people wore grass skirts.

In India we went by a rapid train. The passengers were lean Indian men in spotless white robes. White rice was served at lunchtime. The Indian passengers used their fingers to pick up the rice and put it into their mouths. To this day I have this image coming back to me once in awhile. I could not understand how they could do it with such elegance.

We sailed through the Suez Canal. My mother stressed the monumental work of the Suez Canal (opened on November 17, 1869) and its importance to world trade. However, for a six-year-old girl, it was a relatively narrow strip of water. Our ship eased slowly along the 105-mile passage. Somewhere along the way we stopped at Casablanca.

In Europe I remember having milk and porridge for breakfast. I do not know if the milk was pasteurized. There were about two inches of cream on top of the bottle. The combination of milk and hot porridge emitted a flavor that I reject to this day. I put salt in hot porridge instead.

I remember at 4 p.m. the streetlights in London turned on for a few minutes and then turned off, the same as in Shanghai as a means of telling the people it was 4 p.m. It was already dark. White fog, like smoke, curled around us. Bobbies in blue uniforms with metal helmets, carrying short wooden sticks in their hands were patrolling. They were courteous and helpful. I also remember food stores with rabbits and deer hanging on the exterior walls at the entrances.

In 1930, after the world trip, mother decided to move our family to Peking. (Changes in English pronunciation of Chinese words have resulted in Peking being known as Beijing today.) Everyone told her what a wonderful city it was—the old Imperial City. My father traveled a great deal, so it made no difference where we lived. Mother located a three-story house with central heating and a tennis court. We had an icebox for refrigeration. There was a man that worked at the front gate.

My mother found a missionary girls' school on the east side of Peking for Lucy. She went into seventh grade and traveled to school by rickshaw five days a week. She also took violin lessons with a Russian, named Mr. Orope. (After World War II, Lucy met Mr. Orope in Hollywood.) We lived on the west side of town. In the middle of the city was the Royal Palace and Royal Park. We ice skated on the frozen Royal Lake in winter, and we rowed a boat among the lotus plants in the Royal Park the rest of the year.

My brother Robert and I walked to school with two girls, the gardener's daughter and a girl who lived next to our gardener's court. It was quite a long walk for us, about thirty minutes one way. For lunch, our cook would bring our lunch using a bicycle. After school the four of us would play together. Most of the time we would climb trees or throw around a basketball-sized ball. Robert raised goldfish in earthenware bowls. We had a large cage with eight or nine yellow birds. They were pretty. They chirped whenever I gave them egg whites.

Peking is in the northern part of China; the main food staple is flour. In Southern China, the main staple is rice. Frozen food was not on the market yet. Cooking was simple; if we wanted noodles, we made dough from water and flour. Then we rolled up the dough like a jellyroll and sliced it into noodles. For yeast bread, we used a small lump of yeast dough that was saved from the last batch added flour and let it rise overnight.

Our iron had one handle and two metal irons. One iron with the handle attached was used to iron the clothes, while the other iron with no handle was being heated. When the first iron cooled, the handle was removed and placed on the hot iron. This process continued until all the ironing was finished.

In our garden the peach trees and Northern Chinese date trees were huge and as common as orange trees are in Florida. We also had a mulberry tree. I raised silk worms every year. We would put the silk worms in a shoebox punched with holes and take it to school. Children did this at silkworm season. At recess, we would admire each other's silkworms.

My mother played the piano in the evenings. I remember her sheet music was beautifully decorated. Her music was not in books. My father and mother played duets from opera arias. Sometimes my father played the Chinese bamboo flute and my mother accompanied him on piano. He put glue on some of the holes and drilled new holes to create sounds to suit the Western piano. When he traveled abroad, he would pack his flute. Traveling by ship took considerable time, so he played the flute in his room to pass time. Mother started our piano lessons when we turned six.

Every weekend mother took us to an historic place. The Imperial Summer Palace was built by the Empress Dowager, and modeled after France's Versailles. It was destroyed during the Boxer Rebellion, 1898-1901. The weeds were taller than I when we visited. We went to the original Great Wall. The walk was difficult and uneven. It was built for soldiers and sentries in the countryside on the west side of Peking. We also visited a mountain called West Mountain with temples, gigantic sleeping Buddhas, and ferocious fighting Buddhas with swords in their hands.

The Peking city wall had eight gates. The Peking rugs were made near the gates. Through the gates we often saw a string of four or five camels walking in, chewing their cuds. They walked with a rhythm. Mother bought curios, tapestries and embroideries at the bazaars.

We went to the Ming Tombs, famous for the entrance lined with stone statues of guardian animals and officials. There were more statues on both sides of the road then, looking grander than at present.

In the summer, we went to a beach north of Peking called Bei Tai Ho, located between Peking on the south and Manchuria to the north. Both Chinese and Caucasian professionals spent the summers at Bei Tai Ho.

In the community building there, these summer residents pooled their talents and had programs for all ages, such as hobbies, astronomy, recitals, and concerts. Once we had a well-known cellist from Europe staying there. He played a Bach cello sonata unaccompanied from beginning to end. The audience decreased in number as the sonata proceeded along. I stayed to the end. One of the presentations was "Tales of Hoffman." We typically went to the beach from 11 a.m. to 1:30 p.m. Going home we were ravenously hungry. We ate whatever the cook put on the table.

Our household help went with us to Bai Tai Ho. In the afternoon we played a card game called Pounce. It is like double solitaire, but much faster. The number of players varied from four to eight, depending on who stopped at our house. Those days were fun and carefree.

In 1936, Robert was going to school in Nanking. Lucy was in Baltimore studying at The Peabody Conservatory. My mother wanted to travel with my father. I felt sad because I did not have a home. Instead, my sister Alice and I attended St. Mary's Hall, a boarding school for Chinese girls, operated by the Anglican Church. Soon I met girls in the same boat as I was, and I was happy and fine.

In the summer of 1937, my family came back to Shanghai so that we could finish school there. My mother had all of our things shipped to Shanghai. We lost all of our belongings in transit when Japan attacked China beginning the Second Sino-Japanese War, 1937-1941. After the bombing of Pearl Harbor in 1941, this war joined World War II which ended in 1945.

Robert was at Cornell University. My father was abroad somewhere. My mother rented a home and we lived in the international section of Shanghai. Japanese troops surrounded Shanghai, but did not enter the international section. Citizens from neutral countries like Switzerland and Sweden also lived in Shanghai. None of the residents was harmed by the Japanese.

After the war, my father, who was speaking in the United States, was able to secure scholarships for Alice and myself. In 1946 my mother left China with us so she could get us settled in college. I majored in Home Economics at Syracuse University. Alice went to Smith College and majored in Physics. Lucy studied music at the Paris Conservatory.

In 1948 I met my husband Yoh-Han (John) Pao at Syracuse, where he earned a PhD in Applied Physics. I cooked everything from scratch, not using mixes. I did this because I thought I might teach Home Economics when I went back to China. This was not to be, for in 1948 the Communists took over China and the Bamboo Curtain descended. For a time we thought the rebels, as we called the Communists, would just go away. It was a blessing that my mother came with us because if she had stayed in China, she might not have been able to leave. My father was able to obtain positions teaching Chinese at mid-western universities.

My husband first worked for the DuPont Company in Delaware and later did research for Bell Telephone Laboratory in New Jersey. He then obtained an appointment as full professor at Case Western Reserve University with tenure and became the first chaired professor at C.W.R.U. During the forty years we lived in Cleveland, we had four children: Robin, a graduate of Smith College with a master's degree from Columbia University; John, a graduate of Case Western Reserve University, currently employed as an engineer in Boston; Victor, now deceased; and a son who died shortly after birth. While they were young, I stayed home to care for them.

After they were grown, I traveled around the world with my husband to science conferences. I enjoyed visiting historic sites and museums. During the Nixon Presidency,

my husband went to China to develop ties between Chinese and American scientists. This was my first trip back to my homeland. After meetings, Yoh-Han and I had time to travel as tourists. We followed the Silk Road in the western part of China bordering on Pakistan and Soviet Russia.

Unfortunately, my husband died just one month before we were to move to University Village. I moved here to be near my daughter, Robin, who is married to jazz guitarist, Peter White. They are the parents of my granddaughter, Charlotte. I enjoy California weather, auditing an art history class at California Lutheran University, and taking UVTO excursions to nearby museums.

MY WEST VIRGINIA CHILDHOOD DURING THE GREAT DEPRESSION
BY RALPH SHRADER

My name is Ralph Shrader, and I was born November 24, 1917, in the hills of southern West Virginia near the city of Bluefield, which had a population of about 20,000 people. Bluefield served all the coal mining communities in the southwestern part of the state. The Norfolk and Western Railway ran directly through the northern part of the city. Its thirteen tracks held coal cars until they were ready to be distributed to all parts of the country.

My parents, Hedley and Virginia Shrader, lived in the country and had five children, three boys and two girls; I was the third born.

Other Shrader families owned homes and property up the "holler" from us. (Holler is a Southern term meaning "down the road a spell" or "down in the valley a ways.") The hollow road is now a state road marked as "Shrader Hollow Road." Just across the creek from our house was a one-room school named "Shrader School" on land donated by my grandfather. This little school had five rows of desks and seats, one row for each grade. Our teacher's name was Clyde Ellison; and if a student were bad, Mr. Ellison would throw an eraser at him. And that's not all, he seldom missed. Because of childhood sickness, my mother held me out of school until I was seven-years old.

All the Shrader men and some of the older cousins worked in the coalfields several miles away. My father was a coal mine inspector and was injured on the job when I was an infant. The hospital where he was treated set the bone in his right leg in a manner that caused him to be crippled for the rest of his life. It is said that West Virginians have one short leg anyway so I guess Dad was right at home.

My brothers, Ray and Gene, and I swam, built wooden boats, and fished in the river nearby. Our neighbor, John Hare, a blacksmith at the railroad yard nearby, was kind enough to build me a wagon with wheelbarrow wheels like nobody ever imagined. This wagon was the envy of all the boys in the area. I enjoyed it so much I built a makeshift road down the hill from our house with curves and bumps and even a little bridge across the creek. I was a loner and a racer. I played by myself most of the time. My wagon was stolen when I was seventeen, so I guess it was time for me to grow up.

Those were the days when the Great Depression was really hitting hard and so many people were receiving government assistance. My mother was a proud woman and refused any kind of help. She said, "As long as we are healthy, and have a piece of land, we will not go hungry." So we worked three gardens, raised three pigs every year, milked a cow, and dried and canned fruit from our fruit orchard above our house. Every Thanksgiving everyone in the area got together and slaughtered pigs, made sausage, and salted away meats in the smoke house. One Thanksgiving when I was five-years-old, three of my mischievous uncles grabbed me and put me inside a gutted hog and proceeded to close it up. I'm sure that must have had something to do with the claustrophobia I've had for years! For example, during the six weeks of sonar schooling I had on a submarine before the war, I was very uncomfortable. (Sonar is an underwater device which detects submarines or other objects under water.) Gradually, my claustrophobia dwindled in time.

On fall days we all went berry picking, and mom baked delicious blackberry cobblers. That was also canning time for the berries, peaches, apples, etc. Under the smokehouse we had what we called the springhouse, where we stored all our canned meats, veggies, milk, butter, potatoes and fruits. All the kids took their turn churning the milk for butter. My sister and I belonged to the 4H club and my project was raising chickens for which I received a second place ribbon at the state fair.

We boys cut and stacked wood from the mountain behind our house. Sometimes, when we could afford it, we bought a ton of coal and had it hauled to our place. Coal burns longer than wood and heated the house all night. We had no indoor plumbing, but we were fortunate to have a fresh-water spring above our house where we got buckets of water to carry to our kitchen. Of course, we only had an outhouse for a toilet. After the war, my father and I piped water into our house from that spring. My older brother and I worked in the corn and hay fields during the summer for a dollar a day. Soon a main highway was being built nearby and we earned $2 a day working on the construction crew.

We were bused to high school in Bramwell, the closest town to our home two-and-a-half miles distant. At that time Bramwell was recorded as the richest town per capita in the U.S. The reason was that most of the coal company owners lived there. In 1929, during the early days of the Great Depression, it is said that a number of these owners committed suicide after the stock market crash. The town is now designated a historical town. Many of the fine homes are now used as Bed and Breakfasts. Some have as many as fourteen rooms. It was a rare treat for me to have a five-cent Coke at the famous corner drug store.

Our basketball team was named "The Millionaires." This name certainly did not describe my family or me, however. On cold winter days I walked the two-and-a-half miles home from basketball practice and my hair froze from taking a shower after practice.

Some of my school years were difficult. The rich kids wore dry-cleaned clothes, and I only had jeans. They also brought sandwiches for lunch made with what we called store bought light bread. I had to take biscuits. In my last two years of high school, I envied some girls who were "A" students in typing class. "Somehow," I said to myself, "I must do better." So I found an old Underwood typewriter for $10 and practiced almost every night pounding that thing. By the time we had our final exam, I beat them. This not only gave me pleasure, but seemed to give me confidence. Typewriters in those days were mechanical, and I still have trouble with today's electric typewriters and of course with the computer keyboard as well. I just want to pound them the same old way. Before graduation, our senior class of fifty-one was the first from our school to take a train trip to Washington, D.C. The trip was enjoyable and added to my confidence, like I was now a man of the world.

Since college was not an option, I joined the Navy in November, 1938. During World War II, I served on the destroyer

USS Craven (DD-382) one of a division of four destroyers that escorted the aircraft carrier USS Enterprise (CV-6) one of the most, if not the most, decorated ship of World War II.

Although my hearing was impaired by my proximity to the large guns, I am proud that I was able to do my duty in service to my country in time of war.

One day after I returned home, I tagged along with my brother-in-law, who wanted to see his brother, an employee in a town some twelve miles distant. In those days, I was quite shy around the ladies, but there was something about the receptionist that caught my eye. So after some chit chat and introducing myself, I simply asked her if she would like to attend a football game in a nearby town that night. To my delight she accepted.

Today, Mabel Crouch, and I have been married for almost sixty-four happy years. We have been blessed with three wonderful children, Pamela Yvonne, Rodney Kim and Susan Elaine, four grandchildren and five great-grandchildren, all of whom we are so very proud. We are also thankful to live here in University Village, Thousand Oaks.

MY LIFE IN FRESNO DURING THE GREAT DEPRESSIONBY FRANK J. WELCH

Thinking back over these difficult and tragic years of the Great Depression for our country, I realize that my family and I were very fortunate. We lived comfortably during the "Thirties," and no one in our family was hurt during the subsequent war. I grew up in the small farming town of Fresno in Central California knowing nothing of the poverty that many suffered across our nation. On occasion, however, Mother gave food to transients who called at the kitchen door. I also heard stories of "hobos" in the railroad freight yards.

My father, Frank J. Welch, was a journeyman printer of limited education and a good union man. He had worked for newspapers in Chicago and Cincinnati before coming to

California after World War I. My mother, Lillian F. J. Law, was a widow with a young daughter, Harriette, when they met and married in Fresno in 1925. They bought a small frame house on the eastern edge of Fresno, two blocks from the end of the streetcar line. Several years later on August 5, 1929, I was born followed in three years by my sister, Margaret. Dad was able to provide a comfortable life for the family. We lived frugally and Mother never bought anything that could be made at home. Every week Mother baked bread that was delicious when fresh, but was hard and less palatable by the end of the week. In school I often envied classmates whose sandwiches were made with soft, store bought bread. We always had everything we needed and a few luxuries, but as kids we expected to work for any special things we wanted.

The houses in our neighborhood were all modest like ours. There were several vacant lots on our block, one being directly across the street. These lots and the street itself were the playgrounds for the kids. We had a small lawn in front and a backyard with lawn and garden enclosed by a wooden fence. An apricot tree, which I climbed often, stood in the middle of the yard. There was a one-car frame garage that was accessed from an alley in the back.

Dad lost his job a few years after I was born when the paper he worked for closed, but he was able to find another job, immediately, in the nearby town of Merced. The family followed him and we lived there for two or three years. We returned to our house in Fresno when Dad got a better job with the *Fresno Bee*. I never knew whether or not Dad rented our house while we were away; in any case we returned to the same house. Dad continued to work for the *Bee* until his death in 1949.

Our house had one gas floor furnace in the living room for heat. We kids would stand over it on cold days to get warm. The kitchen was warmed by the gas cooking stove, but the bedrooms were always cold. There was no cooling in the summer except for the open windows. We had an icebox in the kitchen, which an iceman filled periodically with a large block of ice from a delivery truck. The iceman chipped the block to size in the back of his truck, where all the kids gathered to get ice chips to suck on.

Milk was delivered in glass bottles with the cream separated in the neck of the bottle. Homogenized milk was a later development. The bottle was shaken to disperse the cream while taking care to hold the paper cap in place; more often the cream was carefully separated by decanting and saved for other purposes. Notes were placed in the empty bottles each night to tell the milkman which of the several products (whole milk, cream, skimmed milk, buttermilk, etc.) to leave in the morning and how many bottles of each.

There were concrete sidewalks and curbs along our street, but the street itself was oiled dirt. On occasion work crews would grade and oil the street with heavy machinery. Sycamore trees along the parkway provided shade. People raked the tree leaves into piles in the street in the fall and burned them. A great sport for the small kids was to jump and play in the leaf piles. We built "forts" in the vacant lots, really holes in the ground, and had wars throwing clumps of grass with dirt attached that we pulled from the field. They sailed nicely and showered the victim with dirt on impact. Some of the older kids built a racetrack for bikes in one of the vacant lots with the course going over built up hills and through channels dug in the lot.

The younger neighborhood kids walked together about eight or ten blocks to grade school. At that time there were no school buses nor did the parents feel the need to accompany their children. We always had a car, a Model A Ford sedan; but mother never learned to drive. Dad usually walked or took the trolley or bus to work so our car was used mostly for family outings or trips.

Occasionally on weekends, Dad went to the foothills to pan for gold, returning with some flakes in a small vial. I doubt he ever got enough gold to pay for the trip, but that probably was not the true purpose anyway. On other occasions in the spring the whole family drove to the foothills to gather mushrooms in the green fields.

Dad was an avid stamp collector, an avocation very popular during the prewar years. His brother, Charlie, a bookkeeper for mining companies, lost his job in the Depression and asked Dad's help in selling his collection of stamps. Dad complied buying some himself to complement his own collection.

My sister and I had all of the usual childhood diseases and had our tonsils removed at an early age. Some vaccines were becoming available for these diseases, but mother never trusted them and we were never inoculated. We saw a doctor only for serious illnesses, relying on home remedies for treatment of colds, scrapes, and infections.

Mosquitoes were prevalent in the Fresno area, spreading polio and malaria. I contracted the latter and suffered several recurrences of the fever during my teenage years. I rather liked having malaria because it was an excuse to get out of school for a few weeks and I got lots of attention. I never felt bad after the fever subsided; and when the fever was high, I just slept. About this time, a major mosquito abatement program in the area greatly reduced the incidence of these diseases. Later polio vaccines became available to eradicate that debilitating disease.

Chandler Field, the Fresno airport, was a small field on the west side of town. The field was used mostly for private planes, but there were some commercial airliners as well, such as Ford Trimotors and Douglas DC-1s. Most people traveled by Greyhound bus or by train. Both Southern Pacific and Santa Fe railroads had stations in town. It was a big day in 1936, I believe, when the new Santa Fe streamlined train first came to Fresno. It was aluminum clad with very comfortable passenger cars. We went with the crowds to see it and to marvel. I believe it cut the travel time to Oakland to about three hours. Later I was thrilled to ride this train alone to visit my godmother in Oakland.

For fun we kids would walk over to the streetcar tracks and help the conductor reverse the backs of the seats for the return trip to town. It was said that the tracks were removed later by WPA (Works Progress Administration) workers, sold as scrap to Japan, and eventually made into armaments for use against us in World War II.

After we returned to our house in Fresno from Merced, it became evident that the house was too small for our family with a teenage daughter and two active children. Shortly after my tenth birthday, we sold the house and moved across town to a much larger California bungalow style house that was to be the family home for the next thirty years. My older sister was married there in the living room in 1940; Dad and Gran died there in 1949; and Mom continued to live there alone for another twenty-five years until she finally sold the house and moved to an apartment. The house had two bedrooms on the ground floor and two more and a half-bath upstairs. The living room extended across the front of the house. Between the living room and kitchen was a dining room. We had two floor furnaces: one in the wall between the living and dining rooms and one at the base of the stairs. The latter was supposed to heat the upstairs rooms but it was not very effective. On cold mornings we huddled over the furnaces to dress.

Although summer temperatures in Fresno often exceeded 100 degrees, the only air conditioners in houses at that time were evaporative "swamp" coolers. Only a few houses had them. Ours was not one of them. We cooled the house by opening all of the windows in the evening to let the hot air out. In the morning, the shades were drawn to keep the cool air in as long as possible.

The bathroom had a tub with legs that served the entire family. We took a bath every Saturday night. In later years we connected a shower to the tub via a hose and rigged a circular shower curtain that was just large enough to enclose one person. It was snug but worked well. I washed in the small basin in the upstairs bathroom most of the time. It was there when I was about ten or eleven that I nearly caused a fire with my new chemistry set. I randomly mixed two chemicals that reacted with a flash, creating flames and much smoke. Fortunately, I was able to smother the flames before damage was done.

There was a covered cement porch across the entire front of the house. In the back there was a small screened-in utility porch off the kitchen with doors leading to the backyard and to a crude cellar for storage of the preserves my mother made each year. Two wash tubs and a wringer washing machine were on the porch. Clothes were hung on lines in the backyard to dry. Mother preserved fruits, made jams and jellies, and baked pies and cakes. We always had some kind of dessert at dinner.

A grape arbor covered the walkway that led from the back door to the garage in the rear which opened onto a back alley. A tall wooden fence separated the yard from the alley in the back, and there was a shed to one side, which served as a chicken coop for several years. In the middle of the yard there was a large apricot tree and next to the house was a plum tree. On the north side of the house were a naval orange tree and a large lemon tree. At various times the back part of the yard between the garage and chicken coop was used as a vegetable and flower garden.

There was a small lawn in the front of the house. The roof sloped upward from the front to a high peak in the middle and then down to the back. At every opportunity I climbed to the top of the roof and got down by jumping to the grass in the front yard, a leap of about ten feet. The street was lined with large sycamore trees that shed leaves and cotton balls during the year. The street and curbs were concrete. The house next to ours was very small and sat on the rear of the lot with unkempt lawn and dirt in the front. Cars were frequently parked on this yard, and the small kids from the neighborhood played in the dirt. Often in the afternoons a flock of pigeons flew in circles over our neighborhood. Many people raised homing pigeons as a hobby in those days. Each day the pigeons were released to fly free, and after a short time they always came home to roost.

John Muir grade school was a block away on the street behind our house. The desks had a folding seat and a hole in the top for an ink well. Before ballpoint pens, we learned to write with a metal quill-style pen that was dipped into liquid ink and scratched onto the paper. The pens were cleaned up with an ink wipe (a small piece of cloth); a paper blotter was used to clean up ink blotches. As we grew older, fountain pens which had an internal supply of ink replaced the quill-style pens and the ink well. Pen and mechanical pencil sets made by Schaeffer, Waterman, and Parker were treasured gifts for high school students and also for adults. My school desk had metal grill on both work sides. When bored with schoolwork, I made little stick men out of "pipe cleaners" and connected them hand to foot climbing the sides of the desk. (Pipe cleaners were metal wire about six-inches long, covered with cotton fibers, that were used for removing tobacco tar from smoking pipes.)

Fresno was a town of about 60,000 people in 1940. Our house was about two miles north of the center of town. The main shopping street was Fulton with department stores, five & dime stores, and banks. Some of the stores had large signs in the windows proclaiming that they were cooled by Refrigeration. Most did not. The main highway, Route 99, went one block west on Broadway. One block east on Van Ness was a park about half-a-mile square with the classic, domed county court house in the center and a new modern city hall building on the north side. On Saturdays there was a very popular farmer's market along the streets fronting the park. We often bought produce there. The *Fresno Bee,* where dad worked was on the north edge of the central town. He often walked to work, and sometimes when the buses were overcrowded, I walked to the down town movies. Usually, however, buses were the main transportation.

There were several major movie theaters that were well attended by the kids on Saturday mornings and by the teenagers on Saturday nights. Movies were a half-day affair. In addition to the main movie feature, there were newsreels, cartoons, and a second feature. On Saturdays there was also a serial such as Flash Gordon, Sky King, or a Tom Mix western with a different episode each week. At the end of each episode, the hero got into deadly peril only to be rescued the next week. The serials drew the kids back to the movies each week regardless of the feature picture that was showing.

After two years at John Muir, I went to Washington Junior High, which was about a mile east, for three years and then to Fresno High, which was a mile north, for three years. I rode my bike or walked to junior high, but wouldn't think of riding a bike to high school. If I couldn't get a ride in a car, I walked. At sixteen I got a car and seldom walked thereafter. One of my friends was a recent migrant from the dust bowl, an "Okie."

There were two elegant residential areas in Fresno: Fig Gardens on the north edge of the city and Sunnyside on the eastern side. The south side of town was industrial and the west side of town was "the other side of the tracks." That was where the poor people lived. Fig Gardens ended at Shaw Avenue, with fig orchards extending from there to the river several miles out. Van Ness Boulevard going through Fig Gardens was and still is lined with large fir trees, which were decorated with lights each Christmas. "Christmas Tree Lane" was a magnificent sight every evening during the season. Cars with steamy windows from the December chill and filled with people crept along the street bumper to bumper with their headlights off to look at the lights and the displays in front of many of the houses. I have never seen anything to rival this since, except perhaps for Disney's Main Street Electrical Parade.

Radio was the big thing when I was growing up. Television did not come along until I was in college, but we listened to the radio often. Our family got a table model radio about the time we moved to Wilson Avenue. It had several short wave bands that could pick up calls from around the world when conditions were right as well as the standard AM broadcasts. There was no FM at that time. We had an aerial that stretched across the roof of the house. All of the kinds of shows that are now on television were then on radio: soap operas during the day, comedy shows, dramas, mysteries, serials, westerns, music, and news.

In the late afternoon the kids gathered in front of the radio to hear shows like "I Love a Mystery," "The Shadow," and "Sky King." On Sunday afternoon and evening there was Bob Hope, Edgar Bergen, Jack Benny, and Fred Allen. Other favorites were "The Great Gildersleeve," "The Hit Parade," "Kay Kyser's Kollege of Musical Knowledge," and "Amos and Andy." One of my warmest memories is of listening to these shows while driving home Sunday evenings from a day in the mountains. It made the two-hour trip seem a lot shorter. We listened to boxing matches (Joe Louis was my hero.) and recreated baseball games. I became an avid New York Yankee fan from broadcasts of their games. Of course, we never missed Roosevelt's Fireside Chats.

When I was about twelve, I made a crystal set radio. It consisted, I believe, of a small crystal of mica about a quarter-inch across, a fine tuning wire to touch the crystal, an aerial, and ear phones. I never really understood how it worked, but it did. Since plastic did not exist when I was young, all toys were made of metal, wood, or rubber. Bicycles and wagons were pretty much the same as now. Model kits were wood, glue, and paper; "tin soldiers" were metal; and skates had metal adjustable brackets that attached to our leather-soled shoes. They didn't work with the tennis shoes we often wore. The brackets were adjusted to fit our shoes with a skate key. Every kid had a skate key in his pocket. We skated on the concrete sidewalks.

We made many of our own toys. We made wooden guns that shot rubber bands cut from automobile tire inner tubes. The rubber band was stretched from the front of the gun to a notch cut near the back. We used a strip of leather to lift the band from the notch to shoot. We made multiple-shot guns by cutting several notches in tandem. Inflated inner tubes were also used as rafts for floating on the lake and rivers. We made scooters by attaching skate rollers to the bottom of a three-foot long 2 by 4. A fruit crate with an attached handle to steer with was mounted on the other side of the 2 by 4. We also made slingshots by tying a rubber band cut from an inner tube to a "Y" cut from a tree branch. Pebbles were the ammunition.

All of the boys carried pocketknives and I was no exception. As Cub Scouts we had sheathed hunting knives and hatchets for use when camping. Whittling and carving were a common past time. We also liked to throw knives, using trees or the side of the garage or a wooden fence as targets. Sometimes we just stuck them in the dirt. We played a game like "Battle Ship" in the dirt yard next to our house. A ship the size of our foot was scratched in the dirt. We stood with one foot on the ship and tossed our knife to stick in the dirt as far as we could. The ship was then moved to where the knife stuck. The opponent was moving his ships the same

way in turn. If the knife could be stuck in the opponent's ship, it was sunk. Each competitor had a harbor at his end of the field. The first to stick his opponent's harbor won the game. The game took half a day to play! Stories of recent Tong Wars during the 1920's between rival Chinese immigrants and/or their descendants in West Coast China Towns involved the use of hatchets as principal gang weapons. We were thus inspired to learn this art of hatchet throwing and soon became quite adept at sticking our hatchets in tree trunks from ten to twenty feet away.

I graduated from Fresno High School in 1947 and Fresno State College in 1951. Then I went on to Stanford University, where I received a PhD in Organic Chemistry in 1954 and met and married Mary Lou Newell. We moved to Charleston, West Virginia, where I began my career as a research chemist at Union Carbide and subsequently became a Technology Manager for Coating Materials. Our five children were born and grew up in Charleston. In 1971 we moved the family back to Whittier, California, when I joined Avery Label as Director of Research and Engineering in Azusa. After retiring in 1992, we enjoyed travel, games, and family until we moved to UVTO in December, 2007.

DEPRESSION, NOT DEFEAT BY ADINA WILSON

During the Great Depression of the 1930's, I was a child living with my family in Brooklyn, New York. Those experiences left lasting impressions with me, but also taught valuable lessons. I remember my mother and me riding the subway downtown to see the Macy's Parade one Thanksgiving. Later, she took me to see the Rockettes at Radio City Music Hall and later still "Snow White and the Seven Dwarfs" at that same wondrous theater.

I also vividly recall my parents' financial struggles and their efforts to protect my little sister, Beth, and me from too much awareness of their difficulties.

My father, George Wagner, was a contractor, but at that time no one could afford to build or remodel. He got whatever work he could, even once stuffing envelopes for some firm's mailing program. Finally, it was no longer possible to make the payments on our home, so my parents were forced to let it go. Somehow they were able to rent (with an option to buy) a one-hundred-year-old derelict farmhouse sixty miles out on Long Island, in Coram, a small rural community. Dad did what he could to make our new home livable before moving us in.

The house had "good bones" but had no plumbing, no electricity, no central heat and only a ladder by which to reach the unfinished second floor. Our household water supply was obtained by hauling a bucket up from a backyard cistern, and we were introduced to the dubious pleasures of an outhouse. We had kerosene heaters and lamps; and since we were forced to move in the middle of winter, it was cold, both inside and out. We children were appalled at the conditions, and I can remember us sitting on the running board of our old car, commiserating with each other.

Except for weekends, our father had to remain in the city, where a little work was available occasionally. He slept on couches either at his sister's or sister-in-law's and ate when and where he could. When he came home, he continued working to make our old house more modern and comfortable. Our mother, Maude Bornitz Wagner, had almost the full burden of helping us children learn to live in an entirely new style and environment. Although city born and bred, she managed to make our new house a home and helped us adapt to the rudimentary conditions.

My sister, Beth, and I transferred from large city schools to a one-room schoolhouse heated by a potbelly wood-burning stove. We had left classes averaging thirty or more pupils to enter our new school, which had only sixteen students total and one teacher, Mr. Jayne, for all eight grades. Since I was a mid-year rapid advance student, Mr. Jayne helped me do a year's work in six months, which ultimately allowed me to graduate from high school before I was seventeen. During recess we played games in open fields, rather than on concrete-paved schoolyards. All in all in this new environment, I often felt inept and as if I didn't belong. Academically and socially, I was ahead of my classmates and that set me apart.

One of my school day memories involves a schoolmate who was an overblown sixteen-year-old and not the sharpest knife in the drawer. I suspect she was in school only because the law required it. Each year at Christmas time, Mr. Jayne arranged to have his students sing at a nearby "old folks" home. On this particular Christmas, he gently suggested to his buxom-blond pupil that maybe this time she could find something more appropriate to sing than "Flat Foot Floogie with a Floy Floy."

Our family slowly adapted to our new life style. We joined a little struggling church, made some friends, and learned to live with little in the way of amenities. Mother was able to feed the family for $5 per week. She packed our school lunches in used bread wrappers to save money. Being both a creative and a talented seamstress, she kept us girls well-

dressed, often by taking apart old coats or other clothing. She would cut and reuse the pieces to make new apparel for us. Our door was always open, and we shared with others having a harder time than we were.

After Pearl Harbor, the war effort created jobs and my dad, a World War I veteran, found steady work at the Brooklyn Navy Yard. Our financial situation gradually improved and when World War II ended, Dad was finally able to live at home full time and reestablish a building business. Somehow during the bad times, we children never felt "poor" or "impoverished." We had plenty of love and laughter and learned that one can cope, improvise and adapt to almost any situation when necessary.

Our experiences as a family during the Depression years gave my sister and me an innate sense of personal adequacy engendered by the coping skills we learned from our parents. We both went on to jobs and marriage. Each of us have had two children, our own homes, and fulfilling lives. My husband, Mel Wilson, and I aside from our families enjoyed the theater, playing bridge, entertaining, and community involvement.

For myself, I was active in church choir, several clubs, a performing drama group, a bonsai society and primarily as a paraprofessional counselor at Pasadena Mental Health Center, a low-fee organization helping those with limited finances. Serving as a volunteer, I met with clients on a regular basis, both long and short term, under professional supervision. I co-led support groups and co-trained incoming interns and volunteer counselors.

In 2009 my husband and I decided the time was propitious for us to make a lifestyle change, and thus we looked for options. Chance led us to investigate University Village in Thousand Oaks, and the rest as they say, "is history."

SECTION TWO

LIVING THROUGH WORLD WAR II

WORLD WAR II BY JEAN BARDGETTE

On December 7, 1941, we returned home from church and turned on the radio to find that Japan had attacked Pearl Harbor and that we were now at war. I remember sitting in front of the fireplace listening to this news that would affect so many of our lives. I finished high school in the next two years, having a great time. There was a large airfield in Texas, built between Midland and Odessa, to train bombardiers. We entertained many servicemen from the church for Sunday dinner. Through church and with other friends we dated pilots, bombardiers and other service men, also going to USO dances. I often wonder how many of those young men made it through the war and returned home. They would tell us about their homes, families and girl friends they left behind.

After high school I went to work as a receptionist and typist for one of the local law firms, hoping to save money so I could go to college. It soon became evident that this was impossible at the salary of $50 a month. I didn't like office work and was wondering where to go from there. I happened to visit my parents who were at that time living in Jefferson, Texas, and met a young lady

my age who had just applied for the nursing program under the Cadet Nurse Corps at The University of Texas School of Nursing in Galveston. This was a program sponsored by the US Government to train more nurses for the war. One of my classmates from high school was already in the program at Baylor Hospital in Dallas. Even though I had never even been in a hospital, this appealed to me. I applied to The University of Texas Medical Branch at Galveston, associated with John Sealy Hospital, the state hospital for Texas, and was accepted after my seventeenth birthday. My intention was to join one of the service branches upon completion of my studies.

In late February of 1944, my sister saw me off on the train from Midland to Dallas – my very first train trip. I met a nice young soldier on the train, which helped me feel more comfortable with someone to chat with and shorten the trip. I stopped off in Dallas to visit my high school friend at Baylor and learned a little more about what my life was going to be like. Then it was on to Galveston with my two suitcases and two boxes that had been shipped, to begin my new life. We lived in the nurses' residence with most of us sharing a room for two. We carried a heavy study load with our nursing courses being taught by RN's with advanced degrees and all of our science courses taught by the Professors at the Medical School. After six months we received our white caps and started working with instructors or head nurses in the hospital wards. After awhile, we took fewer courses and spent more hours working in the hospital.

By the time we were in our final year we, as senior students, effectively ran the hospital on the 3 to 11 p.m. and 11 p.m. to 7 a.m. shifts, with only one RN over the entire hospital. Many RN's had by now joined the armed forces, many serving overseas. To my knowledge John Sealy Hospital was the only state-operated hospital in Texas at that time. It was a very large hospital consisting of many buildings: Main, Women's, Pediatric, Colored, Psychiatric, Out-Patient Clinic and a small Tuberculin Building. These were set up in large open wards of up to twenty beds each with the nurses' station in the middle. There were very few private rooms as most of our patients were charity cases. One student nurse would handle these large wards by herself with one extra student from 3 to 7 p.m. This was a split shift of 7 – 11 a.m. and 3 to 7 p.m. We all hated this assignment as it really ruined our day.

My class in March of 1943 started with over 80 young ladies with only 25 of us graduating three years later. Many found the courses unpleasant, they were lonesome for home, or just couldn't pass the classes. I remember walking through the dissection lab for the medical students with the strong smell of formaldehyde on our way to our anatomy class and handing different human bones around the class for identification. This was not for everyone. My first roommate washed out at three months. I loved it from the very beginning. I had been raised to do hard work on a dairy farm, so not much bothered me. The courses were interesting and I felt the government had given me the opportunity for an education that I would not have otherwise had. Upon graduation we gave up our blue dresses with big white-bibbed aprons and now dressed in wonderful starched white uniforms with our cute little white caps. We had to pass our State Board Exams before we were truly Registered Nurses. I did not go into the armed forces as the war had ended before I graduated. I did feel an obligation for my education and returned to active nursing whenever my family duties permitted.

My life took another major path in early 1946. The war was over and our servicemen were returning home. On April 1st of that year I had a chance date with a young man returning from his army stint in the South Pacific, ending up in Japan before coming home to Galveston. We were married nine weeks later. I still lacked nine months of school and he was just returning to Texas A&M to complete his education at the time we married. He would come to Galveston most weekends to see me. After I completed my schooling, I joined him at college until he graduated. The rest is history and here we are 63 wonderful years later, a retired couple at University Village.

WORLD WAR II BY JOHN BARDGETTE

I was at Texas A&M, in Sbisa Mess Hall, eating lunch, when an announcement was made over the loudspeaker system that the Japanese had bombed Pearl Harbor. It was 12 noon in College Station, Texas, Sunday, December 7, 1941, or 8:00 AM Hawaii time. This was during the first semester of my freshman year. Not long after this bombing, the United States started the draft to pull in young men for military service. Soon after I passed my 20th birthday, I enlisted in the Army Reserve Corps, October 13, 1942.

Midway through the first semester of my junior year I was inducted into the Army at Camp Beauregard, Louisiana. I was transferred back to Texas A&M, and assigned to #55 S.T. Company, and readmitted as a student of the Army Specialized Training Program (ASTP) to complete the first semester of my junior year. At the completion of this semester I, and all of the juniors, were called to active service, and transferred to Fort Sam Houston. On arrival, we were assigned to Company B, Reception Center, Fort Sam Houston.

Five days later, March 29th, after receiving several inoculation shots and additional army gear, I, and all of the juniors in the Engineers, Signal Corps, Infantry, Coast Artillery, and Cavalry, were transferred to Camp Roberts, California. We were assigned to the 88th Infantry Basic Training Battalion, Camp Roberts, California. The A&M cadets made up almost the entire complement of the 88th, Battalion, Companies A, B, C, & D. The remainder of the battalion's trainees were from Oklahoma A&M and draftees. I was assigned to Company C.

The corporals seemed to enjoy our group because we went out and marched all of the maneuvers the first day and they didn't need to teach us. During the first week, we started training on the M1 Garand 30 caliber rifle. At A&M we had learned about the 1903 rifle. We practiced with field stripping both the M1 and the 30 caliber Carbine for many hours and got to where we could do this blindfolded. Part of our training was at the rifle range. Besides firing, we spent time working the target pits. After shots were fired, and we were given the clear signal, we pulled the target down, put a patch over the hole, ran the target back up and held up a small black round metal plate, on a long pole, placed over the spot where the bullet had hit the target. This showed the shooter and score keeper where the shot had hit. If the target had been totally missed, we waved a red flag, on a pole. This was called "Maggie's drawers". We only fired for record one time and I qualified as a Marksman.

We had a lot of training on the 30 caliber water-cooled machine gun. Our training covered maintenance, firing, and marching with it. Some days we put the machine gun in action, and took it out of action, all day long in the hot blazing sun. Another day, in the afternoon, we took our machine guns up the hill and mounted them in an entrenchment, pointing toward the sky, for anti-aircraft protection. There were two men on each machine gun with 1,000 rounds of ammunition. We were in the foxholes all afternoon and got very hot sitting down below ground level.

The other weapon that we were extensively trained on was the 81-millimeter mortar.

We had several days of putting it in action and taking it out of action. Firing it was a two-man operation. One would aim it and set the elevation and the other would drop the mortar down the tube where its base would strike the firing pin to ignite the propelling charge. It would explode when its nose struck the target or any hard surface. I well remember the weights of these machine gun and mortar components. I was one of the taller privates in my company, so was at the head of my squad, and carried the 51 lb. machine gun tripod or the 45 lb. mortar base plate, depending on which we were being trained on. We carried the machine gun tripod on our backs, on top of our full field packs, with the two legs over both shoulders and mortar base plate strapped to our chest. We were also introduced to the 30-caliber air-cooled machine gun and the 60-millimeter mortar but didn't fire them. I don't remember the weight of these, but they were quite a bit lighter.

We also had gas mask training. I am not sure if our instructors were sadistic or just challenging us to put out more effort when they had us climb the hills wearing gas mask, full field pack, canteen, mess kit, ammunition belt, and carrying a component of a heavy weapon. I know that this was to simulate actual wartime conditions that could be encountered, but this didn't make it any less the heavy work it was. The humidity was so low that I would not feel sweat on my body but would notice salt rings on my fatigues. This was still true with the gas mask on, as far as it affected my body. However, my face was not exposed to the outside atmosphere, and sweat collected inside of the gas mask and dripped out a special one-way vent.

Another interesting requirement during our training was to drink a minimum of water while on active training. We were required to be able to touch the top of the water, with our finger, in our canteens when we stopped for lunch, and when the day's exercises were over. We could drink all of the water we wanted at lunch, and refill our canteens. I understood that this was the camp's commandant requirement, based on his experiences in battle. Despite this, we survived all of this in good condition.

I remember the two extremes of weather that we experienced. First were the cold mornings. The first morning that we fell out for formation in our fatigues I thought I would freeze. I shivered until we got inside the mess hall. The next morning I fell out with my long-handles on and was quite comfortable. As the sun rose I began to heat up and by mid-morning I was burning up. Thankfully, we had a rest break and I shed the top of my long-handles and stowed it in my full field pack. This was the last time I did this. It was better to be chilly for about thirty minutes than to be very uncomfortably hot for hours. The second was the extreme heat of the parade ground. Our machine gun training included both dry runs and actual firing. The dry run training was frequently held on the blacktop parade ground, and this was often after lunch. The blacktop, absorbing the sun, got almost too hot to sit on, but sit on it we did. I don't remember the exact temperature, but one day one of the privates took a thermometer out with him and laid it on the asphalt. It climbed to about 150° F!

About our seventh week of training we received word that we would be transferred to the originally planned training as engineers, Signal Corps and Coast Artillery. The Infantry and Calvary would stay at Camp Roberts. We Engineers would be shipped to our Engineer Replacement Training Center and we were all very happy about this. We felt like we were moving to our own specialty and ready to start Engineer Basic Training. With all of these A&M groups leaving, the 88th Battalion would be down to less than half of its regular complement.

Fifty-eight ex-A&M Engineers boarded a train and headed north to Camp Abbot, Oregon, where we were assigned to Company B, 55th Battalion, ERTC (Engineer Replacement Training Center. We Aggies from Texas A&M were soon referred to as "training cadre" and assigned to act as squad leaders. The training setup here was different. It was the complete opposite of Camp Roberts which was well established and had its training down to a fine point. Camp Abbot was brand new and we were starting its second training cycle, and it wasn't half as strict. We

Aggies were split up and spread between different companies in the Battalion, and put in the barracks with the non-coms.

Our battalion area was new and not built up, so besides training we had to make the walks, roads and all of the necessary things around our company area. All of the ground was volcanic ash that is very light and fine. We sank into it an inch or two, and kicked up a cloud of dust walking across it.

Somewhat like Camp Roberts, we spent several days on the target range but here we were firing only the M1 rifle. Our last day on the range was to fire for the record. This was a terrible day, very cold, with rain and mist most of the day and with the sun peeking through occasionally. We lay on our stomachs, with a shelter half over us, and the rain dripping on our rifles and in front of our eyes. Despite this bad weather, several of the Aggies qualified as Expert, and I improved my score over my Camp Roberts experience and qualified as Sharpshooter.

One morning, while out on a hike, a tank chased us. Those of us that dropped to the ground and rolled out of its way were left alone, but some of the new trainees got scared and ran. The tank kept chasing them. After that we dug foxholes on the edge of a gentle slope, ate our lunch of canned "C" rations, and then started off on an eleven-mile hike. We dug more foxholes and ate our supper, again of "C" rations. With supper behind us we hiked back to camp, just a couple of miles away. All during our training we dug so many foxholes and slit trenches that I lost count of them.

They taught us to use carpentry tools - hammers, saws, chisels, adz, etc. We built tables, benches and saw horses one day. All of this I had learned as a boy and teenager watching and working with Uncle Chet and Uncle Bob, but for many of my fellow trainees this was all new. Later in our training, we built new barracks. Our training cadre provided the plans and ordered all of the required materials and fixtures. These were delivered on two or three trucks. With the whole company working on this, we made short order of getting the trucks unloaded and the building started. We completed the building in just a few days, as I recall.

In late August it started snowing. One day it lasted an hour or more and came down in sheets, covering the ground. This didn't slow our training. We went out and built a road through the forest, cleared the underbrush, cut down trees up to about ten inches in diameter with axes, and larger trees with two-man crosscut saws. These crosscut saws were a new experience for me. This was all just brute manpower without the use of any heavy construction machinery. Another day we received training on bulldozers, road graders and cranes. I had a scary experience on a Caterpillar D8 bulldozer. I started down a hill that was progressively getting steeper and was heading toward a huge tree. I momentarily forgot how to stop it but remembered how to lower the blade, which I dropped, and it dug in and the dozer ground to a stop.

For a few days we learned to build bridges of several types. We built a pontoon bridge across the Little Deschutes River and then tore it down. This required us to get in the near freezing river water that was fed by snowmelt from the mountains. The individual pontoons were floated into position with their keel parallel to the stream and about twenty to thirty feet apart. Bailey bridges units were assembled on top of the pontoons, to form the roadway. The Bailey bridge requires no special tools or heavy equipment for construction. The bridge elements are small enough to be carried in a truck, and strong enough to carry tanks. Each panel, or unit, is ten feet long by five feet high and weighs 600 pounds, light enough to be carried by a few soldiers, and they are connected to each other by pins. Several of these units could be placed side-by-side and also on top of each other. This allowed flexibility to accommodate different weights of trucks or tanks for various span lengths depending on the spacing between pontoons or the spacing between piers that are installed in the river. We had cards that provided the number of units needed for these different requirements.

We also had training with the H-10 bridge units. These were an older, U.S. Army design, similar to those for a Bailey bridge, but they were considerably heavier and required the use of a crane to lift them into position to be pinned to another unit. The Army also had H-20 and H-30 bridge units, but we didn't train with these.

About two months into our training we made a 23-mile hike. The day started with breakfast of "K" field rations in the barracks. During the morning we were attacked by tanks and airplanes, and had to put on gas masks during a tear gas attack. At noon, about 12 miles out, we stopped at a bivouac area, for about an hour. We dug foxholes, and ate another "K" ration lunch. ("K" consisted of three wax-coated boxes, marked breakfast, dinner or supper. "C" rations were prepared foods in pull-top cans.) We hiked for another ten miles up and down hills and stopped for supper of more "K" rations, and of course, we dug more foxholes.   From there we had only another mile to go to get back to camp.

We received training in map reading and compass marches. The officers would assign each squad a multi-leg march with compass bearings and distances for each leg. The squad leader would sight down the direction of the given bearing and pick out a landmark to march toward and count the paces until the distance was reached, and then sight in the next bearing and repeat this procedure until the course was completed and he arrived at the designated ending location. If there wasn't a prominent landmark to march toward, he would send a soldier out two or three hundred paces, positioning him on line. Then everyone would march to him, repeating this process until the end of that leg was reached. The next time, we went out for a night compass-march. The trucks took all four squads of our company to different starting points; but, all of our courses ended at the same rendezvous point. This started out as *a slow go* since it was difficult to spot a landmark in the darkness, and I couldn't send a soldier too far ahead and still see him in the dim moonlight. Despite this, my squad was the first one in. Our last leg was on the compass bearing N 22° E. I realized that this was true geographic North, and the stars were bright with the Big Dipper and its North Star clearly visible, so I didn't need to send a soldier out and line him up on our path.

On another day we received training with explosives, mostly with TNT but some with Primer Cord and with plastic explosives. The TNT that we trained with was in small half-pound yellow blocks, two inches by two inches by four inches. There was a hole in one end of the block where the cap was inserted. Primer cord was a very long plastic tube, filled with an explosive like TNT, and about a quarter of an inch in diameter, and rolled up on a wheel. It could be pulled from the wheel and wrapped around a tree trunk one or several times, depending on the size of the tree. Like the small blocks of TNT, it was triggered by a blasting cap. Plastic explosive is soft and malleable and can be molded around irregular shaped things. Once it is in place, a blasting cap is inserted into it and it is set off the same way as TNT.

Probably the scariest training event of our basic training experience was the Blitz Course. This course ended with all of us crawling on our bellies under live machine gun fire. We were instructed to stay very close to the ground with nothing sticking up above 30 inches. We knew that the machine gun tripods were well weighted to the ground and that the barrels were above a bar that prevented them being depressed below their firing position, but we had heard of one trainee being killed when a defective round dropped below its programmed level, so we were extra careful.

The last part of our training was a 23-mile hike. At midnight the entire company climbed into trucks and were taken to the starting point of our hike. This was about 15 miles northwest of camp. On reaching there we dug sleeping trenches and made our sleeping bags with a shelter half, two blankets and a heavy comforter. I slept nice and warm but I made the mistake of leaving my shoes out on the edge of my trench. The next morning they had a thick coating of frost. The next day was spent laying mines and recovering them, and hiking. All of our meals that day were "D" rations, the hard chocolate bars. That night I kept my shoes in my sleeping bag. The second day we started an 11-mile hike, up and down hills, some with inclines of 30°, in the general direction of camp. We stopped by the river, dug our prone shelters, ate supper. After it got dark, we built a footbridge across the river. When we finished the bridge, we dug another sleeping trench, made our sleeping bags and went to sleep. We didn't get up until well after daybreak. This concluded our Engineer Basic Training. I would say that Camp Roberts trained us to be soldiers and Camp Abbot trained us to be builders.

I boarded the *Searay* and started my first ocean voyage heading for New Guinea. The *Searay* was a new cargo ship that had been converted to troop transport ship. There was a small mess hall where we were served in shifts. Space was limited, so there were no seats, we ate standing up. Meals were served on metal trays with separate compartments. Showers were with seawater most of the time. Fresh water was available about once a week, but then we had to turn it on only long enough to get wet and then soap up with it off, and then back on for a quick rinse. The one and only deck available to the soldiers was barely large enough for all of us to be on it at the same time, and then only if we were all standing up.

Shortly after we put to sea, one of the ship's officers asked for volunteers for guard duty. Normally, in the army, you never want to volunteer for anything, and guard duty was always a boring job. Despite this, I had somehow learned that this was not the typical guard duty and I volunteered. My duties consisted of sitting on a folding canvas stool at the edge of the ship's deck at night and looking out at the sea to spot any lights, which could be enemy ships. This was a very pleasant duty. I enjoyed the solitude and cool ocean breeze for four hours, and I was out of the smelly bunk hole. Beside myself, there were other guards, spaced about ten feet apart, along both sides of the ship. The *Searay* crossed the equator on October 6th and everyone aboard became a member of the "Ancient Order of the Deep". We were all given a document attesting to this.

After a seventeen-day voyage, we landed at Oro Bay, New Guinea. The United States had built an advance base here as a staging area for allied ships, an army camp, and anti-aircraft gun batteries in the surrounding hills. Every day that I was at this camp it started raining at sunset, rained all night long and stopped at sunrise. The first few minutes in the morning, as the rain stopped and the air was clear, I could see the tops of the Owen Stanley Range of mountains to the south.

A large part of the camp was a Casual Replacement Center used for administrative purposes, issuing clothing and equipment and discharging released soldiers. I was assigned to the 105 Replacement Company. We were quartered in pyramidal tents equipped with eight canvas cots. Each cot had a wooded frame above it that supported a mosquito net. This was a damp, tropical area with lots of mosquitoes that really swarmed at sunset and sunrise, and malaria was a prevalent disease. Because of this, we were given Atabrine tablets that we took daily. In a fairly short time we developed a pallor or yellow tint to our skin, which I kept my entire time in the Pacific area. While in New Guinea I developed "jungle rot" that caused very smelly feet and small blisters in my armpits.

There was a large, outdoor movie theater. It had seats of logs. The bark had been removed and they had been split down the middle. The split side had been smoothed and the round side was placed on wooden posts driven into the ground. The movie projection equipment was housed in a small weather-tight building just large enough for the equipment and the operator. Movies started after it was completely dark, and by this time the rains had started. We sat on the log seats with our ponchos pulled up over our heads looking out the ponchos' neck hole and our helmet liners on our heads. The mess hall was a large building with a corrugated steel roof and no walls. It had several rows of long tables about chest high and no seats. Food was served on metal compartment trays and everyone ate standing up. About my first day at this camp, they asked for KP (kitchen police) volunteers and I stepped up. This would get me out of training requirements in the damp jungles and my KP duties were easy. All I did was keep the tables clean. This took about an hour and a half to two hours every meal since the soldiers were served in shifts. Most soldiers were just given a standard amount of each item, but I had more choices in what I ate. I could select what I wanted and the amount that I wanted of the foods that had been cooked, which was mostly of dehydrated vegetables and canned meat. The meat was in large square cans about four inches on each side and about a foot long. The meat was much like an early version of Spam, not very good. This is probably the reason that, to this day, I don't like Spam. One time, while I was on KP duty, the mess hall received a large supply of fresh onions. To me this was a welcome change from our normal dehydrated foods, and though most of the troops passed them up, I ate them, with relish, like apples. KP turned out to be a great benefit on Thanksgiving Day. We had turkey with the usual side dishes of fresh vegetables and real mashed potatoes. However, the turkey necks were not being dished out on the serving line so I ate my fill of them. Everything was really delicious, particularly after a normal diet of canned meat and cooked dehydrated vegetables.

Just a few days after Thanksgiving, I was notified that I was promoted to Corporal and being transferred to the 43rd Engineer Construction Battalion.

I departed from Oro Bay on a C-47 Skytrain. We landed in Hollandia, Dutch New Guinea for a brief stop. From there we flew on to Morotai, Netherlands East Indies, where I joined the Battalion. It was the second oldest construction

battalion in the Pacific, and had four companies; A Company, B Company, C Company and Headquarters Company. I was assigned to B Company.

Morotai was just a couple of degrees north of the equator, and was the final island invasion before the liberation of the Philippines. The 43rd Engineer Construction Battalion was nearing completion with the building of the airfield to accommodate the Army Air Force bombers. My only clear memory of that time was the almost nightly phosphorus bombing of the personnel tents by the Japanese from Halmahera. These bombings inflicted phosphorus burns on the soldiers. I was told that in earlier times the Japanese bombed the airfield, but they ran out of high-explosive bombs. The Allied Forces had cut off their supply lines to Halmahera.

Toward the remaining days of December, the 43rd Engineers' equipment was loaded aboard LSTs (Landing Ship Tanks). LSTs were 380 feet long with a draft of 15 feet at the stern and 3 feet at the bow, and equipped with berths for 217 troops and a crew of 98. They had flat bottoms and no method of stabilization. The bow had a hinged door and fold-down ramp. The LST was sailed into the beach until its bow touched the bottom, the doors were opened and the ramp lowered so each piece of equipment could be driven aboard. They were backed on so they would be

ready to drive off at the invasion location. I don't remember how many LSTs it took to handle all of our bulldozers, graders, cranes, rollers, air compressors, trucks, jeeps and miscellaneous supplies, but I think it was two or three. As each piece of equipment was loaded, and in the planned location, it had to be secured to the deck to prevent sliding as the ship rolled and pitched, which it did in even light seas.

We sailed in a large convoy from Morotai for the Lingayen Gulf Invasion, on the west coast of Luzon Island, Philippines, well north of Manila. The convoy sailed through the mouth of this gulf. Enemy action was relatively light, both on the beach and in the air. However the sea was rough, causing some LSTs to breach, but all of the LSTs that had the 43rd Engineers aboard hit the beach, opened their bow doors and dropped their ramps without difficulty.

This landing followed a devastating naval bombardment, and about 68,000 soldiers of the U.S. Sixty Army landed in the early morning of January 9, 1945, meeting no opposition. A total of over 200,000 troops landed over the next several days and established a 20-mile beachhead.

Our battalion went ashore on January 11th (D+2 or Day Two) for the Lingayen Invasion. Our LSTs were just a very few of all the landing craft going onto the beach. There were many LCIs (Landing Craft Infantry) boats. We immediately set up camp just a hundred yards, or so, from the beach. While this was being done the dozers and graders proceeded inland about a half to three-quarters of a mile, near a coconut grove, and started leveling and grading for a fighter airstrip. Due to the soft, loose sand the privates cut fronds off a grove of palm trees, and many of the corporals, including myself, both directed and helped with this work. These palm fronds were laid down on the graded airstrip. On top of these, pierced steel planks were installed to make the surface matting for the airstrip. The palm leaves were to prevent an excess of sand from being sucked up through the holes in the planks when a plane landed or took off.

Laying the steel planks was going fairly rapidly when I got sick with dysentery or diarrhea, so I don't know how long the strip was or how much time it took to complete it. I stayed in my tent most of a day, alternating between going to the latrine and into the gulf to stay clean. About the end of the day I was taken to the nearby 54th Evacuation Hospital. I don't recall how long I stayed in this Field Hospital, but I think that within a week or two, I was well enough to be moved to the 24th Field Hospital several miles toward Manila. I remained in this Field Hospital until I was fully recovered and ready to be sent back to duty. My dysentery or diarrhea was cured but I continued to have arm pit blisters from the "jungle rot", and the doctors continued to supply me with liquid penicillin to apply to these areas.

The personnel in charge of providing our orders, and arranging transportation, kept wanting to send me to the 43rd Division but I finally convinced them that I belonged with the 43rd Engineer Construction Battalion, which had moved to Manila. They gave me my individual orders, as I was the only one going to the 43rd Engineers. On, or about, February 15th I climbed aboard a truck with a larger group of soldiers going to one or more different units in or near Manila. When the truck reached Tarlac it was stopped by a couple of MPs. They told the driver to return to the hospital, as the road ahead was not secure and subject to Japanese attack. When the truck started to follow these orders, I grabbed my duffel bag and dropped off over the tailgate. I had no intention of returning and taking the chance of being sent to the wrong organization.

As I walked down the streets of Tarlac, I saw a truck with the 43rd Engineers Fleur De Lis insignia on its door. I walked up, told the driver who I was and why I was there, and he immediately agreed to take me with him. He was there to pick up supplies. I helped him and another soldier load the truck and climbed aboard on top of the supplies. We departed Tarlac in the late afternoon and stopped to spend the night somewhere along the road to Manila. It wasn't safe to proceed with the lights on because of the probability of Japanese snipers.

When we arrived in Manila I found that my company had moved into abandoned Spanish style homes or haciendas on the eastern outskirts of Manila. When the 43rd Engineers first arrived here, fighting was still in progress in the north border of the city. They bivouacked in some empty homes that were ahead of the front line, but in three days the front line had moved on beyond their camp area. These houses were quite plush quarters in comparison to our pyramidal tents.

We had three major jobs while in the Manila area. The first one that was assigned to my platoon was started the day after I rejoined it, after leaving the hospital. This job was the repair of the major water line that carried drinking water to the city from Laguna de Bay, the largest fresh water lake on Luzon. It was a 72-inch concrete pipeline that the Japanese had blasted in several places after the U.S. forces occupied Manila. After closing a valve to stop the flow of water, we excavated the area around the damaged sections of pipe, removed the damaged joints, installed new sections of pipe between the ends of undamaged pipes, wrapped the spaces between the new and old pipe ends, built a form around these, and poured fresh concrete to enclose and reinforce these new joints. The nearest source of sand and gravel was in the vicinity of the Mariquina River which was still in the hands of the Japanese. Reconnaissance, while looking for a suitable site, encountered sniper fire, but we found a site where personnel and equipment could be operated and protected from the Japanese. A shovel and bulldozer were moved there along with a number of trucks with machine gun protection. In route they were stopped by a Calvary Recon Group and advised not to proceed, but they were allowed to continue at their own risk. This job was near enough to our bivouac area that we didn't set up an on-site camp.

While bivouacked in the Spanish Hacienda, I had a couple of interesting experiences. One day when I went sightseeing in downtown Manila I passed a bank where someone, probably GIs, had blown a safe in a bank. There were all types of Japanese invasion currency (printed by the occupying force as legal tender), and real Japanese currency, scattered over the street. I picked up a few bills of invasion currency that had been printed for use in the USA. I could have, but didn't, pick up any of the real Japanese currency. I didn't stop to think that it would one day be worth keeping.

On March 7, 1945, after we completed the waterline repair job, Company B relocated to Guadalupe, several miles to the east of Manila, to build a major bridge, using H-20 bridge units for a 360-foot span, over the Pasig River. This river flows from Luguna de Bay to Manila Bay, a distance of about fifteen and one-half miles. This was the first permanent bridge over the Pasig River.

When we arrived at this bridge site, the area had not been fully cleared of Japanese and was considered in advance of the front lines and subject to Japanese attacks. However, we didn't have any contact, not even a single sniper attack. We set up our camp near the northern bank of the river, and started work. This was both a bridge building and a road construction job. Two small barges were lashed together to provide enough buoyancy to support the crane that was used to drive piles, in the river, for the three bents, or frameworks to carry both vertical and horizontal loads. The piles were large untreated tree trunks, stripped of their bark, and about three feet in diameter at the butts and some hundred feet long. The pile driver leads were barely wide enough for the piles to fit between them, and the heads of the piles had to be extensively trimmed down to fit inside the pile driver cap. The crane used a drop hammer to drive each pile. I don't remember how deep the river was at this location, or how high above water the caps for the pile bents were, but I do remember that the southern bank of the river was honeycombed with caves and tunnels that were about eight feet from the floor to the roof and the floor was well above water level, so the caps were probably 20 feet or more above the water level. The caps were 12" X 12" timbers. One of my jobs was to trim the heads of the piling, ready for driving. It took much longer for the crane operator to position and drive a pile than it took me and other soldiers to trim the pile heads.

While the pile driving was in progress, the roadway on the northern side was being constructed. The portion nearest the river was solid rock and required blasting before the material could be removed to get the roadbed to the needed grade. Another job that I did was using the air-driven bit to drill holes in the roadbed for insertion of dynamite to blast the rock. As with the pile head trimming job, there was time between drilling holes and waiting while others loaded the holes with dynamite and blasted the rock.

After about 200 feet of roadbed next to the river was complete, we started assembling the H-20 steel truss bridge units. Two lines of these were assembled on top of rollers so they could be pushed out over the river. The length of these assembled trusses needed to be several feet longer than twice the distance from the bank to the first pier, so that it would not tend to tip and fall in the river as it was pushed toward the first pier. A bulldozer was used to push these trusses out over the river, one at a time. As the end approached the pier, a soldier walked out on top of the narrow truss and hooked the crane's cable to the truss. The crane lifted and held the H-20 truss slightly above the rollers on the bridge cap until it was pushed passed the rollers. The crane operator then lowered it to sit on the rollers.

While working on this bridge I saw two or three dead Japanese soldiers float by. I also explored the caves and tunnels on the far side of the river. The Japanese had occupied these and there was considerable machine shop equipment in one area - a lathe, a drill press and a band saw. There were also abandoned bunks where they had slept. At that time I assumed that the Japanese had dug these but later, when I lived in Japan in 1981-1984, I visited this area and was told by a Filipino resident that this tunnel had been dug as an escape route by the Spanish settlers living in Manila many years before World War II.

On completion of the bridge and road job, Company B returned to Manila to the same haciendas. The other companies of the 43rd engineers had started building barracks for the WACs, and Headquarters buildings for AFWESPAC (Armed Forces Western Pacific). Company B joined them in this job. A couple of weeks later I was promoted to Sergeant and transferred to Headquarters Company. My first job was to draft additional plans for this work and make blue prints for field use. This was an interesting process. After completing drafting the plans on paper, I traced them, with black ink, on clear transparent tracing paper. When the tracing was finished I put it in a frame with a clear glass front, and a piece of unexposed blueprint paper behind the tracing and then put the back on the frame. This was a piece of quarter inch plywood that was locked into the frame with clips. Then I took this outside where it was exposed to the bright sunlight. After awhile the paper turned a bright blue. When it was removed the lines showing the plans were white, and would remain white for weeks before they also turned blue from continued exposure to light.

I was promoted to Staff Sergeant and given the interesting and challenging job of planning the placement of all of the battalion equipment on LSTs for the pending move to Japan. This involved three major elements: maximum use of area available, weight distribution to maintain the ship's trim, and "first needed – first off" logistics. This was an interesting use of drafting and center-of-gravity calculations.

The battalion moved to a dried-out rice field staging area on the outskirts of Batangas in preparation for the invasion of Japan. Just a week after we arrived, the first Atomic Bomb ("Little Boy") was dropped on Hiroshima on August 6, 1945. This was followed three days later with the second Atomic Bomb ("Fat Man") dropped on Nagasaki which brought an end to the war. This was a welcome relief in the big picture, but with nothing to do, and in an undesirable location, we got bored with the long days of inactivity. After almost two months of this, we got orders to load out for movement to Japan. We loaded out on LSTs and sailed toward Japan. We had a rough, rolling trip, having encountered a storm. One of the sheep-foot rollers broke loose, creating a dangerous situation for the men that had to secure it, but they were successful and no one was injured. We sailed into Yokohama, on a bright sunny day, a few days after my birthday. It was a wonderful experience to be able to dock in peacetime conditions, instead of wartime conditions. A wartime invasion would have been bloody, with a good chance that many would not have survived.

From Yokohama we convoyed to Irumagawa. Along the way we passed many civilians. The older people were somber and quite, but the children were curious and friendly. When the convoy stopped and we climbed down from the backside of our trucks to stretch our legs, the children approached us speaking very accented English. This made me feel comfortable. I had wondered how the people would react to us. Irumagawa is a few miles north of Tachikawa, which in turn is just a few miles west of Tokyo. It is fairly close to the spine of mountains that form the backbone of Japan. Mt. Fuji's snow-capped top was clearly visible from there.

On the outskirts of the small village of Irumagawa the Japanese had a small grass-covered, airstrip that had been built in 1937. It was the Air Academy for the Japanese Army Air Force, with the academy in the town. Mostly training aircraft operated from this base, including several biplanes painted orange. When we occupied the base, we saw a mock-up of a B-29 that they had used for training suicide teams on how to disable a B-29. Fortunately, these paratrooper missions never happened.

We set up camp and built corrugated steel barracks instead of pitching pyramidal tents. It was late fall, approaching winter, and was already quite cold. Having just arrived from tropical Philippines it probably seemed colder to us than it would have if we had been there during the summer. A wood-burning stove in the center of each barracks building kept the chill off but never really got them warm. We still slept on canvas cots, but were issued thin mattresses, blankets and sleeping bags. These sleeping bags were thick wool with a zipper opening, and incased in a thinner weather tight cover. So I slept well and was comfortable.

We also built a nice shower with hot and cold water. For hot water an interesting heating system was built. This consisted of several 55 gallon barrels, with the ends removed and welded together, but with the ends left in the two end barrels. These were mounted in a horizontal position on a steel frame. Water was piped into one end and flowed out the other end to the showerheads. Under this line of barrels was a one-inch pipe that was bent in a long "U" shape and mounted below the line of barrels with one leg of the "U" above the other leg. The section of pipe that was below the top section had small holes drilled through the top of that section, and the end of this section was capped. The other end was connected to an elevated drum filled with 100-octane gasoline, with a valve at the exit from the drum. To heat the water the valve was opened allowing gasoline to flow. As it started to pour out of the small holes it was lit. The fire flamed up past the upper leg of one-inch pipe and to the bottom of the line of 55 gallon barrels. This heated both the water and the gasoline, and caused the gasoline to exit the small holes in a gaseous form that burned hotter than when it was in its liquid form. This system didn't take long to heat the water, and once hot, provided a continuous stream of hot water.

The battalion's job here was to improve and lengthen the small grass strip into a concrete runway, 150 feet wide and 5,000 feet long, capable of handling our bombers. However, instead of doing the actual construction work, we provided the engineering, quality control, inspection, and surveying and level control, but used a Japanese construction company, Hazami-Gumi Company Limited, to do the construction work. Earth moving began November 7, 1945. Concrete placement was 12% complete by Christmas Day. I believe that the use of a Japanese contractor was part of General Douglas MacArthur's plan to rehabilitate the Japanese.

Partly as the result of having the Japanese do the construction work, we had a little more free time to explore the area. Being a Staff Sergeant I had better access to the use of a Jeep, and took advantage of this to see areas that I couldn't have seen on foot and public transportation. I remember making a couple of visits to Chibu, a very small village, in the mountains. I and several other soldiers visited this pretty little village. It was physically untouched by the war, very unlike the destruction we saw in Yokohama and Tokyo. The road to this village was unpaved and cut into the side of the mountain and barely wide enough for cars to meet and pass each other. This was a scary drive, but well worth it, to see neat and orderly Japanese buildings that weren't torn up by bombing.

The day before Christmas I received orders to return to the U.S.A. for discharge. Two days after Christmas, December 27, 1945, I, and many other soldiers, boarded the USS Matsonia. This had been a cruise ship of the Matson Navigation Company. It had been taken over by the Navy as a Troop Carrier. We arrived in California on January 5th, 1946, at Fort Ord, on the Monterey Bay Peninsula.

My stay at Fort Ord was very brief, just a few days. About the first thing I did, when I had some free time, was to go to a restaurant in downtown Monterey and order a big T-Bone steak with French fries and a glass of milk. After the army's dehydrated food, it was everything I could ask for. However, my stomach had shrunk so much that, to my disgust, I couldn't eat all of it. My mind is nearly blank on the activities that I was involved with on the base, but I do remember that I had a complete physical examination. Happily nothing wrong was found except my still existing "jungle rot". Soon, I boarded a train heading to Fort Sam Houston in San Antonio, Texas, where I was discharged on January 13th, 1946. The following day I enlisted in the Reserves Corps at Separation Center, Fort Sam Houston, Texas for three years. During my years of service I received the following decorations and citations: Good Conduct Medal, Victory Ribbon, 1 Service Strip, American Campaign Medal, Asiatic Pacific Campaign Medal with 2 Bronze Stars, Philippine Liberation Ribbon with 1 Bronze Star, 2 Overseas Service Bars, Expert Rifle and Qualified Light Machine Gun.

With an independent travel voucher, I took the train back home to Galveston. During my absence, all of the girls that I had known were either gone or married. However, a good friend of mine had been discharged about six months earlier and was dating a Cadet Nurse. They arranged a blind date for me with Ann, another Cadet Nurse. About a month later another friend returned from service and they got him a blind date with Jean Martin. She was the roommate of one of the girls I was dating. A short while later, on April 1st, 1946, I called the nurses' residence to see if Ann would like to go to the movies.

Jean answered the phone and told me that Ann was out on a date. So, I asked Jean if she would like to go to the movies with me. She did. This was the last date I ever had, and nine weeks later we were married.

Jean, at that time, was frequently on evening shift or night duty and I was returning to A&M to resume my education during the summer term. We knew that this would drastically reduce the time we could be together when I could get home. I did return to A&M and came home the first weekend, June 8th, to marry Jean. She continued her nursing education and joined me nine months later. But I did manage to get home nearly every weekend to be with her.

© 2012 John Bardgette

WORLD WAR II EXPERIENCES BY MICKEY BISHOP

I started nurses' training in September of 1941, and in December Pearl Harbor was bombed. I never really gave much thought to getting involved, but when I graduated President Roosevelt was saying, "Nurses, we need you." So several of us signed up, took basic training and learned to march. (I don't know why we needed that!) Then we were off to overseas duty.

We left Camp Stoneman the day before Easter in full gear, including helmets. As the boat pulled away the band was playing Easter Parade ("*In your Easter Bonnet, with all the frills upon it*"). When we arrived at the pier in San Francisco another band was playing, you guessed it, Easter Parade. Our helmets were a far cry from frilly hats!

With 5,000 troops we spent thirty days aboard ship, stopping in Hollandia, New Guinea to pick up our convoy. It was a little scary listening to Tokyo Rose broadcast the exact whereabouts of our ship which she called the "Grey Ghost." When we got to the Philippines, the Japanese were still holding the reservoir around Manila. At first, groups of four received a helmet of water a day to bathe in. (So those helmets did come in handy.) Manila is hot. Fortunately, our engineers managed to dig wells soon. What a glorious and clean day when the showers were turned on!

We could see our bombers fly over and then we were busy with the wounded. We worked long hours in huge tents held down by huge ropes with huge rats running up and down them. We cared for soldiers who were little boys coming out of anesthesia calling "Mom" - and I'd say, "It's OK, I'm here." Isn't it amazing what we can do when we're young! As the mother of three sons, there's no way I could do it today.

We slept under netting or we would have been eaten alive by mosquitoes. On duty we wore high top boots for the same reason. We found time to travel in jeeps over bomb-gutted roads to jitterbug to the swing music we loved. We came home via the Panama Canal to New York. We had to slow up the East Coast because there was another ship at our berth. Every nurse was ready to mutiny when we found out we had to wait for a ship full of British war brides to embark. The sight of the Statue of Liberty was a great welcome home!

I salute those "Little Boys" and my nation that made it all happen in just four years. Thank you, Tom Brokaw, for recognizing it, too.

© 2012 Mickey Bishop

WORLD WAR II BY ELEANOR BROWN

I didn't understand. Why did the United States have to get involved in a war halfway around the world? It wasn't our war, after all. My fiancé, Lee, marched against the war. Lee had seen what the Japanese and Chinese military did to their enemies. He'd been stationed in Shanghai for a year and been caught in the middle of the war for China. He stood on a soap box in the park attempting, with others of like thinking, to convince anyone who would listen of the horrors of war and why the U.S.A. should not get involved in one. Meanwhile, Franklin Roosevelt was trying to convince Congress and the American people that we needed to help England defeat the Nazi and Fascist powers taking over Europe.

We were unconvinced until the unthinkable happened. On a quiet Sunday morning, December 7, 1941, the Japanese (without provocation) attacked Pearl Harbor in Hawaii. The death toll ran into the thousands. The Pacific Fleet was nearly wiped out. That day, "the day that shall live in infamy", as Franklin Delano Roosevelt so eloquently stated, began our involvement in a second World War. There were no longer any pacifists standing on soap boxes or marching with signs. We hadn't wanted to go to war. Now, the war had come to us. Lines at the recruitment centers wound around block after block as young men sought to enlist in every branch of the military service in the hope of getting even with those "Japs". The United States was quickly involved in a declared war with Japan on the west and Germany on the east (sinking our supply ships to England, thus breaking the rules of neutrality).

We were losing men faster than the volunteers were coming. Speedily and poorly trained, often teen-aged boys without the maturity to think rationally were put out on the front lines. Many performed courageous acts of exceptional valor. Many became outstanding leaders. But more were wounded or died. It was the wounds of their spirits that took the greatest toll. Few talked about the war. That is, few talked about the real war. They talked about exploits, being outnumbered or out-gunned, but not about the dead bodies floating on the waves with heads, arms, or legs blown off; not about wetting their pants, fleeing in terror, seeing the blood squirting out of the heads of their dying buddies while they were next to them, helpless to do anything except to cower in a hand-made ditch among the dead and dying and pray that the big guns would stop firing, that the blood which they saw wasn't their own, that the Medic would come in time, that somehow, some way, somebody would get them out of this hell hole! The quiet was worse. Frightening thoughts would come into their heads. Where was the enemy now? Was there a soldier creeping up to this little ditch? It was so dark! And the stench of death was everywhere. It took days before a few men, growing weary of the wait, or going insane from fear, or soberly knowing that someone had to stop those guns, rose to the call and attacked the hills above, courageously killing the enemy to save the lives of their fellow soldiers. Their true thoughts are known only to God.

The U.S. forces had been fighting in World War II for three years on two fronts. Congress had passed the draft. The first to go were single men between the ages of 18 and 26. The next round included married men with no children of the same age. Finally, married men with one child were being drafted. Some men were exempt because their occupations provided for the defense of our homeland. Among those occupations were air traffic controllers, so my husband was exempt.

In 1944, we were living in St. Louis, Missouri when my husband, Lee, received a two-grade promotion. The problem was - we had to move to Cincinnati, Ohio. He made a trip there to find us a place to live. At the end of nearly a week, he almost gave up the promotion because he couldn't find anyone who would rent to people with children. Our children were two years old and eight months old. He finally lucked out and found a woman who would rent her house to us. Her husband was in the Service and she had become ill and had to move. We had been living in a two-bedroom house with rent of $35 per month in St. Louis. Lee's raise was $50 per month. The house in Cincinnati rented for $85 per month! But it was worth it. This was a beautiful two-story house with three bedrooms, located amidst a cluster of seven homes on a hill overlooking the river, and came fully furnished. It even had dishes and silverware - and a cat!

The airport where Lee worked was on one side of Cincinnati. The house was sixteen miles on the other side. Gas was rationed. Lee would drive five miles to where he could catch a bus and then a streetcar to get to work. Our gas ration was insufficient to get Lee to work and for me to do the grocery shopping. But we were lucky! The grocer in the small town where Lee caught the bus, would call me every Monday, Wednesday, and Saturday. I had to have my grocery list ready when he called, and he would deliver! Cigarettes were at a premium. (They were being sent overseas for our servicemen,) Meat and bacon were rationed. Again, the meat went to the military first. The grocer made sure all of

his customers got their share when these items were available. One day he brought me pork chops, even though I hadn't ordered them. He almost got a "thank-you kiss," it was such an unexpected surprise.

When we rented the house there was one condition. We had to promise to vacate the house when the owner returned from the war. We kept that promise. He could hardly believe it when he found that the bottle of Scotch which he'd left in the china closet awaiting his homecoming celebration (right after V-J Day) was still there......unopened!

© 2012 Eleanor M. Brown

BOMBS OVER GLASGOW BY BILL CAVEN
WORLD WAR II

I was born in a tenement ground-floor flat in Glasgow, Scotland, on July 3, 1936, after two-and-a-half days of agony for my mother. July 1st, 2nd and 3rd were blamed for all my mother's pain and suffering bringing an eleven-pound baby boy into the Caven Clan. Mother, Sarah Meikle Caven, was able to provide two additional clan members--my sister, Christine, and my brother, Brian--over the next ten years. I should claim credit for her longevity, since she had to stay alive to keep up our battle. My father, William James Caven, a shipbuilder, was in charge of a crew of men at Clydebank Shipyards.

Saving the Whiskey Ship

Three years following my birth, World War II was declared September 1, 1939. My father was sent to a west coast island called Eriskay to attempt to recover a ship, the SS *Politician* that had been torpedoed by a U Boat on February 5, 1941. The ship did not sink immediately, but it was taking on water. It was only a matter of time before the precious cargo would be lost. The single most important cargo item was whiskey on route to America. The U.S. accepted whiskey as payment for goods being sent to Scotland to aid in the war with Germany. At this time, whiskey was rationed and the island of Eriskay was presently dry. The stranded cargo was a true miracle to the islanders, providing them the perfect opportunity to save the whiskey from mainlanders or other islanders and at the same time do their patriotic duty by saving the ship. About 24,000 bottles were "liberated" before authorities arrived on the scene. While providing the locals with the great entertainment of savoring the whiskey, the rescue also caused a disaster. When they became sober, it was discovered they had forgotten where their prize whiskey was hidden! We stayed on the island for a few months, while my father and his crew repaired the "Whiskey Ship." It was then taken back to Glasgow for further repair and restocking. An official investigation failed to locate the missing whiskey. I wonder if whiskey becomes better maturing underground. Compton MacKenzie wrote a bestselling novel, *Whisky Galore*, 1947 about this incident, and the book was made into a movie after the war. The film was released as *Tight Little Island* in the U.S. because titles naming alcohol were banned in the United States at that time. Most of the film's representation was reasonably accurate.

Glasgow Under Attack

When we returned to Glasgow, I saw what war could do. Some bombs had been dropped in our neighborhood. Two of the tenements had been hit. My father explained why parts of our neighborhood had been bombed. He said the German's target was Clydebank Shipyards, located only a few miles away. When they turned west to fly home, they got rid of extra bombs on the tenements. Air raid sirens became such a mournful, frightening sound that they left us with a DREADFUL, UNSPEAKABLE, PAINFUL feeling of sadness, never to be forgotten. We knew some families were now suffering and the wail of the siren became a depressing sound. As the months passed, more people began wearing black armbands. The armbands identified people, mostly women, who had lost somebody in the war. Sometimes, a woman with an armband would touch my hair when I was playing in the street and say, "I hope, son, that the war is over soon so you don't have to go to Germany."

My uncle, Jim Meikle, was a Spitfire pilot. I worshipped him. When he visited, he shared my large bed and captivated me with tales of his flying. I once asked him if the war would last long enough for me to become a Spitfire pilot, too. He said he hoped it would be over long before I was old enough to fly. I really was so proud of him especially since he flew a Spitfire. Because he downed so many German planes, he was considered a British Air Force flying ace. My uncle Charlie Meikle, brother of Uncle Jim, also served in the military and saw first-hand the newly liberated concentration camp victims. He only told me about it once, when he had had one too many. It was a difficult memory for him.

Each evening the wardens would inspect everyone's windows to be sure no light showed. There was a fine if we had frequent violation notices put in our letterboxes. We also were required to use tape on the glass to reduce the prospect of being hit with flying glass from shattered windows during an air raid. This happened in our street, where two older ladies were hit with flying glass from their windows as they hadn't used tape. One of them died from her injuries.

We had bomb shelters built in our street where people could go directly from their tenements to an assigned shelter. It was a regulation to shut down all lights, cover all windows and get out of the house to the bomb shelter when the siren sounded. Air raid wardens would help residents get into their shelter if the shipyards were being bombed. At first it was exciting getting out of bed and putting on the gasmask and going to the shelter. As the war continued, by 1943 the third year, we stopped going to the shelter and wearing our gas masks as we were fed up with the war. My mom said she would rather die in her own bed since it was cleaner than the dirty bomb shelter.

Most of Dad's crew were at Clydebank and would stay at the shipyard trying to protect the ships from the bombing. During these air attacks innocent civilians were killed in Clydebank. On March 13 and 14, 1941, some 439 Luftwaffe bombers dropped over 1,000 bombs on Clydebank. Over 35,000 people were made homeless, 578 civilians died and 617 were seriously injured. This town was famous for having built the *Queen Mary, Queen Elizabeth, Queen Elizabeth II* and the HMS *Hood*, a large destroyer. Only eight of the 12,000 houses were undamaged. A war memorial was dedicated to the crew of a Polish destroyer, ORP *Piorun*, which helped defend Clydebank docks and the shipyards of John Brown and Company during this Luftwaffe air raid. (Piorun means thunderbolt in Polish.) My father was working in the shipyards during the attack; fortunately he survived. My father's crew built several dummy ships that the Germans destroyed, thus sparing the real ships so vital to the war.

Tenements in Glasgow were like groups of villages. Just as in a village, everyone in each tenement knew who you were, where you lived, your mom and dad, what religion you were and every single thing about you and yours. This closeness crimped the style of the young. We knew that if we stepped out of line, the neighbors would tell our parents, who would promptly "thump us out." We played in the streets, rain or shine. No problem for us since there were no cars. Only wealthy people had cars so we were safe on the streets. The only vehicle that came along the street was the coal man. I remember a joke that an uncle of mine told about the coal man. As the slowly moving horse-driven cart came onto the street, the fellow used to yell, "Coal!" "Coal!" My uncle said that the coal man actually yelled, "Coal for money!" The grown-ups all laughed so the next day I asked my uncle why the adults all laughed. He said, "They laughed because some women didn't have enough money for coal, so they made a trade. He then said, "Ask your Dad; he will explain it to you. " I told the joke at school to the older boys; they explained it to me. Fortunately, I didn't go to one of the sisters who ran the Catholic school as I would have received a notice to take home along with the strap for punishment.

As the war progressed, the number of men in the families working at factories and driving street cars decreased rapidly. Women replaced the men, becoming bread winners while continuing their responsibilities in their homes. Older students joined the labor force as junior farmers on a weekly basis. Sometimes we complained about our hard lot. However, when our teachers or our parents told us about the problems the people in London were facing, we understood our luck. For the most part, we only had rain falling on us, not a steady downpour of bombs.

Wartime in London

London suffered greatly as it was the target for many German air attacks. London was bombed 57 nights in a row. (When I learned that dreadful fact, I felt both guilty and relieved at the same time.)

The London area population had to evacuate over two million people from their homes in 1939 and 1940. People in the London area had to have their cats and dogs destroyed since the government wasn't sure their animals could be fed.

One area approximately 18 miles north of the city became a safe haven for Londoners. It had natural protection since there were 22 miles of caves. Over 18,000 people with families moved into these caves. They built a hospital, play areas for children, showers, laundry facilities and wooden beds. The majority of the cave residents were retired. Many spent their time educating and training the children by establishing a complete school underground. This area was called Chislehurst Caves. Prior to the war, it had been a tourist attraction. During the war, throughout this area road signs were changed and street lights were removed so that these caves could not be found by the enemy. Maps were drawn for the locals and all the cave dwellers to insure that none would get lost. (Germans did land or survived downed airplanes, but they were promptly apprehended.)

The Germans increased their air attacks in 1944. They sent 8,000 V1 rockets to hit London destroying 20,000 homes and killing 25,000 people. The V2 rocket, which traveled at 4 times the speed of sound soon followed. These new inventions were overwhelming in that they were quiet and traveled so fast that planes couldn't stop them. When they reached their targets, the rockets would shut off and fall to earth. These deadly instruments of war were devastating in their destruction. Had the V2 rockets been invented a year earlier the results would have been catastrophic.

Shortages and Rationing

After the outbreak of war, only essential foods were imported into Britain, thus certain products were in short supply. For instance, the population didn't see a banana until after the war. To allow food to be distributed fairly, the government established rationing of scarce commodities beginning in January 1940 by issuing ration books to each citizen from age five and upward. The government continually increased the number of food items rationed so that eventually butter, eggs, bacon, meat and sugar were included. Rationing prevented stockpiling since one had limited access to food products. Pregnant women and nursing mothers were given an extra allowance for food and milk. As wartime food shortages grew, prices also increased, thus by 1943 food cost 25 per cent more than it had in 1939. Bartering and black market trading became a way of life. Sadly, some country folks took advantage of their city neighbors and sold farm products at black market prices.

Other items including spirits, matches, clothes, fuel, and cigarettes were rationed. Gas rationing did not apply to medical personnel. As new textiles were in limited supply, a plain, more utilitarian type of clothing, which used less material, came into vogue. My aunt, Doris Caven, had ordered and paid for a new wool suit just before the rationing started. She felt guilty wearing that suit when it was finished, but since it was the best suit she had, she wore it often.   Coal was rationed to save fuel for industry. Cigarettes were not only rationed, but unknown brands were forced upon the smokers. Most people bought five or ten cigarettes at a time, but the brand selection was decided by the shop keeper. If a person bought five cigarettes, four of them would be Pasha, a cheap Turkish cigarette; and only one would be a brand he liked. Pasha had such a foul smell, people would demand the smoker throw it away. If one dared smoke a Pasha on a street car or bus, he would be kicked off.

While lack of good clothing, fuel and cigarettes might be inconvenient, food was essential. The government encouraged people to grow their own vegetables and raise rabbits and provided instructions. Very few of these ideas worked especially if one lived in the city. Some people were able to put soil in boxes and grow vegetables; however, they had to police their boxes and rabbit cages since the temptation for theft was strong.

In some respects, a family's ration books were more important than money since without a coupon, one could not buy essential items. Once, after purchasing food from my mother's list, on the way home I committed the cardinal sin of stopping to play football (soccer). When the game was over, I picked up the bag of food, looked inside and noted that the ration books were not there. The three vital books were gone. Stolen books meant somebody else was eating our entitlement and we could go hungry. I went home knowing I would be punished on two fronts: one for loss of the ration books and the other because it might take as long as four weeks to replace them. On the way home, I prayed for a bomb to injure me so that I would not have to suffer the biggest spanking I would ever receive. My mother cried while she spanked me and cried again. Then my father came home and finished the job. Fortunately, neighbors and relatives all pooled their resources and used some of their rations to feed us until we received our new books three weeks later. I prayed that some day in the future I would read the paper and see a picture of the thief in handcuffs standing on the hangman's platform.

In 1944 an amazing food product came to Great Britain in a can called Specially Pressed American Meats. This epicurean delight became known as SPAM. It was the single most popular product of its day. There was an American flag on the can of SPAM. Two other amazing foods, dehydrated eggs enhanced with a finishing touch of condensed canned milk, were also sent by the U.S.

By the end of the war, September 2, 1945, Lord Woolton, Minister of Food, warned that rationing would not disappear overnight. The food situation, far from becoming easier, became more difficult owing to the urgent necessity of feeding the starving people of continental Europe. It was many years before life got back to normal. Rationing continued late into the 1950's. Bread and potatoes were rationed until 1948. Sugar rationing ended in 1953. All food rationing ended on July 4, 1954, when meat and bacon were finally derationed.

<u>Learning to Work</u>

Since all able-bodied men were fighting the Germans, farmers were left with little help to tend their farms. Thus food production vital for both military and civilian survival was jeopardized. One enterprising farmer contacted the parish priest of the Glasgow church where he had been married three years earlier. They developed a plan whereby the city youth would escape the terrifying bombing of their homes by helping on the outlying farms as junior farmers. The principal of our school asked the teachers to compile a list of better students among the older children ages eight and above. The principal then made the final selection of student farmers and gave us a complete description of what was required and of the importance of our work to the war effort.

We, both boys and girls, were scheduled to work on the farm Mondays through Fridays, returning home for the weekends bringing some small allotment of food for our parents. At first, we all thought this was fun and got us out of school. We liked the truck ride out to the fields. However, the work was hard: digging and picking various kinds of vegetables, fruits and flowers for the market. Somehow the entire event lost its charm as it was substantially more difficult than we were prepared for, making school a nice relief. We were not given much food to eat: toast and tea for breakfast, a small amount for lunch and dinner consisted of bread and butter, a half of a potato and milk. On top of this, we were expected to keep up with our school work so we would not lag behind our classmates.

Chosen the group leader, I told the farmer that we couldn't work on so little food. As a result, the farmer's wife added an egg to our daily meal. She also brought water to us in the fields. Another unpleasant fact was that we had to sleep in the barn with the animals on the hard ground as our beds. The smell was displeasing, but in spite of our discomforts, we were so tired we soon fell asleep. A curtain was fashioned to separate the girls from the boys to provide the girls some privacy. We continued this routine for about a year. We had definitely learned how to work. Although challenged by our strenuous labor, we were proud of our efforts to help win the war.

Americans

In the latter part of 1943 and into 1944, about 1.6 million American soldiers trained in England and Scotland. They bought many items to send home to family and friends; their purchases had a great effect on the economy of both nations. These troops wrote back home, asking their folks to send care packages to people they had met in both England and Scotland. Some of these troops, both Canadian and American, became enamored with our local lassies. On one occasion, my two cousins and I tagged after an American soldier with a local girl. They had gone into a tenement hallway. Following them, I intruded on their privacy. I asked the American, "Do you have any gum, chum?" He was very annoyed, reached in his pocket and gave me 5 shillings, which bought my two cousins and me a lot of ice cream--a most satisfying outcome.

War's End

By the time I was eight-years old, the war became less overwhelming. Germany's forces had become so spread out that Hitler had a difficult time controlling the various countries he had attacked. Hitler was sure his air attacks on Scotland and England would destroy them and thus eliminate the need for land invasion. He managed to almost control the south of England and London, but was not able to eliminate Scotland's ship building and repair docks.

Fortunately, Winston Churchill managed to stop the Germans from attacking England from the north. British and American troops spared England from a German take-over on land. The fast-flying-attack Spitfire planes became the protectors of both England and Scotland. London was almost crushed and Scotland's docks were almost eliminated. Although physically ravaged, England and Scotland not only survived, but triumphed.

When we heard the word of the War's end, we were jubilant and thankful. I remember that my violin teacher opened her window, and we in the street below could hear her sister playing the piano, to accompany her violin. I called the girls down to dance with us guys in the street. Later when I returned to school, I asked my teacher if I could go to Germany. She said it was impossible now.

Over 7,060,000 German casualties were suffered in the British Isles by Hitler's desire for World Domination. However, 25 other countries had 49,734,000 casualties in their determination to make sure their beliefs would overcome his insanity.

Many Polish families sought refuge in Scotland, settling in Glasgow. They were given prefab house kits, which they assembled in the park near our homes. About 28 of these temporary houses were installed. We local boys were disheartened since their houses were built on our soccer fields. The children attended our schools; and in an effort to help them learn English, we were taught Polish so we could assist our Polish classmates. I helped two Polish brothers learn to speak proper sentences. Gradually, the Polish students' English improved and we spoke some Polish, and so our understanding of each other got much better.

Housing was improved. When bombed-out houses and tenements were rebuilt, they were upgraded to modern standards. These new buildings had hot water and built-in bathtubs. No more would tenement dwellers need to heat water on the stove and use a galvanized bathtub. War time rationing of water and soap was lifted and thus bath time afforded a bit of luxury for war's victims.

America, Here We Come

We were content in Scotland, especially since the war was over, but our lives changed forever when my mother's sister, Rosina, announced that her family was moving to the United States. The two sisters had married two brothers. Aunt Rosina had married my dad's brother, Ambrose. The sisters had never lived far apart and now my aunt and uncle were moving to California. Between their tears, the sisters vowed they would be together again in the U.S. within two years. My mother took in sewing to generate extra money for our trip. I was happy with my mates, school, music and soccer--two years was a long time and a lot could happen. To my delight, I had passed an interview/audition, which allowed me to play my violin in the youth orchestra. When I came home with the news, Mother asked me to play and she sang along with me. She praised me with much adoration.

Later she gave me a list of food selections and sent me to the market. Since I now could play in the orchestra, I walked with joy in my heart. When I returned, Mom wasn't home, but Dad was. I told him how well I had played earlier that day. Dad told me he was proud of my qualifying.   However, he seemed preoccupied.   I then left and played in the street with my cousins, who teased me about being a violinist.   It was complete joy for me. Later in the evening, we had dinner, and I told my dad that I would play my violin in the hallway because it echoed beautifully from there.

Puzzled when I couldn't locate my violin, I came back to the dinner table and asked my mom where my violin was.   She looked at me and said that Dad would explain.   It seemed that my uncle had found a sponsor for our immigration to California, but the deal was good for only nine months.   Thus instead of two years to prepare for our trip, we now had less than nine months.   Mom had sold my violin at a wonderful price and that money would help us pay for our travel to America.

I was so angry that I left home and went to my cousin's house and stayed the night. I had left a note in my room for my mother expressing my anger and the fact that I would be rejected if I didn't practice with the orchestra.   When I talked with the director, he invited me to come back if I replaced my violin.   As luck would have it, I never received a replacement. I was furious at my mother and didn't speak to her for months!   We left for California in October 1948 when I was twelve.

<u>Life in the U.S.A.</u>

We settled in to life in the U.S. My father was employed in a variety of jobs, my mother found work as a seamstress, and we children went to school.   An interesting tidbit-- my mother became the exclusive seamstress for movie star, Esther Williams, making all the swimming suits Miss Williams wore in the movies.

I served in the Air Force and was trained in air conditioning and refrigeration. Interestingly, I spent much of my time on duty in Alaska.   During my service, I took advantage of the opportunity to become a citizen in Washington, D.C.

My mother and her friend served as matchmakers and thus I met and married (April 30, 1960) Ellen Margaret Wilson, She was Maggie to me, a lovely Scottish lass, who was pleased to ride along on my motorcycle.   During our forty-eight year marriage, we had a son William, "Willy" to us, and our daughter, Moira.   A year after Moira was born, we returned to Scotland.   Three years later we moved to Nigeria, where I worked for the Borough's company.   After about a year, we decided to move back to California.

On our return to California, I worked for Ice Capades, personally designing several of their ice rinks around the country.   After leaving Ice Capades, I decided I would like to be my own boss.   We were able to purchase Menton and Johnson, a Burbank heating-air conditioning company.   Our company successfully provided specialized air conditioning systems for many commercial projects including: the Los Angeles transmitters of all three major radio-television networks, the "haunted house" exhibit at Disneyland, a recording studio on the Disney lot, a medical school's anatomy lab, and Jet Propulsion's labs.   With Maggie handling the paperwork, and me designing and selling jobs, together we built a successful company.

Years later, with the children having finished college, we sold the business in 1993 and retired in 1995. Then we enjoyed traveling. Sadly, in 2008 after a valiant battle with cancer, Maggie passed away. I found it difficult to remain in our home without her.

I'd been watching University Village's development and found it appealing. Now that I have been here since December 2009, I've decided this has been a good move. The people and employees make it a loving, friendly place to live. I enjoy the choir, dancing, and writing both prose and poetry and above all, socializing with so many wonderful people. My life to use a Scottish expression has been "bonnie," meaning beautiful. I'm unable to speak when I remember the overwhelming richness of my life's experiences.

ADDENDA
Impact of Wartime on British Civilian Life

The government controlled the entire British population through regulations.

1. The government closed all theaters and eliminated street lights; no exterior lights were permitted during air raids.

2. People were required to carry gas masks and identification at all times.

3. Mandatory blackout of all house windows to prevent any light visible outside was enacted. Fines for non-compliance were assessed.

4. As of January 8, 1940, the following items were rationed: all food products, alcoholic spirits, clothing, cigarettes, matches, sweets, bathwater, electricity, gasoline, soap, shampoo, coal, toilet paper and toothpaste. Wartime food allowance was reduced each year. Petrol allowance was reduced each year. Petrol was always available for doctors, nurses and emergency vehicles.

5. Shopkeepers sold cigarettes to men first and then to women if there were any left.

6. Over half of doctors and nurses were assigned to care for soldiers and persons vital to the war effort. Civilians received limited medical care.

7. Blood banks were established to provide for needs of the wounded.

8. Cardboard coffins were issued instead of wood. It was estimated that 1 in 25 would become war victims.

9. Vehicles were operated with dim lights to avoid being targets for bombers. This regulation caused a high accident rate.

10. Clothes were rationed to the public to allow production of uniforms.

HISTORY'S REDUNDANCY SEP 97
by Bill Caven

If a million hands all clapped together,
You could hear the bombs' explosion.
If they jumped and landed loudly,
The earth's movement would give the motion
of one bomb the Germans dropped
From black skies with screeching might.
Parts of homes blew up those evenings;
People died with a hell of a fright.

After bombing, sounds the all clear
Wailing sirens calling out
It's safe, the worst is over.
Then you saw those lies, heard shouts.
People called out to each other
With relief, they'd made it through,
Then the guilt of those who survived it
Felt, discovering bodies new.

Taped windows, air raid shelters
Gas masks needed for the fray.
All food rationed, life by coupons.
All the men had gone away.
Women touched you smiling sadly
As if contact was rationed too.
As a child confused, I smiled back
Not really knowing what to do.

When bombers left their cargo,
Skies became a burning red.
Poor Clydebank and poor old Glasgow,
Civilian warriors now dead.

May my children never see it
Or feel frightened in their beds:
Buildings burning, people crying,
Black armbands mark their dead.

Are we forced to repeat our history?
Learning nothing from the past.
Do the bombs just all get bigger?
Can no peace be made to last?

At last we created punishment
Against our very strong German attacks.
With the help of God we survived,
Praying as we hoped all wars to end.

Note: Glasgow was repeatedly bombed because of the shipyards and the fact that it was Scotland's largest city. I remember it still.

© 2012 William J. Caven

OL' BETSY AND WORLD WAR II RATIONING BY HAL EBERLE

In 1941 I became the proud owner of a twenty-five dollar car which I named Ol' Betsy. I earned the money for it by cutting grass and doing chores for my aunt at twenty-five cents per hour, so that represents about 100 hours of labor. The tires were worn out with the cord showing through, but it was my pride and joy. My $25 car was a 1932 V-8 classic Ford, the first model V-8 that replaced the Model T. It was for sale because the owner could not get new tires for it. The war was raging in Europe and almost everything was rationed, including rubber. Tires were not available for non-business purposes - but I had a plan. I did not know it at the time, but I guess the solution to this problem indicated that I was somewhat mechanically gifted.

I went to the salvage yard and bought four old truck tires. The tires did not have to hold air but they did need tread because of my intended use. Knowledge from my geometry class enabled me to figure out the necessary size. It was difficult, but I managed to cut the bead off each tire so that just the outer shell remained. When I deflated the original tires of the V-8 they could be stuffed inside the truck tire casing without the bead. When Ol' Betsy's tires were inflated they held the truck tires in place. Thus I had *overshoes* for my worn out tires. They worked very well, and I had my own "wheels" which was a great social asset. I was one of the few high school seniors who did not have to rely on a parent's car for transportation. It was quite a status symbol. Of course, there was one problem. I could not turn a corner very fast or the overshoe would roll off the original tire!

One Friday night, after having had our milkshake at the favorite ice cream hangout, Mary and I were driving around the countryside and decided we needed to park the car to discuss the Pythagorean Theorem. So I backed Ol' Betsy into a farmer's driveway. The driveway was cut between two banks of earth and was a nice quiet place to discuss the sum of the squares of the two sides of a right triangle. During the heated discussion we heard something hit the bank on the right side of the car and a second or so later -- we heard the report of a rifle shot. The farmer had fired a rifle at us and this proved that the bullet traveled at a supersonic speed since it got to us before the sound did. Ol' Betsy made a quick subsonic

departure out of that driveway with the headlights off. It was a good thing the moon was nice and bright. The tires stayed in place since I did not have to make a sharp turn. We had been shot at - and I was not yet in the war!

When I left home for college, I sold Ol' Betsy for $50 - thus doubling my investment. The reason was that it now had "rubber". I do not have a picture of that car with the truck tire overshoes, but here is a photo of a normal 1932 V-8.

WORLD WAR TWO STORIES BY MACON EPPS

I spent World War II as an engineer at Grumman Aircraft Engineering Corporation developing new military airplanes for the U.S. Navy. Although I had four years of Reserve Officer training and a pilot's license, the Air Corp turned me down when I tried to join it in 1940. Once I was an engineer at Grumman, my work was important enough to keep me from active military duty, so I don't have any combat or other military tales to tell. However, the following stories of my impression of Japan's attack of Pearl Harbor and a post-war visit to my home by a Two-Star German General may shed some insights into that dangerous and victorious time in U. S. history.

Day of Infamy

Most Americans of my generation remember where they were when they learned about Japan's bombing of our naval base at Pearl Harbor, Hawaii. It is still vivid in my own memory, as the following recollections show.

It was Sunday, December 7th, 1941, which started out for me as a special day. I was working as a young engineer for Grumman Aircraft Engineering Corporation, in Bethpage, New York, and World War II was going full scale in Europe and Asia. Somehow, the USA had managed to stay out of the war, but we were supplying equipment to the British, including some of the fighter airplanes I had helped assemble earlier. Having finished my apprenticeship on the assembly line, I was now doing design work on newer models and felt good that I was doing my small part to quell Hitler and Tojo. They were the main villains who had disrupted world peace, and were still a major threat

Because of the war, Grumman was expanding its facilities, and the completion of Plant II was one of the reasons it was a special day for me. Grumman and the Navy were having a dedication ceremony that morning for the huge new production facility, and, as a baritone horn player in the Grumman Band, I was part of the ceremony. I was only 21 years old, but in another month I would be 22, so I felt I was coming of age.

After lunch, my roommate and I drove to a small, local airfield to go for a flight around Long Island. I had earned a private pilot's license my senior year in college, thanks to President Roosevelt's "Civilian Pilots Training Program," and wanted to take my roommate up for his first flight. That was another reason it was a special day. It was very windy, so when we got to the airfield we discovered that all flying had been cancelled. While driving back to our rooming house in my new Chevy Club Coupe, I turned on the radio and heard the awful news about Pearl Harbor. We were both shocked, and continued listening to the radio after we got back to our room.

I remember some American Admiral saying something like this: "The Japanese Navy is no match for the American Navy, so we can defeat the Japanese within a few months."

Those were reassuring words; but, as we soon learned, they were extremely optimistic. The bombing triggered our entry into World War II, and I still remember part of President Roosevelt's speech in which he used the term "Day of Infamy."

Now Grumman was a leading manufacturer of carrier-based fighter and torpedo bomber airplanes for the Navy, so our entry into the war resulted in large orders. It also meant lots of overtime for Grumman employees, which was a mixed blessing. The extra money was certainly welcomed since salaries were still pretty meager, and we all had great pride when our airplanes became such a vital part of our victory in the Pacific. At peak production, we turned out 600 airplanes a month in Plant II, a new record for the industry.

However, our long workweek, frequently 56 or more hours, meant that my social life was greatly reduced and the extra hours I was spending on a Master's degree in Aeronautical Engineering became even more difficult. But – what the hell — I was in my early twenties, had no family of my own, and was full of youthful energy and ambition. Somehow, I managed to work those long hours, get my master's degree, and find a lovely young woman to be my bride.

Elizabeth and I were married on May 6th, 1945, and spent the first part of our honeymoon in New York City. On May 8th, we were there for the celebration of V.E. day - Victory in Europe. In August of that year, the Japanese surrendered and the war was finally over. The "Day of Infamy" was replaced by a "Day of Victory."

Grumman was so pleased that it gave all employees a week off with pay. That meant a trip to the Adirondack Mountains and a second honeymoon for us. It was a very happy ending for a sad and tragic beginning.

Now fast forward to 1965. Elizabeth and I visited Hawaii for two weeks, and of course one of the sights we visited was Pearl Harbor. There was still much damage, and I can never forget my feelings when we saw the battleship *Arizona* mostly submerged in the water, and with the bodies of the crew still trapped within.

Much to our surprise, we saw lots of Japanese tourists, even during our trip to Pearl Harbor. We couldn't help wondering why they picked this time of year to visit.

You see, it was December 7th, the 24th anniversary of: "The Day of Infamy!"

Fascinating Foreigner

It's funny how small talk can lead to a great experience. That's what occurred in May, 1954 when I happened to be seated next to John Van Lunkhausen, chief technical engineer for Bell Aircraft Company. I had been elected National Vice President of the Society of Aeronautical Weight Engineers and thus was assigned a seat at the dais during our annual conference, which was held in Buffalo, New York – home of Bell Aircraft.

During my conversation with John, whom I had just met, I asked him if Bell was doing any work on rockets – a subject that had intrigued me since my youth. To my surprise, he said they were. In fact, he said, "We have hired Dr. Walter Dornberger, the German scientist, engineer and two-star general who managed the Rocket Development Center at Peenemunde." I was impressed.

I sensed that John was interested in rockets, so eventually I mustered the courage to ask: "Would it be possible to get Dr. Dornberger to speak to the Long Island chapter of our Society?" To my delight, he assured me it was. So, the following October, I drove to LaGuardia airport to meet Dr. Dornberger. I had invited him to stay in my home in Huntington. He was a garrulous man and spoke good English, with a slight German accent. I asked many questions and he seemed eager to answer them. I remember that he told me something of his work on inertial guidance systems. I was unaware of such work in the U.S. but I reminisced silently about the day another engineer and I had jointly conceived a primitive system using the same principles. Strangely enough, our concept arose when we were wondering how a rocket ship would navigate through empty space. (Regular celestial navigation depends on the earth's curvature.)

He also told me about being on the receiving end of allied bombing. It seems his and many other houses caught on fire and his reaction surprised me. Instead of saving as much of the contents as possible, he saved his favorite easy chair, took it to the curb, and sat down in comfort to watch all his worldly goods become destroyed. He explained that the raids were so frequent that anything he saved that day would be destroyed another day, so he concluded he might as well enjoy the fire!

Suddenly, the significance of the event hit me. Here was a man who, a few years earlier, was a mortal enemy. And not just any enemy, but the one who was in charge of developing the most awesome and dangerous weapon that came out of WWII – except for the A-bomb. I shuddered to think what would have happened if the Germans had developed the atomic bomb and mated it with one of Dr. Dornberger's rockets – especially the V-2!

When the subject came around to Adolph Hitler, he told us things we never knew. He, of course, knew the Führer and met with him many times. Although they aren't exact quotes, here is the gist of what he told me:

Hitler was a genius and, contrary to popular belief, a very good listener. It was his idea to mechanize the German Army. When one of his Generals told him it wasn't possible because his calculations showed that they couldn't depend on imported oil during a full-scale war, Hitler said, "I didn't make you a General to tell me what I can't do; I made you one to tell me how to do what I want to do!" Then he added, "We can solve that problem by making synthetic fuel out of potatoes and other organic material."

As to the good listener part, Dornberger said that Hitler would meet with a dozen or so of his top generals and aides to make major decisions. He would outline the problem/opportunity and go around the table to get each person's opinion. He listened without interruption while each one said his piece. Then he would give a brief summary of each person's position and reasoning, after which he would ask, "Have I fairly stated your position?" "Ya, mein Führer," they would respond. Hitler would then think a few minutes and say, "Here's what we will do," and describe his decision. If anyone objected to the decision he would coldly ask, "Did I misunderstand your position?" Unless the objector came up with new ideas, Hitler would squelch him and insist that his decision be implemented. This method worked very well throughout the war until things got really bad and Hitler started losing touch with reality.

We also learned that Werner von Braun, who was then gaining a reputation in rocketry in the USA, was Dornberger's Chief Engineer at Peenemunde. It seems that von Braun and some of his men liked to discuss space exploration over a few beers after work. Unfortunately, some S.S. men overheard them and promptly arrested them for not going full bore on the war effort. Dornberger came to their rescue by telling the S.S. how important and demanding their work was and that the space talk was simply a means of relaxation. Fortunately for Germany, but not for the Allies, Dornberger prevailed and von Braun and his men kept developing those deadly weapons.

At the dinner meeting, I had the privilege of introducing Dr. Dornberger to about 150 people – about four or five times our usual attendance. His talk was entitled "Rockets, Satellites and Space Ships" and was very well received. After the talk, we adjourned to the bar and were joined by some other Germans who had emigrated to some of the local aircraft companies after the war. It was fascinating to hear them reminisce about Germany and the war, and I was thankful they spoke mostly in English because my German was very limited, and still is.

Dornberger said, "Hitler once told me that he made only two mistakes during the war. One was when he invaded the Soviet Union and the second was in not backing my rocket programs soon enough and more strongly."

When Hitler asked what he could do for Dornberger, he said, "If you would confer Doctoral degrees on Von Braun and some of his top lieutenants, we would all be grateful." Hitler did just that in a subsequent ceremony. Incidentally, Dornberger had no need for doctoral degrees – he had already earned two, a Doctor of Science and a Doctor of Engineering.

Dornberger was in the regular army and not a member of the Nazi Party. The Allies tried to prosecute him at Nuremberg, but Dornberger was too smart for them. He insisted that he had done the same as Allied scientists and engineers. He compared his rocket development with General Groves' work on the A-bomb and with the men in charge of the Russian tanks and the B-29s.

When the Allied lawyers reminded him that he was the one on trial, not the Allied weapon developers, he said, "Very well, I will get three chairs during my trial and assign them to your developers. Whatever you ask me, I will ask the three absentee people for their answer and will use it as my own." The lawyers saw the power of his approach and never put him on the stand.

Several other German immigrants joined our table, and we talked far into the night. I felt lucky to be part of such fascinating conversation. Dornberger spoke highly of the work of the American rocket pioneer, Dr. Robert Goddard. Today, Goddard is generally conceded to be the "father of modern rocketry." Dornberger acknowledged that Goddard's work had been extremely helpful during their developments, and was surprised that the American military had ignored the great potential that Goddard had uncovered. Needless to say, I was a very good listener that night. Eventually, we drove to my home and went to sleep. Next morning, we had breakfast and I drove him to the airport, conveyed my sincere thanks and said good-bye.

Unfortunately, I never saw him again, but what fascinating memories linger in my aging mind!

THE GREAT ESCAPE – June 1943 BY CARMEN JIMÉNEZ FRIEDMAN

In June of 1943, my father (who at the time was Honorary Consul of Spain in Hamburg, Germany) was advised by the Spanish Embassy in Berlin that it could no longer assume any responsibility for the safety of my mother because of her Jewish ancestry, in spite of her being a citizen of Spain through marriage. We were told to leave Germany within twenty-four hours. To this day, I don't know how my mother managed to pack our valuables and ship them off to Spain in such a short time and in the middle of the war. I only remember that we just walked out of our apartment, closed the door behind us, and waved good-bye to a kind neighbor who stood behind her curtain. We boarded a train to Berlin, accompanied by my father. (That was the last time I saw him until 1950, shortly after my marriage to Leonard Friedman, in New York.) After a night in an elegant hotel, we took the train to the Spanish border via Frankfurt and Paris.

France was occupied by the Germans. The train ride took two days and two nights. When we finally arrived in Hendaye on the French-Spanish border, we were confronted by German soldiers who told us that our Spanish passports had expired and that we could not cross the border. How could that be? They were new passports. We later found out that a Nazi who worked at the Spanish Consulate in Hamburg had sabotaged the passports and changed the dates in order to prevent our escape.

Anyway, my mother and I climbed the hill in Hendaye to look for the Spanish Consulate, only to find it closed! Finally, after insistent knocking, a young man, not much older than I, opened the door in his pajamas. I explained our predicament. He said that his father had gone to Spain to celebrate the day of St. Peter and St. Paul, the 29th of June. Nevertheless, he went into his father's office and stamped our passports with the appropriate seals. Mean-while, of course, we had missed our connection to Spain. I was able to borrow some money from a Spanish Navy officer so my mother and I could spend the night at the railroad hotel. The next day we were able to cross the border to Irún, Spain.

Only later did I realize how my mother must have felt during this whole ordeal. Was it luck? Providence? I don't know. I was young and pretty, I guess, and spoke fluent Spanish. The Consul's son was also young, and St. Peter and St. Paul may have been watching over us.

Our lives were saved!

Life in post-Civil War Spain, in 1943, was very hard, especially for two women alone. I went to a business school and learned typing, shorthand and some accounting. Luckily, I got a job as a secretary in a company that did business with Switzerland, and I could use my knowledge of German. Food was hard to come by if one did not have money in order to buy on the black market, or had other connections. My mother's relatives in New York were able to get us visas to come to the United States. Since both my mother and I were born in Germany, we could come under the German quota, which was very large. By the end of 1946, our papers were ready. Yet, there was still another obstacle. My father had survived the war in Hamburg. Communication with Germany was very difficult right after the war but, according to Spanish law, my mother needed his permission to take me out of Spain because I was still a minor. Again, via Switzerland, his permission finally came, and we could embark for the New World.

In spite of the hardships in Spain, we both left there with heavy hearts. It was home, and it had saved us. But, for a twenty-year-old, New York was exciting, different, and offered possibilities for the future that would have been impossible in Spain at that time.

MEMORIES OF WWII IN FRANCE BY GISELE FRIEDMAN

In my physical presence on the blue bubble that human beings call earth, I try to be mostly an ageless observer. Nevertheless, upon the request of an inquisitive mind, I agreed to play with you, curious readers, a memory game. Imagine me facing you on the checkerboard of earthly time. Our common clock is set on the year 1939. I stand on a place of the blue globe called France. Your opposite side (same globe) is called the United States of America. There is a large ocean between our two sides. The ethereal blanket covering us all has no visible limits.

The rules of the game are simple: "no winner", "no loser", you may quit the game at any time without penalty. From my side, I will retrieve some of the memories strongly imprinted in my consciousness, and translate them into your language. From that same place in time, fellow player, you may choose to recollect your own memories, compare them with mine, discover similarities or differences; you may let your curiosity just keep looking at my side, or simply close the book! Anyhow, for me the die is cast. I will keep my promise of sharing my memories of World War II.

1939

My name is Gisèle. I am 16. I live in Roanne, a small industrial city in the Loire valley. A few weeks ago I married a handsome Italian man 10 years my senior. I have very little interest in politics, but I do know, like most French people, about Hitler and the growing turmoil in European countries leading to a declaration of war between France and Germany. But this "drôle de guerre" (funny war), as it is called by the general public, is bringing no real change in our daily lives. Then the shocking, awakening news: the German army is invading France! A few days later, the streets of our quiet little city are filled with tired and terrified people from Belgium and northern France, fleeing from the carnage of war. Their fear is palpable, ineluctable, the first messenger of the growing, nightmarish storm coming our way.

In the following year, 1940, Marshal Pétain signs a treaty with Hitler's Germany. France is divided into two parts. The northern part is under German occupation, the southern part (France libre!) is under Marshal Pétain and a new Vichy government (under German control). General De Gaulle takes refuge in England with a remnant of the French army. The French resistance organizes a clandestine fight against the German occupation forces. Food and goods of all sorts become scarcer and scarcer, giving birth to a black market. Harsh punitive sanctions are taken against anyone resisting German orders and demands. Ration cards for gasoline are extremely rare, so the French citizenry has to quickly learn how to create a new fuel system to power its road transportation. Gasogene (a fuel for automobile engines created by the incomplete combustion of charcoal) is born! What a great opportunity to expand our creativity.

Meanwhile, back home, I find that I am pregnant. Between the growing difficulty of life in the city and my budding maternal instincts, we decide to retreat to the small village where my grandmother lives, and where I spent some of my childhood. Chateauneuf is some 40 miles from Roanne, in the department of "Saone et Loire" and is part of the "free zone". My parents divorced when I was very young, and I long for the comforting presence of a family member. I am an only child. My father has lovingly assumed my upbringing, but I have never lived with him. Since I was two years old I have spent my time with relatives of both sides of my family or in boarding schools.

My father lives in a small village about 35 miles away. He was an underage volunteer in the First World War. He suffered many serious wounds that left him incapacitated. He is decorated with the "Légion d'Honneur" (equivalent to the U.S. Medal of Honor) and gets a pension from the government.

In the same region, near the city of Paray le Monial, I have an uncle and aunt (my godfather and godmother) who live on a small farm owned by my mother's family. My mother and stepfather live in Paris.

Arriving in Chateauneuf, we settle in a small apartment. The grocery store is becoming bare of every day goods. My grandmother becomes very unhappy. Her only luxury, a cup of strong coffee with sugar, is unavailable at any price! She has a small garden and shares some of her vegetables with us, but for butter, eggs, flour, cheese, or any other farm products, our only way is to bicycle to far-away farms, and try to buy, at high prices, some of these products. We do all that with the fear of being caught by the police, having everything confiscated, paying a large fine, and the possibility of a jail sentence.

One of my personal significant happenings took place on such a bicycling expedition. On a deserted small country road, I came face to face with my beloved schoolteacher. We had not seen one another for several years. When I was 8 or 9 years old, I attended the small school where the boys and girls of Chateauneuf learned the fundamentals for the required "Certificat d'Étude". We were seated at our desks, in a large room, facing the blackboard and maps, under the firm and loving supervision of Mademoiselle Marie, our teacher. I was then living alone with my aged grandmother. To escape my solitude, I became an avid reader, and any book would do. I had discovered a very large book, a collection of popular magazines of the First World War. This book was largely illustrated with gory images of the horrible atrocities inflicted by our monstrous enemies on our defenseless babies and women. I remember that during a class of French history, inflamed by my nationalistic enthusiasm, full of my newly acquired knowledge, I fiercely attacked the demoniacal monsters, our longtime enemies, "Les Boches"! After a short moment of stunned silence, Mademoiselle Marie gently explained to me that the "Boches" were men like any others, learning to deal with their individual good or bad tendencies to the best of their ability. Dear Mademoiselle Marie had opened for me a new door of hope for humanity! Her treasure of knowledge was immeasurable.

But that was in 1930, and now we are in 1940. After a very joyful and affectionate embrace, Mademoiselle Marie starts to pour out her anger about the great unhappiness inflicted on her and France by the dirty Boches. As gently as I can, I remind her of the beautiful lesson of understanding and tolerance she had taught me 10 years earlier. Her painful thoughts are redirected for a while toward better possibilities. We laugh and part good friends. Yes, my curious readers, I did reach home successfully with all my precious food, and a somewhat better understanding of our constantly changing human motivations.

We are now in 1941. We adjust as well as possible, we improvise. We also make room for a growing number of visitors. Jewish families from our large cities take refuge in the small villages of our countryside. The Gestapo has stepped up deportation of Jewish citizens, communists, and dissidents. They are sent to labor camps in Germany.

I am also preparing for the arrival of our child. My grandmother has given me some of her old linen bed sheets, perfect for the baby's needs. I visit and make arrangements with the hospital, and maternity ward of our nearby small city, La Clayette. Near the end of June, my father drives me there for the big day!

As you may guess, dear reader, this is another of my significant personal happenings. It has no direct connection with the war. War or no war, babies are born at all times on our blue "bubble". You might enjoy knowing how we proceed in the France of 1941. Maternity care of this period is mainly under the devoted supervision of Catholic nuns. Tradition demands that any new little French citizen is placed under the protection of a patron saint. I have spent months of serious deliberation finding a name for this exceptional little human being who has chosen to come into my life. Faithful to her duty, the head nun asks me what is the baby's name. "His name is Thierry" I firmly declare to the inquiring sister. With a surprised and incredulous look on her face, the nun informs me that this is not a saint's name, and it would not do! She is very determined to educate this 18-year-old mother and protect that poor new child. I am equally determined in my new role of mother to name my child "Thierry". I know this is an old French name, but not commonly in use at this time. Saint or not, Thierry is his name. The unhappy sister is taking my precious little boy to the nursery for his first hours on earth. To placate her, I say that the child also bears the names of his father and grandfather. Both names are duly recognized in her saint's calendar. The night has been long, the labor arduous. Fulfilled by my precious new gift, I happily abandon myself to the magical healing power of sleep.

Late the next morning, the sister awakens me. She is bringing my newborn son for his first breastfeeding. A bright smile illumines her face. After laborious research, she has found out that indeed there is a Saint Thierry, recognized by the church, and celebrated on the 30th of June. My son is born on his patron saint's day. The whole sisterhood enjoys this small miracle! Indeed, I am the mother of a very special little boy. Thierry, no doubt empowered by his notoriety, resolutely and like a pro, drinks his first meal at my fountain of love. What a beautiful world! For now, the war is forgotten.

Back to Chateauneuf, I focus my attention mostly on the needs of my new baby, regular breast feedings, daily baths, changing and washing his linen diapers (no washing machine). I also care for the household and cook on our coal-fired stove for his proud and adoring father. Our living conditions are worsening. It takes great ingenuity to provide reasonably good meals. The end of the year brings very cold weather and new difficulties to keep ourselves warm. Thierry is 6 months old, and breastfeeding gives way to semi-solid food.

Christmas and New Years are coming. How can I prepare their celebration with such lean fare? A gloomy veil has fallen on the traditional "joie de vivre" of our French society. No more balls travel from village to village bringing music and dances to young lovers, no more merry-go-rounds for the children, no more fun rides, shooting galleries, or circuses. There is no more singing to celebrate a lovingly prepared meal shared with family and friends. Where has our laughter gone?

Impervious to this gloominess, Thierry is growing fast. The spring of 1942 welcomes his first steps, his first words, his joyful friendliness towards everyone. The generous nature of our countryside is jubilantly blossoming, inviting us to have a brighter outlook. It is then that we receive the dreaded letter ordering my husband to leave immediately for an unknown destination. Italy is an ally of Germany, and all able Italian citizens residing in France are mobilized by the German army. We pack a very small suitcase, and my husband leaves for a nearby city, where he is to join a group of his fellow countrymen and go to a mysterious destination.

I am abruptly left to fend for myself without income. Neither my aging grandmother, nor my father, can assume an additional responsibility. I manage to go to the farm of my godfather and godmother, where I have been invited to use my talent of dressmaking in exchange for lodging and food. This is an epic journey to be undertaken with an intrepid and fearless little boy, full of life and curiosity. To cover the short 45 miles to the farm requires four changes of public transport, some of them full to capacity, standing room only, in a mixed, sometimes rough crowd. We do successfully reach our goal, and enjoy our well-deserved rest with the affectionate welcome of our family.

In the next two or three days, I plan with my godmother and her neighbor friends how I can sew a new wardrobe for them. All the while, my scalp is developing an unpleasant itching, fast becoming intolerable. Upon the inspection of my godmother, the source of my misery is discovered. My scalp has been invaded by head lice! My godfather responds to my distress and humiliation with amused laughter. He says, "Not to worry, I know the perfect remedy". He then goes to his garden to pick a few leaves of the precious tobacco plants growing there. He boils them in water, and when cooled off, drenches my head with his concoction. For the next hour, I am certain that my head is going to explode with this sudden raging fire. Miraculously, the fire quiets down, and after a rigorous inspection, my godmother declares my head free from its invaders. I marvel at the wisdom of our self-reliant farmers. War disguises itself in many ways. My personal invasion has been vanquished by my beloved and loving godfather.

I spend several weeks designing and sewing dresses and underwear for my godmother and her friends. Their highly desirable farm products give them access to the necessary rare and precious fabrics. Thierry enjoys his newly found power to get the admiring attention of his lady friends. They are charmed by his sunny disposition and the unusual chatter of this not yet two-year-old baby. Thierry speaks to them with perfectly grammatical French phrases. The explanation is simple. Since the first moment of his birth, I have taken great care to speak to him using a simple vocabulary of correct French words. Rather than learning the distorted baby language that most adults commonly use when talking to a baby, Thierry has learned directly to speak using the correct words.

Still, my little man, speaking in grownup fashion, does not know that most of his new friends have spent the last three years deprived of their husbands, sons, and male relatives, either killed or taken as war prisoners. With great courage, they have kept their farms alive and functioning. We owe much to the hardworking food growers of our countryside. By now, Thierry and I have gained a pound or two, and my lean purse has grown a little fatter too!

We return to Chateauneuf. My valiant try at dressmaking in the village is unsuccessful. There is not much fabric there and still no news from my husband. The SOS sent to my mother is answered by her invitation to come to live with them. Early in 1943 I pack our suitcases and take the train for Paris. No one is waiting for us at "Gare de Lyon", our railway station. I am not worried. I know Paris and can find my way to my mother's apartment. We take the metro. Thierry is excited by this new world of people, movement, and noise. Among the crowd of passengers he sees his first German soldiers. He runs joyously towards them with an enthusiastic welcome, "Bonjour facteurs" (Hello mailmen) to the amused surprise of the Parisian travelers. The only men in uniform that Thierry knows are the mailmen of our countryside. This is certainly not the accepted way of behaving in public in our new surroundings. We both will have to learn how to deal with the fine line between the demands of a changing environment and our personal integrity. Tired by our long journey, we arrive at the door of our new refuge. We are warmly welcomed. The affectionate kisses are punctuated by explanations of how they missed our arrival at the station. May I remind you, fellow reader, cell phones are still unknown at this time. To the delight of everyone, Thierry takes this emotional encounter with the natural wisdom of his loving nature. My mother immediately melts under the charm of her two-and-a-half-year-old grandson that she is meeting for the first time. My stepfather shares the joy of everyone. All is well for the moment in this very small bubble of the big blue one.

We adjust quickly to the fast pace of the capital. We join the daily long queues to get our meager ration of food. Women paint their legs with makeup complete with a fine line to imitate the back seams of our unattainable silk and nylon stockings. We wear jointed or solid wooden soles covered with fabric tops of our own making to replace our leather shoes. Our clothes are reconverted many times to give us the illusion of wearing something new. The daily golden crusted bread that we used to enjoy has become a bitter tasting ersatz, made with acorn flour and other substitutes.

I wake up one morning feeling poorly, my skin is the color of a bright yellow lemon. The doctor diagnoses the condition as jaundice, due to severe malnutrition. With good care, I do recover.

Allied planes are heavily bombing German cities and troops. The anti-aircraft artillery resonates loudly. The shrill sound of sirens reminds us frequently, day or night, to run to a shelter. We do not have one in our building, so we have to run half a block down our street to take cover. For Thierry, this is a game to meet new neighbors.

To keep some semblance of sanity in this insane world, my mother and I take Thierry daily to play in the nearby park of "La Tour Maubourg" next to Les Invalides and Champs de Mars. This oasis of nature, green lawns, towering trees, and playground, welcomes the mothers and young children of the neighborhood. My mother is very proud of her beautiful grandson, with his dark brown eyes, peaches and cream complexion, his smiling face, and curly blond hair. Thierry soon becomes a popular playmate of the Parisian children who come to the park.

After many months of waiting, I receive a short official notice that my husband is alive and well somewhere on the French coast. As often as possible, we take the train to Bullion, a large village in the Valley of Chevreuses, some 25 miles from Paris. My mother's sister-in-law and her parents have retired there. We forage in the nearby farms for any food available for purchase. My aunt's husband is a prisoner of war somewhere in Germany. My mother has three younger brothers, one of whom was killed in battle. The other two are prisoners of war.

The war has spread from Africa to Russia. The German war machine faces growing difficulties. Thus, living conditions in Paris are rapidly worsening. Our trip to Bullion becomes increasingly difficult to manage, because public transport is becoming rarer and overcrowded. My aunt and her parents offer to keep Thierry with them for a while. They, at least, have a garden. We accept their generous invitation and return to Paris, leaving my little boy in Bullion. My inner peace is threatened by a raging battle between contradictory desires and feelings. No doubt, Thierry is better off with some good food and the quieter life of the countryside; but, I am not there to watch over his well-being. Communications are practically non-existent now, even letters or telephone. War takes many forms. All are very painful.

It is June 6, 1944. The long awaited news arrives. The Allies have landed on French soil. The calls to shelter intensify. A new effervescence transports the Parisian population. The end of the nightmare is coming - dreams within dreams... We anxiously await the daily news of our deliverer's progress. The German troops are retreating. Then, as the Allied troops advance toward Paris, a general panic takes hold of the population. "We are going to be engulfed in the fire of the raging battles". Allied forces are already close to the Valley of Chevreuses and my defenseless baby. At all cost, I have to be with him.

There is no transport, so I will walk. My parents try vainly to dissuade me from my insane decision. They are sure that the German army will shoot me. Not to worry, I will explain my harmless goal to them. I do not speak German, so I go to a nearby bookshop and buy a French-German dictionary. I do not know the way, so I will ask for directions as I go. I am fiercely determined that nothing will stand in the way of my being with my baby in time of danger.

I traverse Paris on foot and reach the outskirts. I meet a group of young adolescents in German uniform, looking uncertain about what to do or what order to obey without their officers. I also see a much older soldier, at least 40, riding on a bicycle with flat tires. What has happened to the proud German army triumphantly parading down the Champs Élysées? I pass through their lines without a question, a somewhat sad little victory. I have wasted my money on the dictionary.

I continue my walk. The panic has spread to the countryside. Everyone is hiding behind closed doors and tightly-closed shutters. I keep walking, asking the rare persons encountered if I am still on the right road for Bullion. I refuse their generous offers to come with them and take shelter against the impending disaster heading our way. All these good people feel certain that I am crazy. I keep walking, alone on the road.

After several long hours, I hear the steps of someone approaching. A young man reaches me and indicates his surprise at finding me alone on the road. I explain the urgent motivation of my journey. We both are tired, so he proposes to rest at the roadside, and eat some food to regain our strength. To my astonishment, he pulls out of his backpack large, real biscuits, a can of sardines, and chocolate bars! I have not set my eyes on such treasures for ages! My new friend quietly lets me know that the time has come when he can safely share his secret with me. He is an American, spying for the Allied Forces! He is on his way to his French wife and two young children living in a village close to Bullion. He assures me that the American tanks and jeeps will not arrive at my destination before tomorrow mid-morning. He insists that he will not let me walk alone at night. I must come with him and spend the approaching night at his house. He promises to wake me up early next morning, and I can walk the short distance to Bullion before the arrival of his country's army. He explains that the Americans have made a deal with the French army. The soldiers of General LeClerc will be the first to liberate Paris.

After a short rest and a delicious snack, we walk the few miles to reach the house of my first American friend. There is a joyous reunion with his lovely young wife and his two sleepy small children. They graciously accept their tired, unexpected guest. As agreed, I am awakened early next morning, well rested. After a hasty breakfast, a deeply felt and thankful goodbye, I walk alertly on the road to Bullion and my baby son.

I arrive, the village looks dead. My knocks on the door of my aunt's house are finally answered. My aunt looks at me with the incredulous eyes of someone seeing a ghost, but Thierry runs to me. He is so happy to see his mother. His enthusiastic kisses feel so good! One would go to the end of the world for such joy. Everyone in the village is terrified of the impending battle, certain that it will destroy them. Mass hysteria has taken hold. None of my reassuring, newly acquired knowledge, can assuage their fears.

Thierry and I leave them to the protection of their tightly closed doors. We walk a few feet away to the main road. We will be the first to welcome our liberators. Immediately we hear the rumbling noise of heavy vehicles. We see our first jeep and tank. Very surprised American soldiers jump out of their vehicles to embrace us. To their amusement, I greet them with a few words of my high school English. We all share a joyous euphoria. They show me photos of their children and family, left months ago in the USA. Thierry is delighted by all these strong manly arms tossing him into the air. Each group moves on, making way for the vehicles behind in an unending stream moving towards Paris. I know that many of them will have enjoyed this unexpected short stop at Bullion.

I do not recall, curious reader, how long this time of euphoria lasted. I can tell you that when the first inhabitants came out timidly, Thierry and I were surrounded by a small mountain of K rations and packaged food of all sorts. The beautiful white blouse that I had extracted from an old sheer window curtain was black from all the impetuous embraces. Thierry and I were in the daze of a happy exhaustion.

I spend the next few days resting in the greatly relaxed atmosphere of my environment. The only traffic on the main road consists of American vehicles coming and going. We are anxious to know how my parents in Paris have fared during the battle of liberation. I am offered a trip back to Paris by jeep, but they cannot take a child with them. With the firm promise that I will come back for him very soon, I leave for Paris. I arrive in the apartment at Rue St. Dominique. My mother and stepfather are happy to see me. I am assaulted with questions. These have been traumatic times for all of us. May I remind you, curious reader, that since leaving them in a state of anxiety, my parents had no news of my whereabouts nor of Bullion. They were caught up in the turmoil of the capital's liberation. We have the surprise visit of my husband. He comes back from the coast of Normandy, where he has helped the Germans to build their massive defense works against Allied invasion. We have become strangers to one another. We agree, with common accord, to a friendly divorce, another casualty of the war. Finally all questions are answered and we arrive at a clearer understanding of our present situation.

The Parisian's expectation of getting back the conditions of pre-war living is sorely disappointed. Indeed, surpassing our most pessimistic prediction, our bad conditions have become much worse. Everything is at a standstill. None of our public services function anymore, not even the distribution of our meager rationed goods. There is no garbage collection, spasmodic gas and electricity, no transport ~ nothing! Only the war goes on. The new French government is not yet functional. An internal war of different dimensions grips the French citizenry.

Paris is caught up in the unleashing of an intense emotional conflict between political parties. The French resistance forces are now in power. They display hasty judgment and abusive retaliation against any suspected collaborators with the German occupation. We see shameful public displays of inhuman treatment toward this new enemy. I am glad that I didn't bring my little son into this ugly chaos.

Imperturbably, time passes. We survive through the waves of change. General De Gaulle heads up a new French government. Allied forces continue their victorious advance on all war fronts. Basic goods become slowly available again. My mother and I seize on the first opportunity to travel to Bullion and bring back with us to Paris a very happy little boy.

August 14, 1945.

The war is over in Europe! How can one describe the overwhelming cry of joy of the Parisian people? All the church bells of the city ring out, proclaiming the triumphant victory over this long nightmare. Music is everywhere. We dance in the streets. In a delirious effusion of embraces and kisses, everyone is welcomed as a friend. I work hard at improving my elementary knowledge of English. A short time later, in September of 1945, the treaty sealing the final closure of this devastating war is signed.

1945 ~ 1950.

During the next five years, I meet a variety of people working at several different jobs. I work in the Eastman Dental Clinic, serving American officers. I meet Denise, a student in the Dental School of the University of Paris. We soon become best friends. We are both enthusiastically dedicated to promoting friendship and better understanding between all human beings. Denise is a dental assistant. I work in statistics. I learn about the officer grades, their 32 teeth and their dental treatment. I am promoted to dental assistant. This is when I finally win the gratitude and friendship of a female patient. In spite of our efforts, Denise and I have met a cold shoulder from any WAC we have encountered. They see us only as rivals to their own men. My captain is a good, but very rough dentist. I cannot bear his indifference towards the suffering of his patient, Mary, a WAC officer. In no uncertain terms, I remind him that a little compassion would not hurt him, and might help his patient to feel better. Thus, I win the heart of a very good friend, and a new feminine member to our mission of world peace. I also keep my job!

Denise and I are also part of a small group of people who meet regularly at the cocktail hour of Colonel Thrasher and his wife, Mary. This is a curious melting pot where come-and-go officers of different nationalities, musicians, manufacturers, artists, businessmen, dancers, veterinarians, diplomats, and cat-lovers! Mary is completely devoted to her cats. This is a very fertile ground for expanding our social education.

As the war winds down, the clinic reduces its personnel drastically. I find a job at Marcel Rochas, a well-known designer of Paris "haute couture" (high fashion). I assist one of the main salespersons. We sell our one-of-a-kind creations to the international world of the wealthy and famous. We entertain our clients, taking them to our best restaurants, theatres, and night clubs.

I leave Marcel Rochas, having received an offer to take charge of the household of General Mellac in Baden-Baden. The General, a bachelor, is governor of the French zone in Germany. He needs someone to direct the domestic staff, and be hostess to his guests at dinners and receptions. Everything is formal and organized in military fashion. The job is pleasant but rather dull after a while. However, I accompany the General on some of his trips. I discover the beauty of the Black Forest, new people and their traditions.

I meet and marry an American, a participant in the first wave of the Allied Landings. In 1950, with Thierry and his pet turtle, we cross the ocean for New York. We then ride across the vast USA on route 66 to come to Los Angeles.

You may wonder, curious reader, why this part of my life connects with memories of World War II in France. Gory battles and destruction of cities do not stop suddenly. They generate great changes, positive or negative, in the life experience of human beings.

In the cocoon of our blue bubble, on Shakespearean dream stages, human beings play their roles of conquerors and conquered, kings and jesters, devils and angels, to mesmerized laughing or crying spectators.

During the lapse of time in a play, or the lapse of time in our days and nights playing on the checkerboard of our "Blue Bubble", the dream looks and feels very real! On the movie screen of our human consciousness, we can choose to play and replay any joyful or painful memories from any part of our dream. We may also play with their delusiveness. In this world of duality, we tend to choose to see and deal more with division than the equally inherent possibility of connection.

Through the violence of conflicts that take place between nations, or our own inner world of thoughts and feelings, we may learn to see the relationship of all parts of a process, even of process within processes.

After eons of time and changing transformations, we can, like the butterfly escaping from the prison of his chrysalis, flutter on multi-colored wings in the limitless infinite, toward the Creator of all creation.

Friend and curious reader, as promised, I am playing my last checker on our checkerboard of time with you. I wish you success and joy on your personal journey. As for me, I return to play my role of ageless observer on our "Blue Bubble".

Credits

My account of "Memories of World War II" could not have been expressed without the help of many collaborators.

I do give credit to Barbara Warkentien who directed my attention to an ongoing project to gather memoirs of World War Two. The project's aim is to make available the experiences of the few remaining participants of this war to the following generations.

I want to give credit to Jennifer Zobelein for her excellent editorial skills, and to her unfathomable devotion in bringing this project to a successful outcome.

I give credit to my husband, Len Friedman, my loving companion of nearly 56 years. I acknowledge his unquestionable good will and patience in correcting my erroneous knowledge of the English language. I thank him for sharing his computer expertise of 60 years by transforming my longhand writing into the easier reading and greater availability of the printed form.

Credit is due to all the human beings who have shared the Shakespearean stage with me, to act out our personal and interacting roles of the delusive reality of our dreams on our "Blue Bubble Dream Home". I give credit to our spiritual teachers of all creeds, shapes, or colors.

Most of all, and lovingly, I credit the "No beginning and no end Presence" of the Creator of all creations.   © 2012 Gisele Friedman

WORLD WAR II AT NIAGARA FALLS BY TOM GEISMANN

When I was a boy of 13, I earned a full scholarship to a very fine boarding school near Niagara Falls in Ontario, Canada. Along with about 40 other Chicago schoolboys, I was traveling by train to the campus, located on a promontory across from Horseshoe Falls. The train actually made a *flag stop,* right in front of the school's entrance, especially for us to disembark. It was September of 1939, and Neville Chamberlain, the British Prime Minister, was going back and forth from London trying to negotiate with Adolf Hitler.

The next morning, as we were being given instructions on where to pick up our luggage, the Headmaster announced that the United Kingdom had declared war during our trip and therefore Canada was now at war with Germany. We were also warned not to go near the falls as there would be armed guards protecting the power generating facilities.

Right after breakfast we headed off to the depot. As fate would have it, we got lost and ended up in the beautiful park above the Horseshoe Falls. (Remember: Canada being part of the U.K. had been preparing for war for years.) Anyway we were all strolling through the park when all of a sudden we were surrounded by a large group of really old men with raised rifles (1800's vintage) aimed right at us. They could have rightfully shot us because they were the HOME GUARD and we were the intruders. They had been called up because all of the younger men were away, serving in the Canadian armed forces. Obviously, we managed to "escape" and lived to tell the tale. Those wonderful lights, which usually play on the falls, had been turned off the previous night, and they were not turned on again until after the war.

Canada did a marvelous job of weathering the strife of the war, which included the rationing of gas and certain food items. We could come and go over to the New York side of the border as free as birds, but there were soldiers all over the place. There were bivouacs in some areas and we saw many soldiers leaving town in troop trains with family and friends crying and waving just like in Hollywood movies. Niagara Falls Park on the Canadian side was an absolutely beautiful spot, and I do believe the New York side is now vastly improved.

An interesting point is that Canada pegged its dollar against the American dollar so that $1.00 in U.S. currency was never worth more than $1.10 in Canadian currency. This meant that we could get a great chocolate soda, or the best fish and chips I ever had, for only $.10 Canadian. We offered an American dollar, and received a full Canadian dollar back in change!

Those are some of my World War II experiences. Later, during the Korean Conflict, I served with the Army Signal Corps, but that story can wait until another time.

MEMORIES OF MY EXPERIENCES IN WWII BY EUGENE HANNEMANN

Soon after my graduation from High school in June of 1943, I was drafted, and was able to choose the Navy for my service. I signed up on July 6, and left immediately for basic training in San Diego. From there I boarded a transport ship, the Wasatch, to Brisbane, Australia. We crossed the Pacific without encountering any difficulty but anxious to get off the ship after at least two weeks. However, when we came into port, we were not allowed to go ashore but soon sailed to another port in the north. Some of us were put on a troop train to go back to Brisbane. Why? We never knew, but we did get to do a little 'sightseeing' along the way. One interesting event took place during our travels. A troop train of Australian men was heading north, and at one point both trains stopped together to have a meal. Since the Aussies wanted to give their best to the visitors, they gave us the best they had which was lamb, and they ate our beef stew. No one was really satisfied, so we switched food and everyone was happy.

When we arrived in Brisbane, we were divided into groups, some went to other vessels, such as PT boats, and others to shore duty. Typing skills were in great demand and only 17 out of 150 had this ability. Since I was a high school graduate and had taken typing I was assigned as a yeoman (office clerical worker) on the flag ship (FLAG) of the 7th Fleet, which was the admiral's headquarters. Our headquarters were on the 7th floor of the A&P Building in downtown Brisbane. General McArthur's headquarters were on the 9th floor. Some of us were allowed to rent rooms in local homes. I took a room across the river, and rode a small ferry back and forth every day. It was good to get to know many Australians.

Of course I did not see the General very often, but one incident remains in my mind. I had worked late one night and had just got off the elevator on my way home when a guard yelled, 'Hold that elevator!' So I rushed back in and held it, and as MacArthur came strutting in, I punched the 9th floor button. He asked. "Which floor are you going to, son?" Not wanting to tell him I had just gotten off, I told him 7th. He reached over and punched the 7 button, and when it stopped, I thanked him and got off!

Another time I was on night duty and a phone call gave us the news that Admiral Nimitz had just landed from Hawaii and wanted a conference with MacArthur's staff. We really rushed to get things set up. At this meeting the two chiefs actually planned the invasion of the Philippine Islands, one of the first major offensive battles of the War. The general had vowed to return there when he had to evacuate earlier because the Japanese had taken the islands. It would take several months for the plans to go into action. This was actually the only time I met the Admiral. I would like to say that I was in conference with the two highest commanders, but I would have to add that I was sharpening their pencils. (I knew that Nimitz was from Fredericksburg, but didn't know at the time that he and my mother were second cousins.) The first step they planned was to establish a base at Hollandia in New Guinea, which the Australian troops had conquered. When that was accomplished, navy personnel would be transferred by ship or by air. I was able to go on Navy Aircraft.

One of my duties was to hand-carry Classified Material back and forth between Army and Navy headquarters. Sometimes I used a motorcycle, and sometimes took a jeep. I had access to many files, and found that my brother, Wally, was there with the Army. Another fellow and I checked out a jeep and went to find him. When I arrived at his unit on the post I was told that he was not on duty, so I began a search of the tents until I found him. Was he surprised to see me! We had a very good reunion. I was in New Guinea from March to October, and saw him one other time.

During this time in Hollandia, I had a serious dental problem and was sent back to Brisbane for treatment. While waiting for a return flight, a young Navy officer was trying to get a flight to Hollandia, but my orders took precedence over his and Lt. Cdr. Lyndon Johnson waited for the next flight!

On Oct. 20, 1944, the Army went ashore at Leyte in the Philippines. The 7th Fleet supported MacArthur in this invasion. Some of us were left behind to close the base in Hollandia and as soon as the facilities were set up on Leyte, we went there by aircraft. It was a very primitive base; we lived in tents and the weather was hot and muggy. The natives built a bamboo chapel for us, and we had a Navy Chaplain. The Japanese still flew over to harass us.

In May, 1945, the war in Europe was coming to an end. The troops there were being sent to the South Pacific, and I was offered the opportunity to return to the States. I took it. I left Leyte on the transport GT Collins on May 17, 1945. It was a peaceful crossing; only one Japanese Submarine was sighted. I spent most of my time reading on deck - got a very good tan. We arrived in San Pedro on June 6th, 1945, VE Day (Victory in Europe Day). I soon departed by train for a leave at home, before continuing on to my next assignment in Miami Beach FL.

A sailor from western North Carolina became my best friend, and I eventually went to live with his family and attended Western Carolina University at Cullowhee. His girl friend introduced me to her sister, who later became my wife. Another case where the war actually brought an unlikely couple together!

© 2012 Eugene Hannemann

THEY TOOK US TO AUSCHWITZ BY MARILYN KATZ

I was born in Czechoslovakia in 1927. In 1938 the Hungarian government took over our country, so we went to Hungarian school. Then in April, 1944, the Germans came and took us away from our home, only with what we had on our backs. We went to the city, to the factories, but every day people were transported away. We never knew what happened to them. Finally, around the middle of May they took us away, too. They put us in cattle wagons, and before we got to Auschwitz, the train stopped and the German SS came in and they said to us, "Give us all your money while you have it and all your jewelry." We didn't have any money with us, and we had given away our extra jewelry before we left. So they ripped out my earrings, my sister's earrings, everybody's earrings, saying, "You're not going to need any money and any jewelry where you're going."

Around 6 o' clock in the morning we arrived at Auschwitz. We got off the cattle wagon trains, and there was Dr. Josef Mengele, known as the *Angel of Death*. He decided right away if you were going to live or die. They sent me to the right with my cousin. My mother, sister and brother were sent to the left. My mother was thirty-eight years old, I was seventeen, my sister was thirteen, and my brother was four. One of the other girls told my sister that she should follow me to the right, so she left my mother and brother and came over, but could not see us. She could only recognize my voice. I asked one of the girls if my sister should go back and be with my mother because she was too young to work with us. She replied, "My dear girl, your mother is not alive anymore. You should be happy that your sister is with you." All those who went to the left had already been taken to the gas chamber. All the young children, like my brother, went immediately to the gas chamber.

When we arrived, they took away the only good clothes we had and gave us striped clothes. I still can't wear striped clothing today. Also, when my sister and I came to Auschwitz, we had beautiful polka dot outfits - which they took from us. After the war, every time we saw polka dot clothing we bought it - in every color.

They took us to Camp A (they also had B, C and D) the minute we arrived there and gave us a cup of green tea. We couldn't figure out why. Later we found out that they put a powder in it that stopped us from having menstrual periods, and also took away our emotions. We couldn't cry, we couldn't think, we couldn't feel sorry for ourselves. (Even to this day, I do not cry.)

The closest street to our barracks was the hospital where Dr. Mengele was experimenting on twins. About the second day after we arrived, I saw a girl walking on the street and I recognized her. She was an eleven-year-old twin whom I had met before in my town.

I asked her, "What are you doing here?" She said, "I am here the whole week for experimenting." I said, "Where is your sister?" She replied, "I don't know. She disappeared already. She's not with me anymore." The next day, I waited outside because I wanted to see her again, and I did; but in two days, she disappeared too.

Mengele was always experimenting, not only on twins; and, when he was finished, he sent them to the crematorium. I knew another girl named Rosa. One day she was working in the field between Birkenau and Auschwitz with her sister and her friend. Her sister disappeared with one of the partisans and she got a bullet in her breast. One of her friends got a scratch on her eye. Mengele experimented on them, too. Rosa lost a lot of blood, so he gave her a transfusion. He wanted to know if she would stay alive because of his blood. She did. We used to tease her all that time that she had Mengele blood. They never found her sister. The girl who just got a scratch was sent to the crematorium.

There were some people that worked in a gunpowder factory. They weren't allowed to bring anything in or out. Every time they passed the big gate, a band was playing music. The band was made up of people who knew how to play instruments. One day, one of the girls recognized her fiancé on the other side of the electric fence where the men were. When she came back, he saw her too because she used to watch him when she was marching by. So he threw her a little piece of paper wrapped around a stone. She left it in her drawer, but she should have thrown it away so the SS would not find it. He wrote on the little note, "I hope to God that I'm going to see you soon." The next day, the SS announced on the microphone that everybody had to come to the gate to hear the music. When we got there, the girl who got the note, and her friend, were hanging high up, and they cut their tongues out. The SS marched in and told us, "You have to watch. You shouldn't do anything wrong. You shouldn't have jewelry on your fingers and you shouldn't get notes." We knew right away that it was going to be the end. They came with their machine guns and killed those 18-year-old girls.

I knew a lot of girls who were working in a big warehouse where they took off all our clothes. They checked every shoulder pad to look for hidden money or gold. If they found some, the Germans put it in a big box. They didn't find much. One girl had her mother's coat, and she knew there was a ring in the shoulder pad. So she took the ring and kissed it because it was her mother's. The SS woman noticed that she had a ring. The next day, she wound up in the same place - hanging, with her tongue cut off. Then they killed her. They kept telling us that we should watch what's going on and that we shouldn't do those things. Slowly, everybody knew we were not supposed to have anything. Every time that band started to play, we knew that someone had been found out and would be killed.

When they were talking to us, telling us we shouldn't have any rings or gold, or we would wind up like those two girls, I had a gold ring that some lady gave to me because she was afraid to keep it. I was hiding it in the tip of my shoe, but I didn't want to end up like those girls who were hung and killed. There were four nuns in the kitchen. They were there for three of four months because they were Polish nuns and didn't want to belong to Hitler's party.

I started talking to them when I picked up the food for our barracks and said to one of them, "Would you like to have a ring with ruby stones?" She said, "How am I going to take it? I am leaving next month." I said, "Put it in the corner of your shoe." She said, "All right, I will try it. What can I give you?" I said, "I don't care, give me some food." So she gave me a big basket of potatoes, and I took it to the other girls and said, "Anybody who has any jewelry, I can trade it right away for potatoes." Later on, the nun wrote me a note saying that everything went through okay, and she sold the ring.

One of the girls I knew worked in the warehouse where they kept all the clothes. One day I saw her wearing my silk kerchief that our mother gave to us in case we needed it. I said to her, "How did you get that kerchief?" She said, "I was working there and I liked it very much. I saw it on a hanger." I said, "You know, this is mine. My mother gave it to me." She said, "Oh I am so sorry, but I love it, I don't want to give it back." So, we cut it in half. I took one piece and she took the other.

They had a lot of young boys working in the crematorium, but only for two months. After that, nobody came out alive from there. They didn't want people to find out after the war because those kids knew everything that was going on. They picked up all the people from the gas chamber and took them to the crematorium. After we had left, seven months later, they ran out of the gas, so they threw them straight in the fire.

I don't know if some of you know about the Rothschild family in Milano. A lot of Italian people remember them. Before the war, Mrs. Rothschild came to my hometown to visit her father with her daughter Sarah, and her son. She got stuck there because the SS wouldn't let her go back to Milano. So, the three of them ended up in Auschwitz with us. All the girls and women were drinking that tea every morning and every night, and Sarah was drinking it all day long. After a while, she didn't recognize her mother. I used to take food to Mrs. Rothschild across the street from the barracks. One day she complained to me that her daughter didn't know her. It was because of the powder they put in the tea. In Auschwitz we couldn't drink any water because there was rust in it. Anybody who drank that water got typhus. So for seven months we drank only the tea.

Mrs. Rothschild came to me one day. She had seen her son marching with the SS. I said, "Which way was he marching?" When she told me, I knew right away that he was marching to the crematorium to work. I told her that we should talk to Sarah because the SS found out she was from the Rothschild family and treated her well.

Mrs. Rothschild said, "I can't talk to her, she doesn't recognize me. You must talk to her. But one thing I'll tell you, if they ever finish the war, and we survive, you're coming with me, your sister and you, to Milano. You're going to stay with me in the Rothschild castle." I said, "Okay, but let's not talk about it now." So I told Sarah, "You better talk to one of the SS and tell them your brother works in the crematorium. Perhaps they will let him come out alive if they know who he is."

Later on she told me, "Everything is taken care of. You shouldn't worry." I never found out if they let him go out or not, but I do know that Sarah is alive. When I was in Israel 43 years ago with my son, I found her name in the book in Jerusalem. I tried calling her to see what happened to her mother, but I never could find her. However, when we were in Sweden, we always listened to the radio, and they let you know who survived and who had not survived. They never mentioned Mrs. Rothschild, but said that Sarah Rothschild was alive.

We had a girl with us who was Czechoslovakian, and she was pregnant. She didn't know she was pregnant when she came. We tried to hide her for three months. I used to pinch her cheeks so she wouldn't be so pale, and she was very quiet. We used to give her our food and share with her so she had more. We had to put loose clothes on her so that they wouldn't know that she was pregnant. Then one day they found out. We heard that she had a baby, and her three sisters were with her. They wrapped the baby in a rag and threw it in the latrine because it was not allowed, and they would have taken the mother to the crematorium. Later on, when I was in Israel, I found out who that lady was. It was my husband's sister!

Every day they came to select a load of people for the crematorium. My cousin, who spoke perfect German, was asked to work for them because she knew German and had studied it at school. She didn't want to stay with us because she didn't want to see us taken away, but she saw it anyway. About two weeks later, we were taken to the B locker. One night, I heard violins playing. There were about two hundred gypsies there, all playing. They only used to play the violin if somebody died. So I went on top of the roof of the barracks and I watched and listened to the gypsies playing that beautiful music. They also played in the big band by the gate. It was just like going to a funeral, the songs they played. It took two hours to get to the crematorium, then, all of a sudden everything got quiet because they were dead already and the music stopped.

Then one day, they took us to get a tattoo - no more names, only numbers - but it was safer because it meant you would be staying. The next day I suddenly got a toothache.

They had a little hospital and I asked the nurse there if she had an aspirin, but she didn't. So she grabbed me and pulled my tooth out, with no injection, nothing. My mouth was full of blood, and all of a sudden I heard sirens. It meant that Dr. Mengele was coming to the little hospital to look for more people for the crematorium. So the lady pushed me through a little window in the back. I fell and I had more blood all over me. I crawled to my barracks and my sister said that everybody thought that I wasn't going to come back.

We decided right then that we must find a way to leave Auschwitz, after being there seven months. I was always afraid they would select my sister, and we were told that the Russians were coming, the English were coming, or the Americans were going to clear Auschwitz. We decided if they were going to select my sister, I would go with her wherever she went. Then we would try to run away. We still had a few days to think about it, but every single week they came through Auschwitz and took blood from us for the Germans on the front lines. They hated us, but they took our blood for their soldiers. I never gave it to them. I put a little band aid on my arm so they would think that I had my blood taken already. (Yeah, that was how I behaved. I said, "They are not going to get my blood!").

Finally, we decided to go when we had the chance. We were always standing five by five and my sister was always in front of me. In front of her was a lady, a friend of ours, whose name was Heidi. Dr. Mengele came to visit us, and he pulled her aside and said, "Are you pregnant?" She said, "No I'm not pregnant, I was not even married. I am not pregnant." She had a nice bust and he was examining her. While he was looking at her, I pushed my sister so fast that she flew out on the other side. All the transports were leaving Auschwitz. Then, he turned around and said, "Okay you can go." He forgot that my sister was in front. So both of us got away, and I could breathe again.

That was our lucky day, when we left Auschwitz. Seven months, never blue skies, always red skies from the crematorium smoke. They put us in the cattle wagons and gave us different clothes, and we didn't know where we were going. We arrived at Bergen-Belsen, the other hell, but not as bad as Auschwitz. It was November 10th, the day before my sister's birthday. There was a big snowstorm and they didn't know what to do with us because they didn't have enough space in the barracks. So they put up a big white tent and gave us one big blanket. We stayed overnight and the next day they gave us a place to sleep. There were about twelve Dutch girls who came to Auschwitz, and they were with our group. Only later when I saw the movie did I realize that Anne Frank was there with her mother and sister. We couldn't talk to them because they spoke Dutch and we were all together with the Czechoslovakian girls, Hungarian, Romanian and Polish. And they kept to themselves, but the movie showed that she left her diary to some Dutch girls, and they gave it to her father who survived. She never came with us to a different concentration camp. She and her mother and sister stayed there at Bergen-Belsen and died of typhus.

At the end of the war, people left Auschwitz, like my husband's family. The SS took them on the death march. There was snow at that time. Anybody who couldn't walk anymore or wanted to rest a little bit, the SS shot them right away. Only those survived who kept walking.

In Bergen-Belsen they did not have work for us and there was heavy snow. They sent some of the girls to the airplane factory in Bendorf, but they took us to Braunschweig and put us in a stable with a few blankets. Every day we had to go out and clean the streets. The whole city was being bombed.

One day I was out walking in a bad winter snow. On the other side of the street, I saw electric wires. One of the sixteen-year-old girls was telling me that her mother and her brother had gone to the United States with the last ship, but she never heard from them. I felt sorry for her because she was alone, so I let her talk all the time. She said, "They are supposed to send their papers for us." All of a sudden, she said, "You know what? I think I see my mother. What is she doing here?" Later we found out that the ship came back because President Roosevelt ordered it to. Her family went to Cuba, and then to the United States, and then President Roosevelt sent them back to Germany. So all those people came to Brandenburg that day. Then her mother noticed her. So I said to her, "Quiet, quiet. Don't go close to the wire. Don't go close to the wire." But they had seen each other and were so excited they both ran to the wire fence - and were electrocuted. I never forgot that day. I could do nothing. I was pulling her, but she broke away.

Every day we walked two miles to work and two miles back to the stable in Braunschweig. I didn't work. I always went to look for food. Mostly I would find "bomb potatoes" which were like chewing gum. They were potatoes that had been "cooked" by the bomb explosions and then became very tough. One day I found fresh carrots in a basement. My friend was with me and we saw an old German guy checking on his property. He carried a long iron stick. My friend ran away, but I was stuck there, so I hid in a barrel and put a piece of wood on top and waited until he left. Then I stuffed my pants with carrots, but I wasn't allowed to bring them back or I wouldn't be given my ration of soup and bread, as a punishment. I crawled back to the group so they wouldn't catch me. My friend thought I wouldn't come back, so everybody was happy to see me alive. I gave everybody a carrot and kept one large one in the middle of my pants. We returned to the stable and when the SS woman checked me, all of a sudden, she said, "Are you a boy?" "I am not a boy!" I replied. She pulled down my pants and the carrot fell out. So she called one of the big shot SS men, a general with a big stomach and told him in German what had happened, that she thought I was a boy. He laughed so much and said to her,

"Give her double soup!" The SS woman said to me, "I don't remember when I had such a good laugh."

Every day we were working on the street, the bombers came, the American, the Russian, and the English. The minute the sirens came on, all the SS ran underground to the bunker, and they left us on the street. One day when all the SS were in the bunker, I found a church, but it was all bombed except for the steps. I said to the girls, "I have a feeling I'm going to find some food there."

So everybody held the steps for me and I went up carefully. I opened the door and found a box of wafers inside. I came down slowly because the steps were shaking. I lined them up and I gave everybody a wafer in their mouth, the whole box. So we had some food. All of a sudden, when the sirens stopped, the SS came out from underground and asked, "Why was everyone standing around you looking so happy?" I said, "Nothing." I didn't tell them what I found. Then he said, "How come none of the bombs hit you?" I said, "Because they know we are here."

On January 1, 1945, it was very cold in Braunschweig and everything was frozen. We had to go to the station and they had bombs in big boxes that we had to put in the cattle wagons to be sent to the German front. It was so cold that our fingers were frozen and my sister had frozen toes, too. Finally, they said, "It's too much. You did enough work." They sent us back. That night, the partisans found us somehow and there was shooting all around. The SS ran away and left us there. They came back in the morning and told us we were staying there. I always went out to look for food for all ten girls. In that city I found bacon and some melted sugar. One day the SS woman came to count us and said, "I'm not going to come here anymore to count you because I am full of lice." She didn't know I was catching the lice in the snow. I had a silk shawl that I found in a burned-out textile factory. The lice liked the silk, so I would catch them in the shawl and shake them into a little box. Every time the SS woman came to camp, I would open the box. She was wearing a skirt, and all the lice went up to her. So she did us a favor and left.

Then they told us there were a lot of partisans coming and too much bombing. So the next day they packed us back in the cattle wagons, and took us somewhere else. We didn't know where we were going. We arrived at no-man's land. It was an underground salt mine in Bendorf, and the Polish people brought their machines to make airplane parts. We went in there at 4 o'clock in the morning and came out at 9 o'clock at night so we never saw the blue sky again, and our mouths were burning all day long from the salt.

One day, a Polish man who managed the machines said to me, "I heard rumors that after you finish here, they are going to kill you." I replied, "That's okay, I know they are going to kill us whether they win the war or lose the war."

I told myself that I had to do something. Whenever I could, I was always sabotaging. So I put a piece of iron into the first of the connected machines and all of them broke down. I lost three fingernails in the process. They were hanging and bloody. The Polish manager said to me, "You better do something. Go to the bathroom and wash your hands and I'll give you a piece of newspaper. Otherwise, when the Germans see you, they'll kill you because you sabotaged their machines." My sister and I worked on different levels, but we always met at the elevator. She asked me why I was holding newspaper in my hands. I told her to keep quiet about it. When we went back to the barracks, I took off the newspaper and all my fingernails were hanging loose. One of the ladies came and pulled off all my nails, but I never had an infection. Maybe it was the tea.

At least we had bunk beds at this place which was better than the other place where we just slept on the floor. We were there for about four or five weeks, when the SS said that we had to move again since the Russians and the English were getting close. I thought to myself, "Not again. Where are we going to go now?" So they put us in the cattle wagons at the factory, and every day as we traveled they would throw out the dead people. Once they had to stop and put us in a farm to stay overnight, because they had to fix the train tracks for the cattle wagons. We rested one day and then they put us back in the cattle wagons. Another day it was horrible because I checked to make sure my sister was with me and I did not see her. So I turned around and there she was, on top of the pile of dead people. I climbed up the pile to my sister and listened for her heart. It was still beating. Somebody had stepped on her stomach and she fainted, so they thought she was dead. I pulled her down and went to an SS woman and asked for a little water because my sister was dying. All the girls told me not to ask her because she was the worst lady, and that she would kill me. I said, "No. God is above us. He is going to help us." She gave me some water and everybody couldn't believe it, but I took a chance. So I poured the water in my sister's mouth and she opened her eyes and said," What happened to me?" I said, "Nothing, you just passed out." I held her in my arms.

There were gypsies with us, too.   Usually they like to steal. There was a Romanian and a German. We didn't have a kitchen and we didn't have any food. Those gypsies gave us some tea, and at night they gave us uncooked macaroni. Then I was able to find some things on the farm, some cabbage and some green stuff.   The SS said to us, "You're going to be alive too long." I said, "Yes? Oh ok!"

So we stayed two more weeks in the big no-man's land - 3,000 girls. They put machine guns behind every five people and made us dig ditches. We knew they were going to kill us then. All of a sudden, the SS said to me, "You don't know how lucky you are. I just saw a motorcycle with the white flag signaling that we shouldn't kill you." The war was over. Then he pulled away the machine guns and he said to us, "I don't know what we're going to do with you."

I always remembered what that guy in the factory told me that, "They are going to kill you if they don't know what to do with you. Whether they win the war or they lose the war." We said goodbye to each other. I said, "Ok, so we are going to die." But we couldn't cry, we never cried. That powder they gave us was very strong.

They put us back in the cattle wagons and it was like in a dream. We couldn't think, but we still didn't want to believe that they were going to put us in those ditches. The SS woman came to beg us to give them our clothes because we were going to be free now. One lady I noticed was all dressed up in somebody's clothes, but I didn't want to say anything. I was holding my sister in my lap for three days. Then one day we arrived in Copenhagen, Denmark, and all the SS disappeared. They ran away, they left us there in the cattle wagons because they knew it was finished for them. That was May the 1st. We couldn't come out because they locked us in the cattle wagons. About two or three hours later, finally people in the town noticed all the cattle wagons were standing there. When they came to check we knocked on the doors, and knocked on the doors. Then the Red Cross came. They found out what happened, that the SS had left us there and run away. So the Red Cross opened the doors for us. Everybody was so tired, standing all day in the wagons.

They said, "Don't worry. You're going to be free now." Everybody wanted to get out of the cattle wagons but they didn't go because they were too weak. Only I jumped out. I said, "I am going, we are free! I am going home forever." I was always looking for food. Then I saw a lady in a white uniform bringing a whipped cream cake to the cattle wagon. Some girl pushed me right into the cake, so they started licking it off me. They took photos for a news reel and we saw it later in Sweden. Then I went to every store. They opened them for us and said, "You can have anything you want." So I came back and said to the girls, "You want to come? Come on, I'll show you all the stores are open. You can take whatever you want." They couldn't move, so I gave everybody food and I jumped off and went to bring more food. Then the soldiers came and they took us off the cattle wagons. They took us to Copenhagen where there was a farm which had barracks for the soldiers, for emergencies, but nobody was using them. And they gave us - I'll never forget every time I eat it - oatmeal. That was our first food - oatmeal. They gave us a little slice of bread. They knew our stomachs had shrunk because we had such little food. I saw a big stable with a lot of potatoes, but they told us, "No, you're not staying here. You're going to Sweden. You have to stay here for a little while so you can get used to food, but when you go to Sweden you're going to have everything, even milk." We had not seen milk for a year, or fruit, or much of any kind of good food, just a hard slice of bread. We didn't believe it. So I made a little fire outside and cooked potatoes so we would have something to eat on the trip. They put out the fire and told me we would have lots of food. They said to us, "We're going to put you on a luxury ship to go to Sweden."

We still didn't want to believe it. We were free. Because the Swedish government promised to take us, we were the first ones to arrive in Sweden. It took about two hours on the luxury ship. When we arrived, it was something like a miracle. We saw lots of people. All of a sudden, I saw Dr. Schulz from Czechoslovakia. He had been hiding in Sweden. When he heard me speak he asked where I came from. I told him, "From Slovakia." He said, "Do you know, my dear child, who that man was who just shook hands with you?" I said, "I don't know, a captain?" He said, "No, he wasn't a captain. He is the Swedish King, King Gustav." He was waiting for us to get off the ship so he could welcome us. Later on, I went to his summer home and we played Ping-Pong together.

We still didn't want to believe it, that we were free. It took us time to accept that. So they took all of our stuff and we stayed there for the night. We took a shower, washed our hair, and they gave us new clothes. I've never seen such good people as these Danish and Swedish people. They didn't know what to do for us, they were so happy that we were the first transport. They did blood work on everybody, and anybody who was a little bit sick they took to the hospital. My sister and I were okay. They closed all their high schools and middle schools to put us there until they found a place for us to sleep. Whenever we arrived at a new place, the first thing they asked was, "When is your birthday?" I always said, "Tomorrow." So they celebrated my birthday four times that year!

The Swedish people make big parties when it is your birthday; they like to celebrate. Everybody brought flowers, chocolate, everything. We couldn't eat very much because our stomachs were shrunk, but every day we got a little bit more. I went to get food for the nine girls, ten of us including me, three times a day. I stood in a line for breakfast, lunch, and dinner. Every time they gave us the food, we had to take cod liver oil. So I took thirty spoons of cod liver oil every day to get food for the girls. About two weeks later, the doctors were examining me and one of them said, "How come you don't look like you were in a concentration camp, Marilyn? What did you do?" So, I told him. They didn't have vitamins in those days, so it must have been the cod liver oil. Since then, I never wanted to taste it again. I was the first one of 3,000 girls whose menstrual period returned. They celebrated again. Why only me, why not the other girls? Because the other girls didn't eat enough and they didn't take the cod liver oil.

In Sweden, they have a lot of beds in the castles, and the guest houses. So they took us away from the school because the students had to return, and we moved around four or five times a year. For two years we worked in the fields in the summertime, and we would stay in the guest houses. One day I went to the stable and I said to the stable boy, "I would like to ride that horse." He said, "No you can't do that because it's the baron's horse." I said, "So what? I know how to ride a horse. We had a horse back home, we had a big estate." He said, "Okay, I'll let you go just around the block." I rode to the village, and everybody came out to see, "Who is riding the baron's horse?" I was, and they were so surprised.

We moved so many times in Sweden, but finally they put us into school. From then on, I had to go out and find a job because I was nineteen years old. My sister still stayed in school. When we were in one of the baron's houses, the mayor of the city was there. He said that he wanted to adopt the two of us because we didn't find anybody who came home from the war. I knew that my parents were not going to come because they were killed, and my cousins, everybody. So he said, "I want to adopt you." "No," my sister cried, "maybe somebody from our family will come home and we will have all our luggage ready to leave for Czechoslovakia." He said, "You're not going to go."

He was right. One of my friends wrote a letter to the United States and found out that her kids were alive. And that friend called my uncle. That's how he found out that we were alive. Right away the mayor sent us an affidavit and said, "All the luggage that you have there, I'll bring it back for you. You're going to the United States." After two years, they had finally called me and my sister and told us that we could leave, but when we went to the ship on Friday, they told me, "Your papers are okay, but your sister cannot go." I said, "I am not going alone. Either she comes or I am not going." -- Finally they said, "Okay, take your sister."

Then we went on the ship and the captain asked me if I could be his interpreter because a lot of people were from Poland, Yugoslavia, Hungary, and Romania. He spoke only English and Swedish. That was good. I was free to do anything. He treated us like first class passengers. Then he asked if I knew anybody on the ship who had liquor. He wanted a little schnapps to keep from being sick. I knew three sisters with three bottles of fruit-flavored liquor (pear, apricot and cherry) that they were bringing to their uncles in the United States. They were so sick that they did not even get up out of bed. Every morning I went into their closet and took a little bit of the schnapps for myself and the captain. Neither of us got seasick. When we arrived in New York, one of the girls said, "It's very interesting...all our liquor has dried up."

After arriving in the United States, I found out that my father died two days before the liberation, in Mauthausen, one of the concentration camps. Later on, one of the doctors came to me and said, "Your father was always worried that if a strong man can't stand it, how will our kids stand it? They will never survive." He was always worried about me, but I made it. In the picture below of my family, only my sister and I survived.

I met my husband in the United States after he had served in the U.S. Army for five years, and I came from Sweden after the war in 1947. We moved to Miami, and we had two boys. I always tell them that they would never be here if I had not survived. I also have four grandchildren and one great-grandson. Later on, we moved to California. My sister still lives in New Jersey.

© 2012 Marilyn Katz

MY WAR YEARS BY CHARLES KIRCHER

My story started in 1942. I was eighteen years old, raised in San Fernando Valley, California. I grew up during the Depression Years and graduated from San Fernando High School in June, 1941. World War II started a few months later with the bombing of Pearl Harbor by the Japanese on December 7, 1941. I was working at the Vega Aircraft Plant as an assembler and enlisted in the U.S. Navy on August 5, 1942. After being sworn into the service as a Seaman Recruit I qualified for flight training under the V5 program. The Navy sent me home to await a call up to active duty as an Aviation Cadet.

The Battle of Midway had taken place a short time before and the papers said we had won even though our losses were heavy. We were now involved in the Solomon Islands, the Battle on Guadalcanal and the adjacent Naval Battle. I could hardly wait to get involved and the waiting was hard. I showed up at work each evening at 11:30 PM and worked in the main Vega plant on Hollywood Way until dawn. We were subjected to numerous Air Raid Alerts when all the lights in the plant were suddenly shut off. The windows at this time were not yet blacked out so when the lights went out, we just put down our tools and sat right where we were. The work floor was so cluttered that it was impossible to move about.

Finally, in September, I received a letter from the Navy informing me that I was eligible for something called Civilian Pilot Training, if I wished to volunteer. I wouldn't get paid and I would have to purchase a couple of khaki shirts and pants plus a pair of brown shoes to use as a uniform. They would feed me and house me and teach me to fly. I jumped at it! The school was run by Bakersfield Junior College and took place in Lone Pine California. All I had to do was sign up and show up on a specified date and they would do the rest.

Bright and early on a hot Saturday morning I drove my '33 Ford up to the Bakersfield Campus to find a large group of young men, all about my age, and all anxious to go but knowing no more than I. In short order we had all signed the proper paperwork and were ready to be transported. A few of us had cars and I found no trouble getting a couple of guys to ride with me as no one was anxious to ride in the old rattletrap busses the school provided. Up Highway 395 we went and by afternoon we arrived at the High School campus in Lone Pine. The athletic field was mostly dirt and there we found the line of army tents that were to be our home for the next eight weeks. There was not a tree in sight, and only a lone administrator greeted us. He passed out meal tickets to be used at the only restaurant in town and a schedule for ground school and flight school. Half of us went to ground classes in the morning and flew in the afternoon and the other half reversed the schedule. We walked into town for our meals but they had an old bus to provide transportation to the field about 4 miles south of town.

We met our civilian instructor at the flight line for our assigned flight and kept the same instructor throughout the course. The ground school was conducted by a very, very attractive young female pilot. Throughout the training she seemed oblivious to the love sick looks she received from the class of nineteen and twenty year old students away from home for the first time. We were all in love with her I think. We managed to learn about flight rules and regulations despite the distraction.

Our actual flight instruction was much more interesting as we all thought of ourselves as future fighter pilots shooting down the nasty Japs. On our solo hops we all tried to get our planes as high as Mount Whitney but it was just too much to ask of the Luscombs, Aeroncas and Cubs of that era.

As each of us soloed, we received the traditional dunking in Lone Pine Lake. A couple of men washed out but most of us made it through the curriculum and felt that we were now accomplished pilots. Our instructors may have had a different opinion. We endured the cots, the cold nights, the food and the loneliness for we were all part of something that was changing the nation and Americans. We didn't know the big words but were all aware that we were part of a big adventure.

When I completed the course, I traveled back down to Bakersfield and was logged out. I left all my new friends and drove back home to the San Fernando Valley but I felt a vague feeling of uneasiness as I had no idea as to what would come next. I called Vega Aircraft Co. and they said to come back to work for however long I had until I was called up again. Back to the assembly line on the graveyard shift I went. In December I was notified to report for active duty on December 23rd, 1942. I was to bring a minimum amount of clothing as I would have to either ship it back home or throw it away. In those days, civilian clothes were not allowed while on active duty. Report I did, two days before Christmas, to the Federal Building in downtown Los Angeles. We were shipped out that evening on an overnight train to Oakland, CA. and then transported to St Mary's College in the middle of nowhere. Twelve weeks of pre-flight training were in store. We spent the Christmas and New Year holidays in quarantine and were issued uniforms while they converted us from civilians to Naval Aviation Cadets.

Pre-flight training consisted of athletics morning, noon and night with a couple of hours of classroom study squeezed in between the various torture sessions. To some of the high school "jocks" it was a cakewalk, but I was still a chubby bookworm and to me it really felt like a torture chamber. Twelve weeks of football, track, basketball, swimming, boxing, wrestling, calisthenics and military drill nearly did me in but I survived, even thrived. I ate like a horse, lost weight and gained muscle. Before I knew it March had arrived and I had passed all the requirements and was ready for Primary Flight Training. During this time, and in the months to come, we were pretty much isolated and oblivious to world events. Like most young men of nineteen, I was "WAR" would mainly worried about my own problems and somehow felt the wait for me.

Pasco Washington and the N2S Stearman Bi-Plane occupied me for the next four or five months. At that time there wasn't much around the small town of Pasco except barren land with the Snake River flowing through it. It was a perfect place for Primary Flight

Training. They had numerous landing pads scattered around the countryside where we practiced various types of landings. There was a lot of open space in which to practice aerobatics and nothing in the town to distract a young cadet. I was not as it turned out, a natural pilot. I suffered many a down check which then required further instruction and retesting. The pass/fail bar was set very high and it seemed I was always just on the verge of elimination but, eventually, I passed my last check-ride and was considered qualified to move on to the next stage. The transfer from Pasco to Corpus Christi Texas was by slow train in old, turn of the century passenger cars that had certainly seen better days. There were no sleeper cars, just passenger cars with wooden seats and it seemed that we stopped at every siding to let a more important train go by. The food was cold sandwiches and the trip took several long, hot days.

The next five months were spent moving through a series of outlying fields like Kingsville, Beesville, Cabiness and finally, the main field at Corpus itself. We flew in a

number of training planes culminating in the SNJ advanced trainer. I never had much of a problem with the academic curriculum, and didn't here either.

My problems with the flight training alleviated somewhat as it seemed that the more advanced the aircraft was, the less problems I had in mastering it. I had excellent grades in dive bombing and thought sure I would be assigned to a bombing squadron upon graduation. The great day finally came.

On January 19, 1944, I was graduated and received a commission as Ensign, U.S. Naval Reserve and was designated a Naval Aviator. None of my family attended, I was just another number in a pipeline but it was the proudest moment in my life. Along with all the other graduating cadets, I tossed my hat high in the air and, like the others, I had a dollar ready to give to the first enlisted man who saluted me. (With the gradual inflation, I wonder how much a new ensign gives now?). When I saw my orders, however, I was a little disappointed as they were not for Dive Bombers but for advanced training in Fighters. There was to be no leave to visit home but immediate reporting to Vero Beach, Florida where I was to be indoctrinated in the Grumman F4F fighter and in advanced fighter tactics.

The F4F turned out to be an easy plane to fly although we considered it to be slow, especially when trying to gain altitude. I was getting good grades in the various tactics we learned, particularly in the various forms of bombing. The F4F could carry two small bombs even though it was classed as a fighter. One problem with it was in ground handling. It had narrow landing gear that was supported by shock absorbing supporting struts. It was the devil to taxi in a cross wind and a supporting strut could collapse leaving you cocked at an angle, perhaps to be towed back to the flight line.

One day in March on a normal flight in perfect weather conditions, I came in for a landing that I expected to be like any other, when disaster struck! I swerved to the left and then to the right and the plane swung around with the left wing dragging the runway. I wound up off the runway with the nose of the airplane digging into the dirt and the tail pointed skyward. My knee hurt like hell and I had banged my head into the gun sight causing a slight concussion. They carted me off to the hospital where I awoke the next morning. A couple of days later when they released me from the hospital I learned that they were to hold a hearing and were considering the incident a pilot error. I was allowed to view the photographs they had taken of the plane sitting on the runway and it was obvious to me that the left landing gear support strut had collapsed on touchdown (We were taught to always use a hard three point landing). They held the board (Navy lingo for hearing) immediately, while I was still recovering. Things did not go well. I was bitter and belligerent. They were firm in their point of view even though my instructor testified on my behalf. They recommended that I be permanently grounded, my wings taken away and that I be reassigned as an Aviation Ground Officer. Guess who won? Years later I felt vindicated when a study concluded that the landing gear support struts on this aircraft had a faulty design that caused numerous accidents but by this time it was too late for me. I was devastated, my dream at an end, but I was still an Ensign in the Navy that I had grown to love.

While waiting for the Navy to decide where to send me, I was assigned to conduct night landing operations at an outlying field at Ft. Pierce, Florida. Here I learned ground to air communications and control, all the while fighting the swarms of mosquitoes that were common in the area. When my orders came they were to Control Tower Operators School at Atlanta, Georgia as a student. So, as so often happens in the Navy, you pack your gear, say your farewells to the friends you have made and ship out. After twelve weeks at Atlanta, I was designated a certified Control Tower Operator. Ironically, I was never to see the inside of a control tower again! My orders this time were to a Squadron preparing for overseas duty at Los Alamitos California. I was given some time at home after being away for a year a half.

At home things were much different than when I left. At my instructions, my mother had long since sold my '33 Ford, so I was dependent on her '38 Dodge. Gas was rationed, as was meat and sugar. It seemed that everyone was working in a defense industry. My old friends were gone on their own wartime odysseys. My brother was in the Army Air Force about to graduate as a 2nd Lieutenant. My mother had moved to a very small apartment in a different city and was working long hours. This was not the home I remembered, and I almost felt relieved when the time was up and I reported to my squadron.

When I reported in to VC-79 I found that I was not really wanted or needed. There was no open billet that needed filling. They were pleasant enough but had an attitude of "What shall we do with this guy". I wound up as assistant this and assistant that and became proficient at making coffee. The squadron was slated to "ship out" and in a few weeks we were transferred aboard the USS Sargent Bay, CVE 83. At long last I was going to get my chance to go to war. After a stop in Pearl Harbor we set off to join the Fleet in the

South Pacific. The squadron was undergoing intensive flight operations as we were heading for action! It soon became apparent that the ship had no one trained in ship to air communications even though they now had radar and an Air Plot capability.

My skipper agreed to loan the ship an "Air Plot" Officer. That became my job and for the duration of our tour I acted as one of the ship's crew. I was happy for I was now doing something that my training had fitted me for. Our tour, however, was something different. When we joined the Fifth Fleet we learned that we were to be assigned to guard the tanker fleet. For the duration of our tour we were always adjacent to the sea battles, the landings, the large air fights, but we were never directly involved. We cruised, we listened, flew our CAP flights, ate the lousy food, sweated in the heat and humidity, endured the typhoons, and to others went the glory and the terror. Years later when I saw the movie "Mr. Roberts" I felt a certain kinship with him and Ensign Pulver. In the spring of 1945 we were relieved and returned to the States and the squadron disbanded. We had neither fired a shot at the enemy nor had been under their fire.

Now, a Lieutenant JG, I received orders to a CASU-45 at 29 Palms, California. I learned that "CASU" meant Carrier Aircraft Service Unit and that they supported operations of Navy or Marine squadrons ashore. In other words, they operated the island airfields that the Navy captured or set up. When I reported in and met the crusty old skipper, he greeted me and informed me that I was to be his Night Check Officer for the Engineering Department. When I protested, saying that I knew operations but nothing about fixing airplanes, his only comment was, "Did you not hear me lieutenant? Dismissed". I took charge of the Night Check Division and was just smart enough to know that I should place my faith in my Leading Chief. I did, he was proficient, and we were a success. Twenty Nine Palms was just as hot then as it is now. The strip was built of steel mats and the heat was terrific. The aircraft were too hot in the daytime to touch. All maintenance work was done at night. The enlisted men were housed in tents and suffered greatly while we officers at least had barracks but no air conditioning.

The war in the Pacific was proceeding and they were running out of islands to conquer and so we had no idea where they would use our CASU. In July we received Top Secret orders to cancel all leave and liberty and to separate the CASU into two sections. One section was to go in with the marines to set up operations on an unknown airfield, and the second section to join up once the airfield was secured. Where this operation was to take place, no one knew. At this time the Engineering Officer was transferred out and I, being senior, became the CASU's Engineering Officer. I was twenty-two years old and had over one hundred Enlisted men, thirteen Chiefs and two other Officers in my Division. The two other officers, although junior in rank, were "mustangs" and had many more years of service than I. Again, I trusted in those with more experience than I and made sure to always give credit where credit was due.

We divided the CASU into two sections, the first section packed all the gear we felt was needed and when the orders came to move out we were ready. We were transported to San Francisco and there we went aboard a transport CVE (jeep carrier). It was about the first of August, 1945, and we still didn't know where we were headed. It was a Top Secret operation and we were prohibited from informing even our closest relatives as to what was going on. We didn't know anything anyway. We put to sea and the heading was North-

West. After a few days it was apparent that we were in the northern latitudes and the secret destination was disclosed. We were part of an invasion of Hokkaido, the northernmost island of Japan. There was an airfield within a couple of miles of the coastline just inland from a beach suitable for a landing. This operation was not part of "The General Plan for the invasion of the Japanese Islands", but the Allied Command had observed that the Japanese forces were all being transferred south to defend the southern island of Kyushu. If we could capture this airfield it would give our forces a land base to mount airstrikes on the rear of the Japanese defenders. It was a spur-of-the-moment tactical operation that Admirals felt had a good chance of succeeding. We felt like pawns on a large chess board being moved about as the situation developed. We also realized that we were expendable.

In the Navy, it is hard to keep sailors in the dark as to where they're headed. They are used to judging the sun, moon and stars to determine their course. Thus in the middle of August we became aware that the ship was no longer on heading but proceeding in a large circle. We were informed of the dropping of an Atomic Bomb and then a second. When word came of the "Cessations of Hostilities" the ship was ordered to put in to the nearest Naval Base. This was the Naval Operating Base on Adak, part of the Aleutian Island chain. If my memory serves me correctly it was August 24, 1945 and the war was over. Much more occurred and I was eventually discharged. A few years later I rejoined the Navy as an enlisted sailor but all that can wait for another chapter. For now:

THE WAR IS OVER!

© 2012 Charles D. Kircher

CLARA KNOPFLER – Excerpts from her book,
"I Am Still Here" – My Mother's Voice, **Copyright 2007**

My memories of childhood go back to when we lived in the little village of Cehul-Silvaniei, Transylvania, in Northern Romania. In 1939 and 1940 war started in some parts of Europe, but it affected us very little. There were discussions in our house; my uncles told us news about the war of Hitler and the anti-Semitic actions of the Iron Guard. The grownups looked worried and insecure about the future. They listened to the radio and tried to understand the reactions of our government.

One Friday evening my father returned from the synagogue and told my mother about a man who had escaped from Poland and told outrageous stories about the Nazi regime's atrocities in his country. Jews were the target of their torture. Fortunes, jobs, and houses were taken, synagogues were burnt, and groups of men were taken away – he did not know where.

The members of our congregation did not want to listen to the outcry of a Polish stranger, but he pleaded with us to believe him about how the Nazi menace was threatening their seemingly peaceful lives. He urged us to unify and develop some kind of resistance, or to escape our country as soon as we could. But the Jews of our village could not think about leaving their little shtetl. Wars come and go, they said. Anti-Semitism always was and always will be. If we are good, working, studying, praying people, God will help us and our families stay together. And Hitler will fail.

However, my parents soon lived in a constant fear that we sensed each day. They knew our future was foggy and insecure; my father's shoe business slowed and anti-Semitic feeling was growing like poisonous mushrooms in the forest. In the summer of 1940, the Iron Guard initiated pogroms against Jews and we were very frightened. Then the Hungarians occupied Cehul-Silvaniei with a great parade. Soldiers marched and cavalry rode through the center of our little village.

The problem that preoccupied us now was our immediate future. Every day was full of new edicts against the Jews. In cities, these instructions were posted in the streets and in the post offices where everyone could see them. In my little village, the town crier would be preceded by a drummer who would read the orders of the mayor. One day the village drummer appeared in the center of the main square twenty yards from our house, beating his drum so all could hear. When the people surrounded him, his drumming ceased and he began reading: Jews should not congregate, go to restaurants, or to market before 10 a.m. and they should return home no later than 5 p.m. We began to live in a constant nightmare, worrying and wondering what would happen next.

Even the Hungarian population worried about the outcome. The mayor enforced dictatorial rules and encouraged spying on neighbors, especially those who were a "Jew friend." Those who were Christians had been warned that if they socialized with us they would be punished. We could not even meet secretly. We were afraid of being denounced and we cared about the safety of our Christian friends.

The authorities had confiscated all the radios and the newspapers and were lying in order to hide the truth: that Hitler had been losing the war since 1942. His army had suffered its first great defeat in Stalingrad and never recovered. What we did not know was that Hitler would exterminate almost all of Europe's Jews.

In March 1944 Hitler's army invaded Hungary. A week later my brother came home from his school in Budapest, completely devastated by the events that had taken place in the capital. The Hungarians had sold their country to the Nazis. On March 28, 1944 we were all home. All Jewish children and relatives had to return to their families. April 1, 1944 was The Day of Fools, except for us. It was the day we learned that every Jew would have to wear a yellow star. My mother had to sew it on our coats, jackets, and other clothes. On April 6th, we put them on. It was horrible. I felt like a leper who knows that he does not belong to this society and whose existence is harmful to friends or acquaintances, even if he only greets them from a distance. Since we were not allowed to be out until 10 a.m. to go to the market, there was nothing left to buy because the fresh vegetables, milk and dairy were already sold. We had no telephone and no radio. We were cut off from the world. Jews were to be forever isolated from human interaction.

One of the rumors was that entire families would be taken away from home to an agricultural camp. We would work in the fields during the harvest period, collect the crops, work in mills, and send food as soon as possible to the soldiers who were fighting on the Eastern Front, and everywhere else where Hitler hoped to occupy more territories. After the end of the battle of Stalingrad in 1943, no one believed that he would win, but his orders stood.

There was no indication of what we could take with us. All our valuables already had been confiscated by the Hungarian authorities. We had been given no receipts for what they took: gold, silver, foreign money, stocks, bonds, insurance papers, and foreign investments. Everyone's life savings were taken away without an explanation except one: "Jew." We heard about other villages where Jews were already in ghettos – two or three families in a room with one bathroom, or none at all. Finally, we heard that our deportation was imminent. The authorities would give us at least three days before our departure. The tension was tangible and our anxiety grew in the days that followed. Then the Hungarians told us we had two days to prepare. We were told to bring food, but not perishables: flour, sugar, jars of fat, oil, marmalade, yeast, eggs, potatoes and a little smoked meat. No milk, cheese, or butter, because there was no refrigeration. We were also told to bring blankets, pillows, and enough light clothing for two or three weeks. It was the second of May, but the nights were still chilly and often rainy.

The next day they surprised us, and of course we were not prepared, but they did not care. We were given half an hour to get ready and were then taken to the train station. From all the Jewish houses, two hundred families had joined us in this stop and go, sad, tragic, and hopeless march. When we arrived at the station and saw the train wagons, we rushed up the steps because we were exhausted from this terrible, humiliating march and we wanted to escape the looks of our neighbors. We helped the old people first; then lifted their luggage after them. We carried heavy backpacks and wore three to four layers of clothing. There were just a few benches inside the wagons, and we teenagers sat on the floor or on our backpacks.

Late that night we arrived at our destination, a huge brick factory that was empty of bricks. The commander of this camp was the infamous Jew-hater and sadist named Krasznai, our former village mayor. The brick factory was our ghetto. Eight thousand people were living there like badly treated animals. We were packed like sardines, and only blankets were hung on concrete posts that separated entire families: each section was about ten feet wide and six feet long. One petroleum lamp provided light for three to four families. There was no bathroom, washroom, toilet or running water. To wash in the morning, we walked one kilometer to the river where we collected water for cooking and carried it in two pails to balance our walking. How many barrels would we need to quench the thirst of eight thousand people? We were thirsty all the time; dehydrated from the heat and the salt we used to add flavor to our meager food. The administration provided soup at noon, but it was so bad that many families opted for one potato per person and some fat with which to prepare it. We had a frying pan and some matzo that we brought, just as our ancestors had when they fled from Egypt.

My friend Ervin was ordered to dig a trench for a latrine, but he rebelled and confronted the gendarme saying that he was willing to construct an enclosed toilet, but not such a shameful and subhuman place. The enraged guard ordered him to be tied to a high tree branch by his arms until he was no longer able to endure the pain and fainted. Then he was cut loose to set an example for all. I thought nothing worse could happen to us. We were hungry, thirsty, humiliated, and without hope that our conditions would improve.

One day we were told to pack a small bag, and to choose its contents carefully. Everything else was to be left neatly in the brick factory to be stored until we returned, they said. We did not know what was waiting for us, but we did not think it could be worse. We walked to the train station like a herd of animals, and were prodded to go faster. Then we saw the cattle wagons. We thought it was incredible that these wagons were to be used to transport human beings. Before we were moved onto the train there was another search of our bags, pockets, underwear, panties, and bras, by women who volunteered for this important job. They did their work thoroughly and rudely, some of them penetrating our bodies to search for diamonds or money that might be hidden. It was humiliating and painful.

Secrecy was one of the weapons they used to prevent panic and rebellion. The guards did not tell us where we were going, when exactly we would leave, or how long the trip would last. If we asked any of these questions we were severely punished. The guards' words to us were always peppered with cursing and condemnation. "The Goddamned Jews want to know everything, even their futures," they laughed. There was so much hatred and sarcasm in their constant yelling, that I begged those around me to stop asking questions. In this way we could pretend to ignore the importance of these matters. We could not trust the answers they gave us, anyway.

The trains we had seen were cattle wagons. Seventy people were piled into each wagon. There was not enough room for so many people to sit down at once. Sleep was impossible. In one corner was a big pot, like a garbage can, where we were supposed to relieve ourselves. The Hungarian gendarmes locked the doors from outside after they piled the old and sick together into the wagon with the young and the babies. We heard the heavy iron bars clicking, and then the huge lock closing.

Three days later when the train stopped, a guard opened our wagon and I asked him, "What is the name of this town?" He replied, "Auschwitz. You'll never forget it."

My father took my brother by the arm, looked back at us, waved lightly, and smiled as if to say, "See you later." I could not see his warm eyes because it was dark and we were already being pushed to step out of the train. This is my last picture of my father. I cherish it and keep it vividly in my memory. This unique human being was good, honest, and loving. After the men were all off the train we again heard shouting, and were told to move faster and leave our luggage on the platform. This time they did not say that we would be getting anything back. Everything was chaotic. There was shouting, crying and confusion. Guards with dogs surrounded us. We were told there was to be a selection. We were so numbed by the events, we followed without asking anything. Then a strong SS man, armed and holding a stick in his hand like a great orchestra conductor came towards us. He pointed the women right or left without saying much. To his right he directed the old women, younger women holding children in their arms, and those holding children by the hand. Sometimes he pulled a child from a woman and pushed it into the arms of an older woman. At the time, none of us knew his reason for making the selection. We just speculated that the young women would work while the older women would watch the children.

Then it was our turn to be selected. Mama and I were pushed by this powerful, smiling, and cursing giant into a line of adults who were all over fifteen years old and appeared strong enough to work in slave labor camps. Josef Mengele (we found out later) was the man who selected us. He had good eyes even in that dim light. He did not waste a second to argue or to explain why my mother was pushed to his left while all the other women on our wagon were directed to his right. We did not know that this little motion to the left meant life and a chance to survive.

After twenty minutes of marching on the stony road, we saw a somewhat different barracks with a light at its entrance. We were directed to enter this building, one by one in a long line. Then we were ordered to undress completely, and to proceed to the next room holding only our shoes in our hands. Five women worked feverishly shaving the women's hair. My fine, dark, warm-brown wavy hair reached my shoulders. I was ordered to sit by a woman who pointed her finger to the first chair. Tears streaked my cheeks as she continued nonchalantly shaving, circling the crown of my head. In those five minutes I felt violated and stripped of my femininity forever. I ran to my mother, but she did not recognize me, so naked and shaven was I. later on we found out how much better it was to be bald because it prevented lice from infesting our hair for a couple of months.

This first night in Auschwitz our column was ordered to march in the darkness of the night and we stumbled here and there on the hard pebbles. By this time, we were dead tired as it must have been 2 a.m. or later. We passed a huge barracks with closed doors. Then we got to one that had an open door. We could not see or hear anything; when our turn came, we entered and were stunned. In the semidarkness, we saw hundreds of bodies lying close to each other on the floor. We were ordered to occupy the empty parts of the floor where we were to sleep until morning. Our group consisted of at least six hundred newcomers. But we had no sooner lain down than we felt thirsty and many of us needed toilets. Mama and I walked out, trying not to step on anybody's head as we moved to the exit. Outside in the pitch dark we looked for latrines, but there were none. When we couldn't hold it any longer we found some grassy spots where we crouched and emptied our bladders. We used some long leaves for toilet paper, and it was horrible. We ran back and settled silently wherever we could find a spot on the floor.

We were awakened by a loud voice. This was the 5 a.m. roll call. We went outside. Nobody had slept well and we all complained of the hard floor and how impossible it was to turn over with so many bodies pushing for a little more room to extend their tired arms and legs. We were warned to be quiet, stand still, and wait for the roll calls. SS women moved in front of our lines counting by fives and forming us into groups of hundreds. It took long hours to organize this flock of miserable women. Then somebody came with a bucket, paint, and a brush, and put numbers on our backs. I had **51455**. We escaped the tattoo, used only for those who stayed longer than a week in Auschwitz. The paint had to dry, so we had to stand there longer, and a rumor spread that we would be given breakfast. One by one we went back to the barracks and took our ration of bread, one plastic dish for coffee or bran soup, and a wooden spoon. The other inmates warned us not to eat all our bread because that one thick slice (one inch) was our allotment for the whole day. Wondering what would happen next, we asked the girls who had come there before us. They urged us to accept any work that was given to us, just to get out of Auschwitz. They warned that this was both an extermination and a concentration camp. Of course we did not understand fully what this meant, and we were so preoccupied with the present misery, filth, heat, thirst, hunger, and diarrhea that we could not think of anything else.

By what was probably the seventh day, we were told that we would get some work, that we had been of no use for a week, and had just eaten and taken up space in the barracks. We were taken on foot to the train station about five miles away. There we were herded into cattle wagons, as before. As the train continued to roll on the tracks, the monotonous noise seemed to be rhythmically repeating my thoughts, which were always: *let us live, let us live, let us live*. Where we were going and how we would stay alive, I did not know. If we had known that the Allies had landed in Europe and the Russians had encircled Hitler's occupied territories, we would have had some hope and inspiration to go on and stick it out. But we were kept in the dark, as good news for the Jewish people was well hidden.

The train was rolling still when the wagon doors opened on an astonishing view: gray sky, gray yards, dark gray barracks and not a soul in sight all the way to the gray horizon. A siren sounded and SS men in green uniforms stepped out from the barracks. They walked to our train to meet the new supply of two-legged animals who would produce the necessary goods for Hitler to win the war. They yelled and pushed us into rows of five and directed us to the barracks of this place. When we entered, we were surprised by its cleanliness and by the wooden two-story bunks with some blankets on them. The SS woman, in her harsh voice, said, "This is not a shit-house like a Jewish home. Here we have German neatness and discipline.

At five o'clock the next morning, a siren woke us. It was dark outside, but there was a lot to do. We rose quickly and rushed to the cold shower room where we washed without soap or towels; then we put on our clothing to dry. Luckily, it was June and warm outside. Breakfast finally came, but all we could see was the long line for coffee, one piece of bread (for the day), and some bran cereal that was thin and tasteless, although sweetened with saccharin. This was the breakfast served in all the concentration camps, and left us hungry for the rest of the day. We were given ten minutes to eat and drink and get back to our place in line for the march to our workplace.

Fifty yards from the barracks was the road we were to travel for three months. It consisted of broken-up Jewish gravestones. We had to step on letters or very short words that we could decipher. Walking on these stones was like stepping on our grandparents, our families, our fellow human beings. We felt as though we were desecrating the Ten Commandments and we thought of the instruction to respect our elders so that we might live a long life. At that time, however, we did not want to live a long life. We were preoccupied with our constant hunger and only hoped to eat a whole meal once more, to sleep on a normal bed, to clean our teeth with a toothbrush, and to shower with soap and a towel. The road was about two miles long and we were not allowed to speak, to share our thoughts or feelings.

From six o'clock at night until six in the morning we dismantled huge batteries and placed the components into four piles: aluminum, wires, copper, and the residue of the batteries. The precious material was sticky, dark, and rubbery and had to be scraped from the walls of the blackened aluminum. We were to scrape every bit out so the Nazis could use it for gunpowder. We were later told that ammunition was the most important and most necessary product for winning the War. In the morning, another group came at six and left at six in the evening. We were advised to follow orders and work if we wanted to live. Our leader was an older man who did not wear a Nazi uniform and looked kindly. He was not frightening and did not carry a gun or a rubber stick. He did not yell, but was firm in his orders. His assistant was a German Jewish woman who was strict but willing to explain our complicated work. After all, recycling was very important in the poor German economy of 1944.

We worked without any break until ten or eleven at night when it was still light in Riga, almost like daylight, but when the darkness came, we were ready to fall asleep. By midnight we were so sleepy we could not hold our heads up. The leader called me to his desk. I was frozen with fear and stood in front of him trembling. The old man looked at me with understanding eyes. "You little girl," he said in German, "you must sing." I remembered a Mozart song, a Schubert song, and a love song by Lehar, but I wasn't sure if I could remember the lines correctly. He said, "When dark sets in outside and you feel that your regular sleeping time has come, start singing. Even if the people around you do not know the words, they will hum the melody with you and this will encourage them to sing along. They will join you and they will not fall asleep. They will work. Otherwise, I will have to beat them every night to keep them awake and force them to produce."

His good intention to avoid using physical punishment was the first spark of humanity I had seen. Maybe not all Germans considered us animals and slaves, I thought, so I immediately responded and told him I would sing. At the end of the night, the old man secretly gave me a few slices of bread that I took to my group of six and shared with them. It was more valuable to us then than a million dollars, and I was very proud of it.

One night, the Russian bombers came. They started early, and many more circled around our camp. They brightened the whole sky with "Stalin candles," settling, it seemed, on the top of our barracks and telling us, "We are coming! Soon you will be liberated from the darkness and misery, though you cannot escape now." Nazi airplanes chased "the candles" away. The Nazis wanted to destroy the Russian planes in their last efforts to win the war. No bomb ever fell on our camp. The Russians must have known that this was a prison camp holding Jews and non-Jews, so they did not aim at us. They showed up almost every other night, but the more they came, the crueler the Nazi guards became. The Nazis took all their frustrations over losing the war out on us as if we were to blame – pushing us harder and cutting our bread rations daily. Soon we learned that the Nazis were emptying Kaiserwald because the Russians were approaching. The young and healthy would be selected and transported by ship somewhere to work.

There were a few among us who already knew that we would be taken to Riga's harbor to embark on a merchant ship. The shipyard looked like a big city to me; there were huge warehouses, small houses, and many military tents. Our marching line slowed down and turned towards the biggest ship. Forklifts were moving up and down, carrying merchandise to the ship's upper deck. When I looked around I realized how big a crowd we were – eight hundred people, at least. Where would we be put? We did not stay on the top deck, but were led down until we were three or four levels under the sea. In each area, there were three tiers of fifty to sixty beds and each of those was to hold three women. We were on the ship for about three days, and it was dark all the time. There was one light bulb on the top of the three tiers of sleeping compartments and steps where we would go around, looking for a toilet or some place to empty our bladders. It was also a chance to breathe some fresh air, which we badly needed. More and more coughing was heard in the sleeping area; we were suffocating. Those who survived the trip landed in Danzig and we couldn't believe how beautiful it looked. There were flowers with huge petals in every hue, some growing on low bushes and some on high trees. They were growing all along the river that flowed into the sea where our boat was. We were pushed into the bottom of a small boat. The trip from the harbor to Stutthof lasted about half an hour.

It was September 1944 when we arrived in Stutthof, an important center for concentrating, selecting, and exterminating Jews, but we were not aware of this when we got there. On the surface it was neat and orderly: plants grew around the barracks. Stutthof was a concentration camp for transient prisoners where we were deloused, disinfected, and selected for further work. They made us stand in line, wet and itching from the chlorine-filled water, waiting for clean clothing. You should have seen what was thrown to us: ripped and ruffled, but disinfected from the last week's transport group. I received a green satin cocktail dress fitted for size six, so I had to open the seams to be able to wear it. I also had a pair of panties and full-slip in which I slept. It was ridiculous to think that these were my only clothes for five months of digging trenches, repairing shoes and cutting trees in the forest.

The third day our group was ordered to pack up, form our lines, get our ration of bread and lard, and walk to the train station. The train station! It was about three miles from the camp, and when we saw the train we couldn't believe that it was for us. Regular third class passenger cars with wooden benches we hadn't seen before! There were toilets between the cars and a mirror above the sink! When I saw my face, my one-inch uncombed hair, my yellow teeth, and my low-cut satin dress, I started to laugh hysterically.

The train rode on without stopping for two hours before slowing down in front of a small station – Dorbeck. In the far distance we could see small houses with red tiled roofs, and we knew it would be a long walk. We were told to wait for our dinner and for materials for tents, which we had to pitch if we wanted to sleep in them. When the straw arrived, we realized this tent would be our home for days or weeks, even months. We slept on one blanket, and used another to cover us. If one of us turned, the nine others had to turn too, like spoons in a neat kitchen drawer. We were so tired we almost always slept like logs.

At sunrise the next morning we started our new assignment. We picked up shovels, axes, and spades, and began marching five kilometers to the fields where we dug anti-tank ditches, and other obstacles. The Red Army tanks and the Russians were supposed to fall into the traps that we dug for twelve hours daily until sunset. There were different kinds of trenches in Dorbeck. We dug one kind one yard wide and two yards deep which spanned in length, zigzagging for kilometers without any break. Every morning we found the territory pre-marked by engineers we never saw. That September there wasn't too much rain, but October made up for it. The dirt from the ditch was always wet and heavy.

Between Rosh Hashana and Yom Kippur we got orders to pack up our belongings from our tents. We marched many miles to a place called Guttau in East Prussia.. Here we moved into big, new, prefabricated tents made from wood panels in a hexagon shape made for one hundred people. At the end of October the cold weather set in, and by 6 p.m. it was dark. The Russians were close by and we could hear the cannons during the night. We knew that the war was coming to an end, but did not know if we would live long enough to see it. We had no newspapers, radio, or contact with other human beings.

One day in the beginning of November, Mama felt weak, but she didn't dare stay in the camp. It was around midday when I heard the young Nazi who supervised our work yelling at my mother to work faster. When I heard his stick hitting Mama, I jumped out of my trench without thinking that I could be killed. I only thought that I had to protect her. I faced him within twenty seconds and confronted him full with my anger.

"Stop it!" I shouted. "Don't hit my mother. This woman works twelve hours a day with the terrible food you give us, in rain, in frost, in the same clothing that she wears every day for four months. And you hit her? Don't you have a mother?"

He stopped, flabbergasted, red, and speechless. Then he pulled himself together and answered, "Yes, I have a mother, but she is German, not a Jew." Then he turned around and left without a word. We all worked full of fear the whole afternoon. What had I done? But I didn't regret my interfering, even if I would be punished. The next day at noon the boy suddenly appeared and came straight to our ditch. He had a carrot in his hand and pointed it at me. "Eat this," he said. "It has vitamins in it." Then he gave me half of a cigarette and said, "Smoke it. You will be less hungry." He turned around and left and we never saw him again.

I couldn't believe my eyes. It seemed I had reached this boy somewhere in his soul that had not been brainwashed by Nazi ideology. I had found some human feeling that was buried under his distorted education. To the future generation, I say, "Don't give up on human beings especially when they are young. They can change evil into goodness. If you cannot do it alone, get a friend or friends to help you in your battle for a better society."

One Sunday, a big bag of leather packaging and pieces of sole and rubber arrived in the camp for the mending and repair of our shoes which were in such terrible condition that no one could go out to work. When I heard this, a quick thought rushed to my head. This work must be done inside. My father was a shoemaker and I would be able to do some things, mother even more, and perhaps with this work we could survive. I raised my hand and pulled on hers and my quick thinking probably saved our lives. The SS man asked some questions such as where did we learn this, and we said my father taught us. The materials they gave us were probably thrown away by some shoemaker in Poland. The pieces were too small to cover the holes, but we sewed them together and cut up usable pieces from other old shoes. In one of these shoes Mama found two gold coins that she saved. After the liberation she was able to exchange them for medicine I needed that saved my life.

Towards the end of 1944 we heard rumors of our leaving the camp to go to another place to continue the digging. There were now only two hundred women who could walk, out of the one thousand who left Stutthof in August. One of the tents was full of dead bodies that we could not bury because of the frozen ground. We and the other shoe repairers worked twelve hours a day to prepare for the needy in an eventual evacuation.

January 19th came with a roll call earlier than five o'clock. Mama was weak but very excited because she knew it was my birthday. When everybody was busy counting us, she pulled out a package wrapped in newspaper from under her two layers of blankets.

"Happy Birthday, my darling," she said. "I want you to know how happy you have made my life all these years, and how grateful I am to my God for your existence." Inside the newspaper was a "birthday cake." It was three portions of bread put together in layers with margarine in between. She had not eaten her portion of bread for three days in order to make this for me. It was the greatest present in my life. We did not eat the cake because there was no time. We were ordered to get ready and begin marching on the road that we had used to go to the trenches. We could hear the loud roar of the cannons behind us. Now we knew that the Russians were coming.

On the third day of the march we reached a farm where some of us were pushed into the house to cook the SS some food. We found a tiny pantry containing enough food for a small family who had either run away, or was still hiding somewhere in the house. Later, we woke up in the middle of the night and heard a big discussion in the kitchen. We heard one SS asking what should be done with this herd of sick people. After a while an answer came from another. "Let's burn them." Two others shouted, "You're crazy! The whole region will smell of burning flesh." Another suggestion came, "Let's shoot them."

Then we heard Old Papa's voice. (He was a Nazi, but we called him Old Papa in Hungarian, because he was kind to us when the other Nazis weren't around and made a big difference in our lives.) He said, "That's the worst idea, to waste ammunition on them. How will we protect ourselves when the Russians arrive? I would leave them here in the middle of nowhere, and we should leave this place as soon as possible."

There was dead silence after this. We tried to listen, but we fell asleep again, exhausted and hungry. When we woke up, the sun was shining and there was no trace of the SS. We were alive – without guards! We were free! It was January 21, 1945, somewhere in the middle of nowhere, and we were on an empty farm abandoned by the Germans as they ran away from the Russian soldiers.

The sun was shining and the skies were blue. We heard the noise of a motorbike, and very soon a soldier appeared. We all ran towards him. He stopped and looked very surprised, this unshaven, dirty, tired, young Russian soldier. He kept saying something like, "Others are coming, too. We will win this war soon, and everybody will be free of Nazis. But watch out – they are hiding everywhere." He didn't know who we were or why we were so sickly and skinny! We were the first Jewish group he had met, and we looked like skeletons. He left us the, and nobody else came the whole afternoon. The next day more soldiers came, but they couldn't help us either. They were hungry, too. One soldier showed us a map, pointing out the area where we were and where Transylvania was. It was Hungary when we were deported; now it was Romania. What was going on there right now on January 22, 1945, we did not yet know. It was still war. He showed us a road that would lead to a village. Mentally, we were ready for any walk towards home, but physically, it was impossible. There was no more food, no washing facilities, and everybody was getting sick. We needed medicine, doctors, and care

Three days later our group of fifteen made a decision to leave the place and explore new territory. We hoped that we would get home to our families, of course, but we couldn't believe that our grandparents could have survived these atrocities and forced labor. We put on all the clothing we had. We put straw in our shoes to keep our feet warm, and walked easily on the road – talking, laughing, and singing, with no SS around, free and hopeful that something good would happen to us.

It was a three-month struggle to reach our home, with many incredible experiences. In the town of Neumark we saw beautiful tree-lined streets in front of pretty brick houses with flowers in the windows. But there were piles of books burning in the streets. This was the disaster caused by the Germans who burned everything rather than leave anything behind for the Russians. I couldn't look away from the beautiful burning books: Heine, Goethe, Thomas Mann. I can still remember the golden titles on the books in the flames. What a crime. People looked at us with curious eyes. They didn't know who these sickly looking girls were with uniforms on, numbers on their clothes, running for their lives.

Our days and nights were very similar for many days in February. We walked during the day and slept in attics, stables, or empty farmhouses at night. If we were lucky, some villagers were kind and gave us some thick warm soup with dried beans and barley, cooked with a smoked bone that gave it a great taste. Nobody kept us more than two or three nights, however, and we didn't want to stay either. We were getting impatient. More Russian trucks were on the road. If they were headed south, they picked us up for a couple of miles and we were content.

In one town we heard about a train that was going to Lublin, and we could get on for free. There was a kind of Jewish community service which gave us papers, individually, that stated we had been prisoners in Nazi camps and wanted to get back home. I kept this paper until we reached Transylvania and then ripped it into one hundred pieces.

When we finally arrived back in Cehul-Silvaniei, we were the first women to come back to our town after surviving the Holocaust. The news of our arrival preceded us, and a lot of people, onlookers and neighbors, were gathered at the entrance to our house. They told us how sorry they were for us all this time. No one asked anything of us, our appearances reflected the suffering of our long journeys. But when we entered our empty house, our hearts almost stopped beating.

Everything had been taken except the heavy carved wood dining room set, our piano, and two beds. We sat on the bed motionless until our tears started to flow. Now we realized that what we missed were not our things, but our *home* and the warmth of our comfortable, simply decorated house.

Early the next morning, my friend Ildiko knocked at the door. We looked at each other and she cried and embraced me. She pointed to a dress that she had folded over her arm, and said, "I knew you would come home. Here is your sweet sixteen dress." It was navy velvet and had a lace collar. "I saved it from the truck that carried away all your stuff. I put it among my dresses so no one would know that it belonged to a Jewish girl." It was punishable to hide Jewish goods.

How tragic and comical it was to have my velvet dress and no other clothing to change into, but her action had a more profound message: it was the sign of true friendship regardless of the difference in our religions. This gave me the faith to believe that not everybody hated us. She took a risk to make me feel cared for, and she expected me to return to life as it was before the Nazis. She was smiling and crying with joy to have me back. She had all kinds of plans for me: she would lend me a tennis racket, books that she had read in the last year, notes from her junior year of high school, everything that she could to help me with my schooling and well-being. For me this was the first light I had seen at the end of our dark tunnel.

The next day there was another proof of friendship. Joseph, the son of my father's former employee, came with a big box in his arms which he lowered to the floor. He hugged me, embarrassed because he was an eighteen-year-old boy, and I was a maturing girl. When he opened the box, I saw my accordion! I jumped up and down with joy to see this dear friend who brought me my treasure. He had picked it up on the street when the soldiers emptied our house, hiding it in the ground for three months until the soldiers left our village. The box was in shambles, but the accordion was in great condition. Before we left Romania in 1962 I gave it to Joseph's son. This meant so much to us. Mama and I could believe in friendship again in spite of the hatred that the Nazis and Hungarian fascists inflicted on our village.

It was the end of April and the war was still going on. On the previous January 21st when the Russians liberated us, we realized that we were no longer prisoners, but also that there was no peace in Europe. Now, the Russians were still pushing the enemy out of their homeland and the Germans refused to realize the fact that they would not be conquering the world. On May 8, 1945, the Germans were officially defeated and World War II ended. The radio was blasting the news and the whole village was celebrating. I was already working as a clerk in the village hall, thanks to a former classmate. I earned very little money, but I received coupons for flour, soap, and petroleum for lamps. This was a great help.

The days, weeks, and months passed. No good news came of our family. Thirty-seven members were missing, including my father and brother. We could not, and did not talk about it freely until we were in the United States. It was too painful and no one would listen to or believe our words. But I knew deep in my heart that the time would come when I would speak up as I had promised my dying camp mates – that I would tell the world the truth and make it my mission as long as I lived, so that it will never happen again.

I am nostalgic when I think of how hard my family worked to create a comfortable future for us; how they hoped to make our lives less difficult than theirs. My father had saved the equivalent of five hundred dollars for each of us years before the Holocaust, during the Romanian regime when anti-Semitism hindered our education, but not yet our business. When Mama and I returned, we searched for the money. Mama knew it was buried in the garden somewhere in a pharmaceutical jar, but for weeks we could not find it. Then a neighbor helped us locate it, measuring the steps that my mother remembered. He found it and dug it out – a life saver.

In 1998, when my mother was 100 years old, she spoke these words in an interview on German television:

"I survived to prove that Hitler was all wrong. He could not annihilate our people. I have one child, my daughter who survived (she was pointing to me). She has only one son, and now I have two great-grandchildren. They will have many children, and my people will go on for another 5,000 years! Jews did not die in vain. They have left traces in history, medicine, science, music, art, as in all aspects of human life. We survived to prove to Hitler that we are here forever!"

© 2007 Clara Knopfler

RECALLING MY EXPERIENCES IN PANAMA AND GUAM DURING WORLD WAR II BY KENNETH B. LARSON

When I arrived in Washington, D.C. from my previous job in Goshen, Indiana, on a Sunday morning in early March of 1941, I found a beautiful, very busy city during the day and a quiet, "roll up the sidewalks" place at night. I had recently passed a Civil Service exam and was starting my new job in the U.S. Treasury Department next to the White House. I found lodging on 21st Street, just off Pennsylvania Avenue.

From that first day in Washington, I had no idea that the remainder of that year would evolve into what later seemed like two years squeezed into just a few months. It was also a time when the developing war was on everyone's mind. Uniformed military crowded the streets, and the new military draft drawing was pending. I made two trips to Michigan in the used Chevy coupe I bought, the second trip to show off Mary to my family. That was because Mary and I were courting regularly and I could see that we pretty much were in the same mind about each other with lengthy talks about our future. We enjoyed long bicycle rides around Haynes Point by the Potomac River, Sunday trips into the Blue Ridge Mountains with the Sunday School Class, and exploring new places in town. But the war was always there in our minds to dampen our enthusiasm.

Mary, born in New Haven, Connecticut, was raised there and in Brooklyn, New York. At the time we met, she lived in nearby   Maryland with a family she knew. Her father had died suddenly on a street in New York City when she was just 16, right in the middle of the great depression. As a result, and with no income to live on, she and her mother, her older brother and younger sister were forced to disperse and live with family or friends. Later on, Mary became a telephone operator in downtown Washington, D.C. where many of her calls were to the White House and the Pentagon. After the war started, armed guards stood watch at the entrance and on the roof of the telephone building – a vital facility.

Meanwhile, the war situation in Europe was getting very serious and the U.S. Congress had passed a law to draft men into the military. I registered for the draft and discovered that I would probably be called within a few months. What to do? Fortunately, I heard a rumor at work that the American-owned Panama Railroad was looking for someone to work in a National Defense job in the Canal Zone. I checked it out. If hired, Mary would follow me there as soon as I found an apartment. We were already engaged, and we would get married there where she could certainly work, probably as a telephone operator. I applied, was accepted, and on November 26, 1941, I sailed out of New York City harbor on the S.S. Talamanca - a nice combination passenger and cargo ship which, along with its sister ships, made regular weekly trips to Jamaica and Panama. Mary would follow whenever I was ready.

I arrived in Cristobal, Panama, and found a small but thriving bit of old colonial life. I was met at the dock by a young man in a white suit and we were driven away in an open, fringe-topped surrey mounted on a model A Ford chassis. Housing was in short supply so I was assigned to live in an old, tropical style frame building originally used to house workers when the canal was built. I had a nice, older roommate, an engineer of some sort from North Carolina. The place, a bit crude, was just up the street from where I worked and I liked it.

Panama at that time was a socially and physically divided country, there being no roads over the mountains to connect Panama City on the Pacific side and the smaller town of Colon on the Atlantic side. The only way to travel from one side to the other was by the U.S. owned Panama Railroad or by boat through the canal. And oddly enough, the Panamanians on the Atlantic side spoke mostly English while those on the Pacific side spoke Spanish. Furthermore, the canal does not run east and west as one would imagine. Because of Panama's lazy "S" shape, the canal actually runs southeast from the Atlantic side and emerges on the Pacific side further east of where it starts on the Atlantic side. This mind-confusing situation to a map-loving guy who always knows where North is was something I never adjusted to in Panama.

I lived on the Atlantic side in "Old" Cristobal in the very northeast corner of the ten-mile-wide Canal Zone where the French started and failed to build a canal and where the Americans who succeeded maintained its port and administrative duties on the Atlantic end after the canal opened. In addition, a cluster of foreign shipping offices, including German, Italian and others, were nestled in a tropical garden area nearby. Most of them were padlocked and closed because of the war. I worked in the Port Captains building next to the docks which jutted out from a stubby mile-wide peninsula into the huge bay off the ocean. Old Cristobal shared its narrow strip of land on the left side of the peninsula with the Panamanian town of Colon which occupied all the center part of the peninsula. The small remainder on the far side of Colon was leased from Panama by the U.S. for the "New Cristobal" village where most of the Atlantic side American employees and their families lived along with a fine garden hotel, a school, a church where I sang in the choir, and a hospital.

The Canal Zone was a very racially segregated place. The blacks and Panamanians were "Silver." Whites were "Gold." All the facilities, post office, toilets, drinking fountains, club houses, commissaries, etc. in the Canal Zone were completely segregated. Actually, all got along very well.

I enjoyed life in Panama, my free railroad passes helped me to explore the area quite extensively and my job in the Port Captains building was interesting. Otherwise, I could go on and recite the multitude of experiences I had down there, including having gone swimming in both the Atlantic and Pacific oceans in one day. Instead, I'll concentrate on how the war affected life down there. The first big event happened just a week after I arrived. While playing tennis on a quiet Sunday morning I learned that the Japanese had bombed Pearl Harbor. Was the Panama Canal next? Where were the Japanese subs?

For those of us in the Canal Zone that evening, the war started when they cut all electrical power and we not only were in the dark but were cut off from news. Battery radios were usually not strong enough to hear outside of Panama - and Panama had no news. Fortunately, I had brought with me from the U.S. a new battery powered Motorola and I found that evening that I could get a Miami station on it. So I hurried down to our clubhouse (meals, movie, barbers, etc.) and soon had a crowd as we huddled in the dark around that little red box to get the latest news. Meanwhile, a 3-iron shot away, Colon stayed as bright and gaudy as ever. Damn it all, they weren't at war, so they didn't need any blackouts. By the next day, we were at war, the Canal Zone went on a war footing and all the plans Mary and I had made were cancelled, even though I already had an apartment lined up so she could come down and join me.

So people settled down and were assigned to civilian home defense jobs while the military stiffened itself for expected attacks from Japanese submarines off the coast. Eventually, as the situation cleared up, we got our power back and things sort of returned to normal. The exception was the almost complete stoppage of all but an occasional vessel from Argentina or other non-combatant country at our docks. Soon the Navy ships took up a lot of the slack and their frequent stops allowed time for their crews to go on liberty and enjoy the R & R benefits available in the bustling tourist traps in Colon.

Those Navy crews taking liberty in Colon had to pass through a "Prof" station located at the border. There they received advice and warnings about the town, and they had to prove they had condoms – or were given some if they didn't. That they needed them was proved to me a few times when I took a shorter route to New Cristobal and the church there for early evening choir practice. That route took me up the street past all the prostitutes, they on their side, and I on the other side forbidden to them. One time when the Navy was in town, to my surprise as I walked up the street past the prostitute area I saw a lineup of sailors waiting their turn to go in the far end of one of the long brothels, and others coming out the other end, finished with their latest R & R activity. Then later on, after dark, I returned home from the choir practice by way of Front Street and passed the "Prof" station where the sailors had to go through a sterilizing procedure if they admitted to visiting the ladies of the town. Some of the sailors, usually young kids, would be so drunk they had to be carried along by their more sober buddies. Even so, they helped win that war. Today, I would compare them to college students and their infamous binge parties.

As that year of 1941 wore on, and with the war cranking up, it became clear to me that Mary and I weren't destined to live in Panama. So I arranged to terminate my job at the end of my year, assuring the government that a female could do my work just as well. I contacted the D.C. draft board and received their assurances that I could come home, get married and have a month or two off before I would enlist in the Navy. That done, I flew to Miami on December 7th and took the train up to D.C. two days later. Mary was waiting, marriage certificate in hand, wedding ring, my new suit and all the arrangements made at church for our wedding on the 11th. I should interrupt this personal side of my story and report on what I visualized as the mood and efforts toward the war in the U.S.A. at that time.

The war became the primary event in the lives of most citizens whether they were directly involved or merely bystanders due to age or other self-preservation needs. Scrap iron drives, war bond campaigns by movie stars and others, ration cards for sugar, gasoline and other scarce items due to the war, became part of everyday life. Auto companies and most other manufacturers had converted to producing for the war effort, and the newsreels at the movies were often the reason for going. It was a scary and worrisome time for families with men in the service. Women were starting to be accepted in certain military jobs while they took over a lot of the work in the nations' farms and factories. The goal was to win the war; not much else mattered. An exception, perhaps, would be the national disgust as certain labor unions threatened or actually went on strike for benefits they could see as available because of the shortage of trained workers. And, of course, there was the usual clamor by a few who preferred peace at any cost and the few who illegally dodged the draft one way or another.

The war also produced the terrible tools of war that decimated whole cities in Europe and Asia at a horrible cost of lives by both military and civilian populations. But that was the cost forced on us by those who introduced such terrible tactics, and in the end it proved to be the only way we could win both wars, in Europe and Asia. Reflecting back on the need for such dedication to war it is evident that our lack of such dedication by our country in the Korean, Vietnamese and more recent conflicts proves that action based on limited monetary budgets, lack of national involvement and false beliefs as to the value of negotiations will not win our wars efficiently and at less cost. That was proven with rules for General MacArthur in Korea where he defied the politicians when he decided he needed to attack to win, only to be fired by President Truman for disobeying orders, which MacArthur certainly did do - and we still haven't won that war.

But back to my and Mary's story. Just the week before my return from Panama, she found an apartment (supposedly impossible) by sitting on the steps of the newspaper office on a Saturday night waiting for the first Sunday edition to come out. When it did she found a favorable ad, called, got the owner out of bed, hurried into Maryland and took the place. A week later we were married and the next 20 days were to test our resolve, again.

On Monday following our wedding, we went to my draft board, as promised, and checked in. All was in order except for one thing. Unknown to us, while I was flying to Miami, President Roosevelt had cancelled all enlistments. The army was having trouble getting men because everyone was enlisting in service branches they believed to be more favorable. So, I had two options, I could be drafted into the Army or I could go with a Navy officer from the downtown enlistment center and, based on our correspondence, I would be allowed to enlist that day in the Navy. An hour later I went through the physical line in the Navy Recruiting office, took a test, signed enlistment papers and was immediately made a 3rd class petty officer. Then the "good" news, I was ordered to report back at 7 the next morning ready to join a draft of recruits being sent to California. Stunned, we went home. I was physically sick, but Mary was the rock she always has been and the next morning we were there. Another physical was required – my ears were blocked – and we were sent up the street to an ear doctor to have them cleaned out. He did, removing big plugs of ear wax the size of a pencil eraser. Returning, we ran into an apology, "Sorry, your draft has already left! You'll have to go home and wait for further orders!" We floated home, ten days before Christmas. A few days later I received orders to report and be bussed up to Bainbridge, Maryland, a new Naval training center. That was not too far from Washington. We were elated.

At Bainbridge on December 21, 1941, another physical showed that I had a hernia. A couple of days after Christmas I found myself in the big Naval hospital in Philadelphia where they operated on me. It was the 31st. That year was over.

Several weeks later after recuperation I was sent back to Bainbridge, went through boot camp and was ordered to "Ships Company" to become one of 12 enlisted men assigned to the startup of the 5,000 man training schools program which was the reason for the new base. I quickly set up an office to handle recruit leave and liberty. Mary soon joined me, pregnant by then. We lived on the base and she got a job cashiering in the officers mess hall. Our son was born in January, 1944, and the following year I was finally released for other duty as the training came to an end. The Navy was fully manned and winning. Promised an assignment of my choice, I was shipped to Camp Shoemaker, east of Oakland, in a freight car converted to a troop carrier. Then I went on to Hawaii by ship. There I heard that I would be getting my choice, sea duty, and would be assigned to the cruiser flagship of the Commander of the Ryukyus Islands, the southern sea area between Japan and China. Sure I was! My orders came and I was assigned to Admiral Nimitz' headquarters in Pearl Harbor – way down underground in the communications department. I hated it. A sign appeared on a post there asking for volunteers to go to the Admirals' advance headquarters on newly captured Guam. I signed up, was flown there on a big Navy transport plane and assigned to Nimitz' radio shack just outside of his office. By then I was a Yeoman, first class, one of eight Yeomen mostly of lesser grade assigned to a Quonset full of radiomen. Why? Because, the officer in charge explained, we would be working with top secret messages in plain English, and it had been determined that Yeomen were next to officers in intelligence! With that we found we were privileged because our office was out of bounds for all except the duty officer who came to pick up and deliver to the Admiral the messages we had processed. Our office was in a small corner of the big Quonset where the eight of us rotated two at a time around the clock, 24-7. Our duty was to process radio teletype messages through the Admirals' top secret code to English encoding machine. I made Chief Petty Officer while there. Meantime the war was heating up until the morning when the Admiral posted a picture of an exploding atomic bomb over Hiroshima. The war was soon over and I was on my way home, a 3-week trip by ship to San Francisco and another week by train to Chicago where I was discharged.

But all the above about my personal Navy experience says little about the situation on Guam during that last year of the war against the Japanese.

When I arrived on the high hill over the demolished town of Agana on the coast of Guam, Nimitz' new base was raw and ready. Bulldozed out of the remains of the fortified Japanese positions where the Japs had tried to stop the U.S. invasion, the Seabees had constructed several long two-story wooden buildings in a rough rectangle for the headquarters facilities. Nearby, they built a circle of cottages for the officers. Below the headquarters area on the ocean side of the hill they laid out rows of Quonset huts, both the smaller barracks size and the larger for warehouse and enlisted men's mess hall. A coral road wound down the hill to Agana. The coastal road went east toward the big, new airbase and west a short way to the flat, marshy area where a couple of docks has been constructed for ships. In the shallow waters beyond the shore line were the sunken remains of tanks and landing craft that the Japs had hit from their high positions above during the U.S. invasion. It was like a miniature of the Normandy invasion area in France.

My first few days there, when I had time, were a bit gruesome. I prowled through the brush and rubble at the top of the ocean-facing bluffs where I could see the remains of skeletal bodies, long belts of unused machine gun ammunition and other such material, including green Japanese mortar shell cans containing beautifully color-coded shells - all neat, clean and ready for use. Some of the bodies, I suspect, were Americans because of the helmets lying next to them. The body retrievers were busy, but not all areas had been cleared. I also prowled back of the hill we were on, a jungle-like area with evidence of Japanese camps – a few of them still used by some of the Japanese soldiers who refused to surrender and lived back in those hills for years after.

But the big picture of Guam in that last year of the war was its growth from the big bomber airfield already in use when I arrived, to the new headquarters on the hill and the huge stockpile of supplies that built up on those reclaimed marshes and around the big docking areas the Navy had installed on the flat west side of the Island. Those supplies were intended for the expected invasion of Japan. To come around the bend of the hill after I had been there a few months was breathtaking. Where there had been nothing, there were endless rows of crates, piles of Quonset hut framework, all kinds of trucks and rows of Quonset huts filled with more perishable supplies and working personnel. Then there were the floating dry docks and piers accepting cargo from huge transports, and big trucks and lift trucks whirring here and there in a frenzy.

I also observed another, sad, event on Guam. I went, like some others, to the little beach by the palm groves beyond Agana, along the coral road through the area where the Marine camps would come and go. But one time I found a much larger camp spread through the palms, with busy, busy Marines getting ready for something. A few days later I returned to the area and found that all the Marines were gone. Days later came the answer - we had invaded Iwo Jima. Later we learned that this particular battalion of Marines had suffered huge casualties in that invasion. Such fine young men – and boys. It was part of the cost we paid to win that war.

Other memories of those days soon after I arrived on Guam were from my duty hours. On occasion, Admiral Nimitz would go to the barren area not far from my view out the window to practice his pistol skills. And just beyond, from our unlimited view from our office window of the north part of the island and the ocean around, we could see, during early morning shifts, the squadrons of B-24s struggling to gain altitude before heading south to bomb the Japanese-held islands between Guam and Australia. Later, the big B-29s took off at dawn to bomb Japan; and if I was on the evening shift I could see them return. Their next day "intents" were revealed by some of the messages we handled, and we could identify their takeoffs with our own eyes.

Meanwhile, on a personal basis, it was nice living on Guam. The weather was easy – except for the couple of typhoons that came through. And we had good GI mail service (censored), a base newsletter, a big baseball field and an amphitheater on the side of a hill. They even started to dig a swimming pool, but the press heard of it and the hole, next to our beer hall Quonset, became the place to throw empty beer cans.

Then the war was over, and when I look back on it now I appreciate how lucky I was with the assignments I had been given in spite of my desires. I was one who came back, unharmed, more educated and able to pick up again with Mary and our son. Life in this country hurried back to normal, ex-GI's crowded the universities with their G.I. Bill of Rights awards, and the country settled down, unready for the next war – Korea. The Chinese and North Koreans assumed it would be a pushover to take all of Korea and put it under the Chinese/Korean Communist style of government. We put up a fight for a while, but will that war ever end? Not if we aren't willing to take it on and finish it like we did with WWII.

I ENJOYED THE NAVY BY GENE LORE

At the age of 22, I went to work for Lockheed. Also about that time, President Roosevelt started the Civilian Pilot Training program by which a person could obtain his private pilot's license, so I took advantage of that opportunity. I was trained in a 50 horsepower, 2-passenger side-by-side airplane, called a Luscomb. I flew around the local area of San Fernando Valley.

At the time of the attack on Pearl Harbor, I was in charge of a production tool crib in the metal department (providing templates, router blocks, drill-jigs, etc.). We supplied all the tools for forming parts for the P-38 aircraft and the Hudson bomber. This gave me a deferment from the draft, but it was my intention to serve in the Army Air Corps. Some of my friends at Lockheed wanted to join the Naval Aviation Cadet Program and I decided to go with them to Los Angeles. As it turned out, I was accepted and they were not. One was color blind and the other, I think, was not tall enough. Then I was sent by railroad, a five-day trip, to the University of Georgia in Athens for pre-flight training. Half of the course was physical and the other half was class work.

The first question they asked when we got together was if there were any non-swimmers. There were several, including me, so I spent my physical training time in the pool learning to swim four different strokes (overhand, sidestroke, breaststroke and backstroke) and also how to stay afloat for ten minutes.

After that, I was sent to Huchinson, Kansas, for primary flight training. I flew a biplane called the N2S, made by Stearman. Its simple steel tube fuselage and wood and fabric wings made it a durable trainer capable of taking lots of abuse.

It had a single engine, two wings, and two open cockpits. The instructor sat in the front and the trainee sat in the back. We were out in the open so we wore leather jackets and leather pants lined with wool, and a helmet and headset. First we learned different types of landings (normal, full stall and low approach). Next, we learned acrobatics--loops, slow rolls, snap rolls, split "S" loops and Emelmans (which meant rolling out at the top of a loop). This was invented by a World War I flying ace. I was the first one in my class to pass acrobatics, but then I got the flu and spent the following week in the hospital. When I recovered, I finished the final stage of formation flying and left with the first class.

After completing primary flight training, I started basic training in a Vultee aircraft, a SNV Valiant, a basic trainer aircraft. Jokingly, it was nicknamed the Vultee Vibrator because it was not sturdy enough for acrobatics.

This was a bigger, heavier airplane, single wing, and we were not exposed to outside weather due to its sliding canopy. This airplane was just used for landings and takeoffs as a transition into the SNJ trainer. After passing basic training, I then had a choice of becoming a multi-engine or single-engine pilot. I chose the multi-engine and went to Pensacola, Florida, where I flew the PBY patrol bomber, which was strictly a sea plane made by Consolidated Aircraft. The Navy used them for patrolling.

First, I was assigned to Patrol Squadron VPB-116 as a co-pilot. The crew was comprised of three officers-- patrol plane commander, co-pilot and navigator and nine enlisted men. A full crew would include nine enlisted men, a plane captain, asst. plane captain, ordinance man, radio man and those who manned the different turrets--nose gunner, top gunner, tail gunner, and ball turret. The Navy was interested in long range patrols. The main gasoline tanks held 2,450 gallons. We flew with 900 additional gallons. The plane had four bomb bays; the front two held 450 gallons of fuel, the back two debt charges. The design weight was 56,000 pounds, but we were flying at about 60,000 pounds, creating a very critical condition during take-off. We had to monitor the amount of gas constantly to be sure we had enough for our missions. We flew our patrols at 5,000 feet, which could take an hour to obtain.

We operated in the Central Pacific, first out of Eniwetok in the Marshall Islands and then out of Tinian in the Southern Marianas. From there we ran 2,000 nautical-mile patrols in enemy territory–1,000 nautical miles out and 1,000 back every three days. We patrolled the first day, rested on the second day, and prepared for the next patrol on the third day. We had 18 crews and 12 aircraft. We lost two crews during that time--one to enemy action and one to a lost engine on takeoff. After a 30-day leave, I was returned to Kansas, where I trained to be a patrol plane commander, I was reassigned to a new squadron and expected to return overseas in a much-improved version of the B-24, a PB4Y-2. As it happened, I did not return there because the war ended after the Japanese surrendered. I was released to inactive duty, having spent three years on active duty.

After the war, I returned to Lockheed for a short time and then went to work for Los Angeles Department of Water and Power, known as DWP. I worked for the power section in the Owens Gorge, where DWP was building three hydroelectric power plants along the Owens River. After several months on this job, the Navy needed Navy Aviators to train cadets; so I volunteered to return to active duty as an instructor. DWP gave me a leave of absence to go on my second tour.

After a few months of training aviation cadets, I was grounded because I could not pass the vision test; but I stayed on duty as a ground officer, assigned to Naval Air Station (NAS) in Memphis, Tennessee. My next duty was at NAS Kodiak, Alaska, as the aircraft maintenance officer. After spending two years there and then being returned to the States, I was re-assigned to a P2V Patrol Squadron as the aircraft maintenance officer and deployed back to Kodiak for six months. Since the Navy was shrinking in size, I was returned to inactive duty.

After retirement, I signed up for the Weekend Warrior Program, consisting of duty one weekend each month and two weeks in the summer. For every five years of this program, I earned one more year of credit that I needed for retirement. I retired with twenty years of service as a Lieutenant Commander in the U.S. Navy Reserve. I had made 49 combat patrols in enemy territory and was awarded seven air medals and two Distinguished Flying Crosses. (One air medal was awarded for every seven combat patrols and one DFC was awarded for every twenty flights.) I received these medals by mail afterwards. I think that the reason for this was that the decision was made after I was released to inactive duty.

I still have my Navy cap with the inscription Blue Raiders VPB 116.

I enjoyed my time in the Navy and met a lot of interesting people.

After my naval career ended in 1964, I returned to the Department of Water and Power as a land surveyor and worked on the second Los Angeles aqueduct for most of my career. I retired in 1979. During this time, we lived in Thousand Oaks. My children in order of age are Steven Eugene, Clark Elliot and Holly Sarah. The boys graduated from Thousand Oaks High School, while Holly went to Westlake High. Clark was an outstanding tennis player. Steven, a welder, was artistic and created many iron sculptures. Sadly, both of my sons passed away when they were 42-years-old. Now only Holly and I remain. I enjoyed both my careers. I continue to play pool regularly and I moved to UVTO on August 28, 2007.

RECOLLECTIONS DURING WORLD WAR II BY MEL LOWRY

I was born in the mining town of Butte, Montana - home of the Copper King. We were a mile high and had mines a mile deep. Butte's primary higher education was at Montana School of Mines, but I went to Butte High School. We lived in a one-room apartment and I used to earn money by selling newspapers. The only excitement I remember was all the Newspaper Extras covering the attack on Pearl Harbor and the aftermath. I would go from bar to bar at 5 AM and sell for five cents each all the papers I could carry. Finally, to avoid working in the mines and to remove myself from Butte caused me one day to say to my mother. "I am leaving. Do you want to go with me?" We went by train to Oakland, California, where we had some relatives. Neither I nor my mother ever regretted that decision.

Soon after moving to Oakland, I got my first real job in the mailroom at the Moore Dry Dock Company. This job was ideal for a young man to have. I was the only male in the mailroom. Most of the young women (girls) were busy making mimeograph copies of all the endless paper necessary to run a ship yard. My job was mostly to deliver mail in and around the whole shipyard. I had a motor scooter, so I could ride all around the shipyard, from wood shop to metal shop, unsupervised. I learned how a ship was made and was witness to many launchings from a Dry Dock.

One interesting thing I remember happened as I was making a delivery of paper to a small carrier in for repair. As I climbed on board there were some welders right in front of me. All of a sudden, one of them lifted up the safety helmet and lots of long hair fell out! I was looking at, and almost touching, Rosie the welder – or, as one of the more popular songs of the day said - *Rosie the Riveter*.

© 2012 Mel Lowry

MICHAEL MARK – SURVIVOR OF THE NAZI HOLOCAUST

My family lived in Velke Kapusany, a village in Czechoslovakia. It was mostly a farming community, but my father owned a clothing and tailoring shop. The men of our extended family worked there and we all lived in one large house, adding rooms as needed. At one time there were at least 15 of us living under the same roof. There was no indoor plumbing or running water, but we had a well. It was primitive, but we were happy. My father was well-liked by our Christian neighbors, so during the Hungarian occupation his business was not taken away – although more than 90% of the other Jewish businesses were. Czechoslovakia was a democracy before World War II. The Germans occupied part of it in 1938, and then the Hungarians moved in and became German allies. In March of 1944, the Nazis occupied all of Hungary. Immediately, the 800,000 Jews were required to wear yellow stars.

Shortly after, we were told to get our belongings into a bundle that we could carry and be ready to leave our homes. We were taken by train to a nearby city and then forced to march into an empty field which was a brickyard. There must have been 30,000 to 50,000 Jews there. We slept on the dirt and waited, thinking we would be taken to work on farms in Germany. We waited for two to three weeks. It was terrible. Then we were told to get ready and they marched us back to the railroad station. Babies were hungry and crying. Old people tried to help, but they could hardly walk, they were so weak from lack of food and water. At the station, as far as we could see, there were cattle cars. They packed us in and we tried to stay with our families.

The journey took three days and nights, but we had no idea where we were going. We saw signs in Hungarian, and then in Polish. When the doors finally opened, it was dark outside, but there were lights. The Germans were yelling at us to hurry up, chasing and hitting us. They told us to leave everything. We still didn't know that we were at Auschwitz. I tried to stick together with my older brother, Ernest, and my father. They marched us into a giant building and told us to take off our clothes. Our heads were shaved and we were given a so-called shower, and by the time we came out we had only shoes and eyeglasses - no clothes. Then they gave us striped "pajamas" and little round caps and took us to the barracks. The other prisoners told us that anyone not selected to be a slave would be gassed and burned. Jews were packed into the gas chambers like sardines. When they opened the doors, the dead were still standing up. It was very frightening. The only way I slept at night was from pure exhaustion. We were not tattooed with a number at Auschwitz because, as it turned out, we were not there long enough. My brother, father and I were taken to Erlenbusch in Germany. There, we learned to put paper scraps from cement bags between our bodies and our pajamas to keep warm.

Lying in the barracks at night, I would dream of being a bird so I could fly away and be free. The Nazis, however, had a different view. Their motto was: "Arbeit Macht Frei" – which means "Work makes one free." However, everything was about survival. They only gave us soup and a slice of stale bread so we would have enough strength to keep working. It was summer, and beautiful outside, but I was a prisoner. Several times a day, they chased us out of the barracks so they could report how many of us were alive or dead. The ones who couldn't get up were dragged into a corner on the straw, given nothing to eat. In a day or two, they gave up, and were gone. The chances of survival were zero, but we lived, month after month.

One day, we heard heavy artillery fire not far away. It was near the end of January, 1945. German soldiers were evacuating us from the makeshift concentration camp, Erlenbusch. Surrounded by barbed wire, the camp was made up of small tents with straw on the dirt floors. I was nineteen years old. Along with the other prisoners, my father and my older brother Ernest and I were herded to the Buchenwald Concentration Camp where we remained for about a month. I thought if the Allies could win the war, that's the only way we would be free.

On the move again, we were marched down city streets. We could see German civilians, packed and on the move. They knew the war was coming closer. We just hoped each day that we would be free, but we were led to the next miserable place, the Flossenburg Concentration Camp, high up in the mountains. The cold of winter was even worse than starving. People held each other to keep warm, but everywhere they were dying. When you hold another prisoner and he's cold, you know he's gone. We stayed in places where there were so many dead the Nazis didn't know what to do with them. The prisoners piled up the bodies in latrines. It was almost impossible to stay alive. They didn't let us sleep more than four hours at a time. They worked us very hard and gave us very little food. My father became so weak that he finally died. Suddenly he just collapsed, like the rest of them.

Ernest and I stayed together, but there was no food or water. We were picking grass to eat and chewing on snow. Then we were locked up in a barn, and I had no strength. I told my brother, "I can't walk tomorrow." But the next day the Germans chased us out of the barn into the forest. I saw two soldiers standing off to the side, talking. Then I watched them take off their uniforms and put on civilian clothes. They deserted. Later on, we saw American soldiers approaching in tanks. They saw what we looked like – lice eating us alive, skin and bones – but we were free! Only a handful of us were left – different nationalities, Hungarian, Russian, walking slowly towards a farm. We begged for food, but we could hardly digest anything except potatoes, bread and soup. If people were given the wrong food, they got sick and died.

When I returned to my family home after the war, there was nothing. All our furniture and possessions had been stolen. Ernest and I were the only immediate family members left out of many. For a while, I thought my mother, Blanka, was alive. She had been taken to Auschwitz with us, but we became separated during the "selection" process. After the war, a Christian neighbor received a letter from her saying that she had been liberated, but became ill and was taken to Sweden by the British where she was hospitalized. Her letter was gracefully written in Hungarian. To make sure it would be delivered, she used two addresses on the envelope, one for Hungary and one for Czechoslovakia. I wrote to her and waited weeks for an answer. Her brother, my uncle, arrived in the town and contacted the Swedish Consulate in Prague. We finally found out that she had died on September 11, 1945. She was 41 years old, surviving about five months after the end of the war. Later we learned that she had been liberated from the Bergen-Bergen Concentration Camp in Germany. At least she has a gravesite that we can visit – unlike my father and six million others. Her headstone is the only connection I have to that part of my family. I finally gave her letter to the United States Holocaust Memorial Museum in Washington, D.C. so others can read it.

I was determined to move far away after the war, where nobody knew me. I wanted to change my religion so that the next generation would not have to go through what I endured. My choice was to live in America or Australia. Finally, in 1949, I was cleared to come to the United States. I spoke no English, but I had skills. I arrived in New York with nothing. A cousin put me on a train to Los Angeles to stay with some other relatives. Everything was fine. I learned English and earned $1 an hour as a tailor. Later on I had to register for the draft as the country became involved in the Korean War. Eventually, I was shipped to Germany where I served two years as an interpreter, since I spoke Czech, Hungarian, German and English. I wasn't an American citizen yet, but I had a good feeling about serving this country. I changed my surname to Mark after returning home, and I went into business with my brother, Ernest.

It used to be hard for me to talk about my experiences during the Holocaust. I could not speak about it for 40 years. Then a psychiatrist friend convinced me that it would make me feel better. Finally, I agreed. It took a lot of courage to put myself back into that time. Now I tell my story to university students and they are profoundly touched. People listen to me and it makes them wonder how they would have reacted to the kind of adversity I faced. Would they have had the same kind of fortitude, or would they have caved in? Would they be bitter, or would they make something positive out of their circumstances? We cannot control what happens in our lives, but we can choose how we respond.

I have a wonderful family. My wife and I have been married for 57 happy years. She was born in New York. We have two children, a daughter and a son. We have four lovely grandchildren. God bless America!

COMMISSIONED AS A GENTLEMAN BY TOM MAXWELL

It is September, 1943. This is the life! I am already trained in mechanics and instruments. I learned the Morse Code and the identification of aircraft with only one-hundredth of a second to decide.   Here in San Marcos I am to learn navigation, astronomy and meteorology.   Now with officer training over and the basics behind me, I am really going to learn something with a purpose. Our barracks are in good shape; they have furnaces and the beds are not crowded together like they were when I was an enlisted man. A bank of phones is lined along the road into camp, just a stone's throw from my home, a two-story barracks.

We fly in AT-7s two or three times a week with two crews to each plane. The flights are long enough that we usually spend the night at some distant destination and then repeat our assignment the next day on the return to home base. My job here is to track the plane's course by dead reckoning and also by starlight (celestial navigation), Long Range Radio Navigation (LORAN), and by orienting our location on the map when there is a view of the ground, or by radio directional signals. One of my instructors had used radio reckoning on a mission over Asia. On his return flight, he homed in on the signal supposedly coming from his home base. Unfortunately, he was 180° off course. Either he was reading the compass backwards or the Chinese had rigged a signal the same length as his home base but in the other direction. In any case, he flew into the heart of China and ran out of gas. The plane went down. He parachuted safely but was captured and imprisoned. Eventually he escaped and was able to return to the U.S. where he became an instructor. He developed a fixation on using dead reckoning on all flights and repeatedly gave us warnings about the dangers of using radio fixes.

Looking back, I realize that I still had no commission and was occasionally asked to do some menial duty. I remember cleaning showers in the quarters of the dental officers two different times. I don't remember if the assignment was punishment for some other infraction with our group or whether it was meant to keep me busy.

One day, I was not feeling well but was assigned to make a night flight. I felt really sick, but it was too late for sick call. I was afraid that I would become so ill that I would need to be hospitalized at some far distant landing field, so I went to the day clerk and appealed for mercy. I was required to report to the hospital for a diagnosis. Later on, when the medical officer examined me he listened to my list of symptoms and decided I had appendicitis. They operated on me and during the third day of recovery I was sent down the hall for calisthenics and placed on KP duty. During the second week of my hospital stay, I was in line for R & R, possibly in Hawaii. I asked if I could simply go home to recuperate. It had been two years since I had seen my family. "If you can get a pass from your outfit, there is no medical reason why you could not do so," was the reply. The only danger would be if I had to make a parachute jump which might open up the wound or pull out the stiches. So, the sick leave was allowed. I hitched a ride with two pilots flying to Des Moines - taking a parachute with me all the way home and back. From Iowa, I took a train to Chicago and then to Canton, Ohio, and a bus to Akron.

Because of my two weeks in the hospital and two weeks in recuperation at home, I fell too far behind my class to graduate with my pals. I waited another three weeks for the next class, and spent another month to complete the program. Finally, I received that single gold bar designating my commission as a Second Lieutenant. It was a rating without much prestige and I found myself often referred to as a "shavetail." However, my wings were pinned on my jacket in a crowded auditorium amidst wild cheering and much collective shouting.

A few days later, I received my orders to move on and was given five days to report for duty at Lowry Field in Denver. Only fourteen of the class fit into the category of having a background in mechanics. We were needed as flight engineers. After some training, I was sent to yet another school and left early in the morning, April 15, 1945, for Roswell Air Base in New Mexico. The very next day I took my first flight in the biggest plane the Air Force used at the time - the four-engine B-29. My schedule called for a seven-hour flight every other day with take-off time alternating between 0300 and 1530. I was told it would be ten days before I would be assigned to my permanent crew. My pilot and co-pilot have had only four flights on the B-29, and I was supposed to catch up with their training without flying extra hours. When we met, they threatened me by saying that I had better know the ship because they sure didn't! We were all beginners but we learned quickly during the following weeks. I realized that if I failed, not only might we lose the plane, but I might not fly again, nor ever get home again.

My assignment on the B-29 was to sit behind the co-pilot facing sideways towards a large instrument panel with a bank of voltage regulators and a set of throttles to use regulating engine speed. One emergency maneuver was for the flight engineer to be ready to blow out any fires on the four engines by pushing the appropriate throttle forward. Another emergency action had to do with the voltage regulators. If one of them malfunctioned or got too hot, I had less than one minute to remove it from its mount to prevent a fire inside the plane. The first emergency did occur on our final flight, the night we soloed as a crew. We had two engine fires, lost all four engines for a while and then restarted one. The pilot feathered the engine on the first fire; I blew out the second fire by accelerating the throttle. That was the only engine left when we landed.

Another responsibility for the flight engineer was preflight inspection on the ground. I would make certain the wheel chocks were removed, check the gas and oil caps, the sock on the *pitot* tube (which measured wind speed), and the locks on the flaps that keep them in place. I would look for cracks in the fuselage, check the inflation of the tires, and test the rudder for mobility. In the air, I kept track of fuel consumption and the weight distribution within the plane. If we used all the fuel from the tanks on one side and none on the other, it would disturb the balance and make it difficult for the pilot to keep the plane right side up.

Since our planes had already served their time in combat, many of them were splattered with bullet holes. We could not pressurize the cabin, the plane was unheated, and it was very cold when we flew above 10,000 feet. Frequently, our second-hand training planes would malfunction and our flight would be cut short. Several times, the planes had serious difficulties and the survivors had to be rescued by ground crews. Although Roswell Air Base was my home, really my home was in the air inside one of those B-29 planes. Since very other flight lasted all night, I would be in the air three days out of five. On the other days I worked on repairs. I went to church in Roswell every Sunday when I was not in the air. Some church family would invite me to dinner, and that was a delight. I wrote home often, mostly in preparation for reentering college to continue my studies towards becoming an archeologist. I withdrew two math books and another Chinese book from the base library and learned how to count to ten in Mandarin. We knew that when our training was finished, we were slated to go to India to fly supplies over the hump. If our plane went down, we would land in China. I thought it might be useful to know some words in the language of southern China.

Our B-29 solo flight took place at night on the twelfth of August. That evening we had two fires and lost three engines, landing with only one still running. We were not sure whether our plane had been rigged to test our survival skills, or whether it was just worn out. Nevertheless, we handled all the emergencies and landed safely. During that last flight, we kept tuned to the short wave radio instead of the intercom. We knew that two atomic bombs, carried by planes just like ours, had already been dropped on Hiroshima and Nagasaki. Essentially, the war was coming to an end. Japan would soon surrender. Perhaps this would be our last training flight. We went to bed about three o'clock the following morning still uninformed. When we woke up, the announcement had already come. The war was over!

I was so delighted, I went straight to the day room, obtained a three-day pass and left for town. I stopped at a clothing store and bought a red and black striped shirt to add some color to my drab khakis. Meanwhile, everyone was restricted to the base as a ploy to avoid any riotous behavior in town. Two days later, I made my way back to the base and was accused of being AWOL. Actually, I had a verifiable permit for my leave of absence.

Within a few weeks, I prepared to leave Roswell and move back home. I had a real itch to go to India, and even inquired about re-enlisting but discovered it would be for a minimum of three years. I would have gone for six months, maybe, or even a year, but not for three. I left the Army for good on October 7, 1945.

© 2012 Tom Maxwell

THE WAR YEARS BY CHARLES MORTENSEN

Tears were in my mother's eyes that May day in 1943 as she stood on the back porch watching me get in the car for my father to drive me to San Fernando where I joined the other enlistees for our trip to Ft. MacArthur in San Pedro, California. By the end of the first week, uniforms had been issued, shots jabbed in the arm, and the first introduction to army discipline inflicted. I quickly learned that the end of your uniform belt always went through the buckle to the left, and that the field jacket always was worn buttoned – no casual wear in the army.

Those of us not on weekend KP received passes, so in less than one week in the service, I was on my way home to Van Nuys. That "Big Red Car" transported me from San Pedro to downtown Los Angeles where I transferred to the San Fernando Valley "Red Car" line that crossed the valley and ran down Sherman Way to my corner at Sepulveda Boulevard. By mid-afternoon I was home. As the weekend closed, I was grateful my Dad had sufficient gas coupons for my folks and special girl to drive me back to Ft. MacArthur.

Before too many days, I joined with others for the train ride to Camp Roberts, California, and what turned out to be twelve weeks of basic infantry training culminating in a two-week bivouac in the wilds of the countryside north of Paso Robles. Most of us in our training unit were eighteen and nineteen years of age, some with high school and/or

college ROTC experience, and some were part of the Enlisted Reserve Program who were sent on later to Fort Benning, Georgia for officer's training. Some were a bit older, a very few were married, but whether draftee or enlistee, we were together – for training, KP, close order drill, calisthenics, Saturday morning barracks inspection, tactics, night patrols, the rifle range (yes, even though left-handed, I had to shoot right-handed), and all the other elements of basic training.

Weekend passes provided needed breaks from the rigors of training, and since many of us were from Southern California, we took advantage of them whenever we were eligible. From Saturday noon to Monday morning reveille we hit the local nightspots (very few and far between) drove to San Francisco, or traveled back to Los Angeles. Fortunately, some buddies had cars and lived in the Los Angeles area. We all had a number of passes home during that summer, frequently arriving back at Camp Roberts very early Monday morning with the result that many of us with similar weekend excursions found it difficult to stay alert and attentive during training activities that day.

With the end of basic training, some of us were destined for the Pacific Theater of Operations, others for Officers Candidate School, while another group of us (I among them) was selected for the Army Specialized Training program (ASTP). We were then transported to Santa Rosa, California, and after about six weeks of orientation programs and introductory college courses at the junior college, we were all transported to Kansas University in Lawrence, Kansas to enroll in basic engineering classes. While attending there for the next five months, I was inspired by the instructor in American History and Institutions towards a career in teaching. Even with the emphasis on the sciences and mathematics for most of our classwork, the army program included two hours a week for this one class.

By the spring of 1944, the army determined that greater numbers of infantry were needed, rather than A.S.T.P. classroom engineers. As a consequence, all of us at Kansas University found ourselves on a train assigned to Camp Gruber, Oklahoma, home of the 42nd Rainbow Division, which was General Douglas MacArthur's command in World War I. There I found I had been placed in the A&P (Ammunition and Pioneer) Platoon, Headquarters Company, 3rd Battalion, 222nd Infantry Regiment.

That summer, those of us in the A&P platoon learned about the care and use of all the tools and equipment from shovels, picks, gunnysacks, explosives, and so forth, that were our responsibility for use by the 3rd Battalion. We trained again at the rifle range, carried out mock battles, participated in night maneuvers, learned to drive a personnel truck, and took our turn at KP and guard duty. Eastern Oklahoma in the 1940's did not offer much other than the town of Muskogee and the city of Tulsa. While passes were available, most of us spent what free time we had on base.

It seemed no secret that we were destined for Europe. We all had two-week furloughs to go home, and during this period I became engaged to that girl back home, Martha Mollett – the best thing I ever did during the time I was in the service. All of us with service experience can relate to the morale surge that came when we received letters from home, from parents, friends, and a fiancée.

Now back at Camp Gruber, all energies focused on preparation for European deployment. By early November the division designated as *Task Force Linden* went by train to Camp Kilmer, where before long we boarded a troopship headed by convoy to land in

Marseilles, France. The two weeks of zigzagging across the Atlantic had its moments, boat drill every day, seasickness for many, but fortunately no U-boat alarms, and we made port December 8, 1944.

Our first introduction to France consisted of camping out in the countryside, a barren, rocky, cold, windswept piece of real estate not too far from Marseilles. There, in the afternoon, we set up our shelter – half pup tents closely spaced one from another, all lined up in military fashion, even with a company street. That first night, one lonesome plane (said to be German, but never properly identified) scoured the sky for a short time before disappearing. By morning, now in drizzling rain, orders quickly issued directed us to disperse our tents all over the hillside. So much for our efforts of the previous day trying to present a neat, well-organized, infantry bivouac!

The cold, blustery, weather seemed to last the entire time we were on the hillside, so much so that there were volunteers for KP duty. The tar-paper sheds that housed the field kitchens were the only warm, dry, shelters to be found. Before too many days, however, we made our way to the rail yards to board "40 and 8" boxcars, so named for their capacity to hold eight horses or forty men. We knew that the horses were accommodated far more readily than forty men, and furthermore, it did not take much imagination to conclude that

horses more likely than not had been the most recent occupants. We also speculated that many of the cars dated back to WWI.

Fortunately, with all our barrack bags and equipment, reduced numbers of us were assigned to each car. These cars, over the next several days, transported us to the area of Strasbourg, France, and the active war zone. Many of us experienced combat for the first time that Christmas day of 1944. Little did we know of the desperate battle waged at Bastogne, and that our task force relieved the more seasoned troops ordered to stem the German advance.

While in Strasbourg, our platoon leader called us together with the news that we needed to take on the responsibility of the ammunition supply for the battalion – after all, the <u>A</u> in A&P stood for ammunition. One of our three squads would take on that duty. Now then, the rule of thumb in the army is that you do not volunteer; you wait until you are assigned. After a few moments of silence from those of us present, for whatever reason, I spoke up and said I would give it a try, and suddenly I was a sergeant in charge of the ammo squad.

Before long I learned that two trucks with drivers from the motor pool, two-and-one-half tons each, would be assigned to our A&P platoon for the purpose of hauling the ammunition to wherever it was needed by the 3rd Battalion. Our squad's primary task was filling the two trucks with hand grenades, boxes of bandoleers for rifles, shells for side arms, trip flares, a bazooka, 60 and 81millimeter mortar shells, and the like, and then maintaining the proper inventory.

During most of January and February into mid-March we were stockpiling ammunition for distribution to our defensive positions, but in March the major push into Germany began. After living in abandoned buildings, deserted homes, and forest dugouts, suddenly we were riding in our two ammunition-filled trucks at the rear of the advancing convoy. (After all, no one wanted those trucks very close.) When we stopped for the night, whenever we could we tried to locate barns large enough to accommodate the trucks. On more than one night the squad slept right in with the dairy cows. Other nights, we camped in sheltered areas safely removed from the fighting front only to join up the next day at the rear of the convoy now composed of walking infantry, jeeps, tanks, and mobile cannon carriers. Of course, whenever possible the troops hitched rides on whatever sort of army vehicle would take them. On occasion we drove at night very much aware of the close ground and air support between the advancing infantry and the P-61 Black Widows as we made our way through those burning towns caught up in the path of war.

In this fashion, our ammunition squad traveled with the 3rd Battalion of the 222nd Infantry Regiment from the forests of Eastern France and the Maginot and Siegfried lines into Germany, crossing the Rhine at Worms on the way to Würzburg. From there it was on to Schweinfurt, Fürth and Munich. Our combat experiences ended on our way to Salzburg, Austria, before we could make contact with the westward-advancing Russians forces. We had witnessed the long lines of surrendering German troops on the roads walking to the west as we drove east through sections of the Black Forest where in many instances clearings had been cut away from the road to house military supplies, especially ammunition. Some portions of the autobahn had served as runways for aircraft, but were now vacant. We all sensed that the German surrender was imminent.

With the conclusion to the war in Europe we now became the Army of Occupation with the task of relocating displaced persons, guarding military installations, representing the United States in the Four Power American sectors of Vienna and Berlin, and anticipating our return home without dwelling too much on the thought that experienced troops were still being mobilized for the invasion of Japan.

Fortunately, the war with Japan closed in August, so that we could now experience some freedom to travel on military passes to various parts of Western Europe – Paris, Rome, London, Berlin, and Vienna – and begin to see the land free of the war's turmoil. The 42nd

Division actually organized what amounted to a junior college refresher program in Zell am Zee, Austria, taught by officers and noncoms who had some teaching or professional experience. As a student, I enjoyed four months there before the program had to close due to many students and staff now eligible to return to the United States.

I had seen the destruction inflicted on small towns caught between defending and advancing forces, the devastation to major cities subjected repeatedly to day and nighttime bombing, and the dislocation and impressments of innocent people who had done nothing more than live in the advancing path of armies. I had lost comrades to death and injury, and I had survived five months of combat without injury myself.

In a personal assessment of the almost three years in the army for me and for so many others, it was a time of sudden maturity, an awareness of duty, an assumption of responsibility, a reliance on the support of our fellow soldiers, and an appreciation for the qualities of discipline, leadership, and valor. If in my career as teacher and principal a modicum of success has been achieved, I can credit that in large degree to lessons observed and learned during my time in the service.

As for the person you become – husband, father, family man, friend, neighbor, worker, contributor in some fashion to society – all experiences play a part in your ambitions, desires, character, attitudes, career, and beliefs. I count it my good fortune to have grown up in a loving family, one where religious ideals and church participation counted, a home where education was valued and encouraged, and one where sharing in the outdoor life fostered fond memories. I treasure my younger brother and his dear family – that younger brother who long ago shed being a pesky kid during my early growing years.

The young woman who wore my engagement ring and I have been married 65 years now, and our son and his family, and our daughter and her family, are well established. We enjoy seven grandchildren and fourteen great-grandchildren. Somehow we have weathered life's small, annoying, exigencies, and the golden years shine brighter each and every passing day.

MY WORLD WAR II BY RALPH SHRADER

I graduated from high school in 1938. The great depression was still in full swing, jobs were not to be found, and college was not an option. I vowed never to work in the coal mines because I wanted a better standard of living than those jobs could support. Some of my options were the Civilian Conservation Camps (CCC), a public work relief program for unemployed men, or the Work Projects Administration (WPA), another government program for job training, or joining the military.

At that time a man I knew asked me if I might be interested in managing a small service station that he owned. I was always interested in automobiles so I accepted the job and worked at it for about three months. But times were hard, people didn't have money to buy gas and oil, and I decided I needed to find something else. I remembered seeing a poster that said "Join the Navy and See the World", which sounded exciting to me. My brother was already in the Army as well as so many other young men. So, on November 8, 1938, I went to Richmond, Virginia, and signed up for a four year tour in the Navy. Four years turned out to be almost seven years, because when the war spread to the Pacific, the Navy kept me for another three years.

From Richmond I was put on a train to Norfolk, Virginia where I spent three months in "boot training". I gained about fifteen pounds and was feeling good even though the training was intense. After training, we got orders to board a transport that took us to Guantanamo Bay, Cuba. Shortly after arriving there, a chief came up to me and said, "See that destroyer over there, that's your new home." You can imagine a kid like me leaving home for the first time and being told that big ship was going to be my new home! The ship was called the USS Gridley (DD380), a destroyer. Immediately I was assigned to the deck force, which meant scrubbing decks, painting the bulkheads and just keeping the ship in order. Painting everything above deck and the entire sides of the ship seemed to take more time than anything else. As soon as you got the painting done you would immediately start scraping it off again, putting on a coat of red lead, then a coat of battleship gray. A couple of weeks later a chief came around and asked if there was anyone who could type. Fortunately, I had trained myself on an old Underwood typewriter while in high school, so my abilities paid off. I got a job in the ship's personnel office and eventually made Office Manager.

About a year later, I was transferred to the USS Craven (DD382), a sister ship of the Gridley. My income was $21 a month, and I immediately made an allotment of $5 a month to my parents to help them with their bills. Each time I made advancement in rank, I would increase that amount.

We trained in the warm waters of Guantanamo Bay. Occasionally, we had time to visit other islands, such as other ports in Cuba, Jamaica and Haiti. Several of us visited the Bacardi Rum Distillery, where I had my first drink of rum right where it was made. Soon our ship was on its way to Boston for the installation of more wartime equipment. On the way north, we hit our first big storm while in the freezing waters off Cape Hatteras, North Carolina. The pitching effect of the ship splashed the frigid water over the ship until ice covered it several inches deep. We arrived in Boston Easter morning and it was snowing.

While in Boston, I enjoyed my first Big League ball game at Fenway Park. I also went to New York City to see the 1939 World's Fair. In those days, that was a real treat. After that, the City of Wilmington, North Carolina invited our ship to a three-day celebration of the city's birthday – a taste of good old Southern hospitality.

Then I really was off to "See the World". We went on to the Panama Canal, San Diego, Long Beach, Hollywood and San Francisco where we enjoyed some good times. It was now 1940, and while we were in Long Beach there was one of the biggest storms ever in California. While two-thirds of the crew was ashore, most of our ships broke anchor and had to go to sea. Some of the streets there were flooded with ocean water. The people of Long Beach were just wonderful, and put us up for the night.

Our next destination was Seattle where our ship was equipped with radar at the Bremerton Navy yard. After a few weeks, we were on our way back to San Diego, which would now be our home base. For several months, I really enjoyed San Diego and Southern California while doing extensive training in and around the Navy's San Clemente Island. Suddenly our ship received orders that we were going to Pearl Harbor. So we got underway and soon we began a lot of training in and around the islands of Hawaii. I enjoyed the islands very much for the next several months, traveling and seeing the area and spending time on Waikiki Beach.

Needless to say, "Seeing the World" came to an abrupt ending in Hawaii. Our ship was supposed to go into dry dock at Pearl Harbor for routine service. The USS Shaw (another destroyer) lost a propeller and had to go in instead. Sadly, the USS Shaw was destroyed during the bombing eleven days later. The day was November 26, 1941, and we suddenly got orders to leave the harbor and join the carrier Enterprise along with other units of the fleet. The crew was unaware of where we were going or why. The history books now tell us that we were heading to Wake Island to unload dozens of fighter aircraft from the Enterprise. The trip took us eleven days there and back. All this time we were on "General Quarters", with watches of four hours on and four hours off twenty-four hours a day. (General Quarters is a shipboard command used in drills and emergencies to ensure that movement around the ship is minimal and orderly. All personnel have an assigned station and task when a General Quarter is sounded. The entire trip was navigated on a zigzag course. Could we have been looking for the Japanese fleet at the same time? The crew never knew.

As we were approaching Pearl Harbor on the way back from Wake that morning of December 7, 1941, General Quarters rang out and the captain announced "Pearl Harbor is being bombed".

We later heard that Wake Island was being bombed at the same time. I can tell you only what you have already seen and heard as we entered Pearl Harbor. It was a horrible sight. The first thing I recognized was the belly of the battleship Oklahoma sticking out of the water. To me it first looked like a submarine. To our right, the Navy Air Base was engulfed in flames. On up the channel were the rest of the battleships sunk and aflame. The smoke and the fire and the smell were just terrible. Navy personnel were being pulled from the burning oil in the water all up and down the harbor.

Immediately our ship was ordered to go further in and dock, and all hands worked all night loading supplies, fuel and ammunitions. So, we were underway for our first day of war, December 8. We left the next morning by 4:30 a.m. to search for enemy subs that were thought to be outside the harbor. My General Quarters station that day was to man the underwater sonar machine, which I had been trained for, to detect submarines. We made a lot of runs on what appeared to be subs and dropped numerous depth charges, but it was unclear at that time if any were sunk. Since the bombing, the big question was, "Are they going to attack again?" We surely expected them to try and invade Hawaii.

I had communicated often by mail with my family before Pearl Harbor, so they knew where I was. I was told later that my mother was frantic. Communications were censored, and she didn't hear from me for over a month after the bombing. Our mail would arrive from another ship by "pulley" on a wire from one ship to the other. It would take weeks to receive mail from home.

As time went on, part of my job during battle was delivering the captain's orders to all departments of the ship by phone. Everyone else wore ear plugs for protection from the noise of the guns. I couldn't use ear plugs or cotton because I had to hear what the Captain's orders were. In time I realized that this was the beginning of my hearing loss.

My memory has slipped for many periods of the war, but I do remember about nine months of escorting troop and supply ships to the Solomon Islands. One moonlight night, dozens of Zero aircraft attacked us. It was quite a battle and lasted at least three hours. We were very successful, and most of the planes were shot down. I can still see plane after plane hitting the water and exploding in a fireball. I don't know how many aircraft were destroyed, but it was a lot. It is possible a few of them were able to return to their ship or island. One of them headed directly at our ship and dropped a torpedo. It apparently had instruments set for larger ships and didn't explode. I could see the wake of the torpedo go straight under my station on the bridge.

Often we would anchor at night close to an island called Tulagy. One enemy plane, which we called "Washing Machine Charley", would fly over every night at midnight and drop a bomb simply to keep everyone awake. One night a piece of shrapnel hit one of our men in the butt, and I can still hear him yelling. His name was Hertado; fortunately he was not seriously hurt. As a matter of fact, not one man on our ship was ever killed by enemy fire. There were, however, deaths caused by accidents. For example, our ship and three others of the division were the fastest ships in the Navy at that time. One day we were doing top speed and ran directly into a huge wave, and as we came down into a second wave it seemed like hitting concrete. I surely thought the ship would break apart. The number one five-inch gun turret was crushed and three men were killed. Other accidents over the years killed four more. Amazingly, shortly before the war ended, our divisions of destroyers were classified as unsafe because of the very thin hulls. Yet they survived years of war! All were later sold and scrapped for parts.

Those were the days when we sometimes listened to Tokyo Rose on the radio with her propaganda. She would try to make the men homesick and otherwise dampen their spirits. But we didn't take it seriously and just listened to the music for entertainment.

For the rest of the war my memory just comes in spots, such as the battle of Midway when we were guarding the carrier Enterprise. The Enterprise was one of the most decorated ships of the war. It was recognized that the Midway Battle was the turning point of the Pacific war, which, as far as I can remember, lasted at least three days. It was a long and difficult battle.

At one period, we had orders to return to Pearl Harbor for some repairs, and everyone aboard was fitted with cold weather clothing. We were expected to head to the Aleutian Islands where a battle was going on. I think this scared me more than anything yet. How long could one survive in that ice cold water? Sooner than expected, the Americans won that part of the war so we lucked out and didn't have to go.

If there is such a thing as a "good" memory in this war, it was when we were detached from the Enterprise to join the carrier Hornet. This was when Jimmy Doolittle's B-25s were launched to bomb Tokyo for the first time. That was an exciting time. I thoroughly enjoyed watching all sixteen of those planes successfully get off the deck of the Hornet. We had watched hundreds of smaller planes take off from the Enterprise, but the B-25s were much larger and this was the first time they had taken off on a carrier. Launching those heavy aircraft required high speeds for the carrier and a heavy head wind. We were there for protection and, if necessary, to pick up pilots in case any had to ditch. Luckily, all sixteen were launched successfully.

Shortly before the war ended, I had to go back to Pearl Harbor for four months of school in order to pass my next test for promotion to Chief Yeoman.

After school was finished, I was shipped to Treasure Island in San Francisco Bay to help discharge Navy personnel from the service. You just can't imagine the feeling that came over me when, after some five years in the South Pacific, the beautiful shoreline of San Francisco appeared before me. I had been away from home for almost five years with only two weeks leave.

My sister Elsie happened to be stationed in the Coast Guard there in one of the high-rise buildings and she invited me up for dinner several times. We sure didn't have food like that aboard ship! I never enjoyed a city so much. After many thousands of Navy personnel were discharged, I released myself on September 15, 1945, and went home.

Back in West Virginia, I tried to find myself again (as many were trying to do as the war ended). To my surprise, things were tough. No jobs seemed to match the type of experience I had gained in the Navy. Needless to say, years were lost insofar as jobs and schooling were concerned. In trying to decide what to do for work, the only thing that seemed to interest me was an opening for a job in the parts department of a Buick dealership - which I accepted. After two years in the department, I was promoted to Manager. In the meantime, I had been doing some dating and along the way I met my true love, Mabel, and we were engaged. My wife-to-be finally picked a date to be married, which was January 4, 1948. One of the first things we decided as a couple was, never buy anything unless we could pay for it at the time (no credit), and we have done this the rest of our lives.

The money I sent to my parents while I was in the Navy was returned to me when I got home. None of it had been spent. Thus, my wife and I had money to start our first home. We lived in our new home for the first two years with minimal furnishings. We bought things as the money was available. Since then we have moved and built five other new homes. I cannot remember a month that we did not save a little. Now we are retired and able to live in the beautiful University Village of Thousand Oaks, California.

As it happened, I returned to the automobile business. My wife had been working for the manager of a GMAC office in town. During a conversation with him one day, he mentioned being interested in opening up a new Buick dealership in another town close by. It turns out that this little incident brought on about thirty years of work in every aspect of the business. Unfortunately, my hearing loss began not long after the war was over and gradually worsened more and more until 1977, at which time the stress of it was making me ill in many ways, causing me to retire.

While I was in the automobile business, my wife was employed by three separate colleges and universities, the last one being California State University, Northridge. She retired in 1989 after nearly thirty years.

We survived the 1971 Sylmar earthquake, and then our home was almost destroyed by the 1994 Northridge earthquake, so we decided to move and build a new home in Thousand Oaks, California, which we enjoyed for twelve years. Then we moved into an active, senior community, University Village, in October, 2007.

Mabel and I have been married for sixty-four happy years. We have been blessed with three wonderful children, four grandchildren and five great-grandchildren. We are so very proud of all of them.

REMEMBRANCES OF WORLD WAR II
BARBARA ANNA BEYER WARKENTIEN

<u>Introduction</u>

Certain memories from my childhood are so vivid it seems they occurred only yesterday. Yet time does sometimes erase one's thoughts and before that happens, I want to have a record of them for myself and to share with my sons, Stephen and Karl. I was born in Agoura, California, February 5, 1932, to John Karl and Myrtle Jane Simmons Beyer. When my parents moved to California in 1930, they lived for a year in The Reyes Adobe. Shortly before I was born, they moved into the adjacent "little brown house." When Ventura Boulevard was expanded to become the Ventura Freeway, this house was moved to Thousand Oaks, now the "little white house" located on North Oak View Drive between Thousand Oaks Boulevard and Los Feliz Drive in Old Town, Thousand Oaks. My father often pointed out the house, for it was important to him as it was the first home he and my mother had entirely to themselves

In the fall of 1939, the family moved to a five-acre parcel nestled against the hills, where Hillcrest Drive and Skyline Drive intersect today in Thousand Oaks. At that time Hillcrest Road curved to join Ventura Boulevard. I have only a vague awareness of our first two years on the farm other than that my father did not think one-half mile was too far a distance for us to walk to school. I didn't agree since I thought climbing two hills in the heat, carrying books and a lunch pail was a real burden.   My first clear memory is of Pearl Harbor.

PEARL HARBOR COMES TO THE BEYER FAMILY

Sunday, December 7, 1941, began like any other for the John Beyer family in quiet, rural Thousand Oaks, with Sunday breakfast prepared by my mother, Myrtle. Her biscuits and gravy are still the best. After washing the dishes, Mother, my brother George age 7, my sister Myrna age 3 and I (Barbara) age 9 got ready for Sunday School and walked the two short blocks from our home on Hillcrest Road to worship in a small building just across Ventura Boulevard (now Thousand Oaks Boulevard). My father stayed behind to attend to some chores around our small farm.

On arriving home, Mother went in to prepare dinner. George and I went out to create a world of fantasy with our father's saw horses and Myrna was off playing with her cat. All of a sudden our neighbor, Mrs. Wiseman came rushing over, crying excitedly, "The Japs have bombed Pearl Harbor, ships were sunk, hundreds are dead...we're at war."

I followed her into the house with George right behind, yelling for me to come out and play. He didn't know what war was and figured that is was just another excuse of his older sister to get out of playing with him. Now, I didn't know what war was, either, but I knew it was something important, when my father turned on the radio. He **never** listened to the radio in the middle of the day, and then when my mother quit cooking and sat down to listen too, well, then something pretty bad was at hand.

I guess we ate, for my next memory is of sitting outside in warm sunshine with a clear blue sky above. My mother had brought us out to our regular fall Sunday chore of shucking the corn that we had grown during the summer. Later we would shell it so the chickens would have food during the winter.

My father joined us later, but he just stood there, spoke quietly with my mother. He appeared dispirited, seemingly powerless to act or move. Now, I still didn't know what war was, but I knew it was something horrible, for my father was always in control, he always knew what to do, and he was always busy doing it. Eventually, he just walked away.

We went on with the corn. Later that day we discovered a hen's nest filled with eggs. The Wiseman's cow had a calf and baby rabbits were born. My mother took these simple events as symbols of God's assurance that He would provide for us in the uncertain days that lay ahead. He did.

Today, fifty years later I still feel the warmth of the December sun, I still see the uncertainty in my father's eyes, I still hear my mother's words of faith, and even now, I recall being puzzled by this bad thing called war happening on such a beautiful day.

(I wrote this for a Thousand Oaks *"News Chronicle"* Saturday, December 7, 1991 (Page B-3) feature on the fiftieth anniversary of Pearl Harbor, called a Day of Infamy. Readers who were either in the U.S. or in the military, but were not at Pearl Harbor were invited to share their memories of December 7, 1941.)

FACING WARTIME CHANGES

As usual the sun came up on Monday, December 8, 1941; as usual my mother cooked breakfast, my father left for work; George and I went to school; and Myrna, who knows? She probably played with her cats. In other words, war or no war, our lives followed our regular routine that day. I do have a vague recollection of being in my class room at Conejo Elementary School and hearing President Roosevelt's powerful "Day of Infamy" radio address to Congress calling for declaration of war.

The government had a war to win and all Americans were both challenged and required to make sacrifices. Rationing of commodities such as sugar, coffee, shoes, butter, cheese, tires, gasoline, heating oil, and nylons was quickly implemented via rationing books and gasoline wind shield stickers for vehicles.   For us on our small farm, food rationing wasn't too much of a problem. We had milk, butter, chickens, pigs, beef and always fresh or home canned vegetables and jellies.   Because we were very poor, our major grocery purchases were limited to coffee, flour, sugar, pasta, a few treats and supplemental items. In his concern for our family's food supply, my father figured we could survive without the coffee, pasta and treats, but sugar and flour were necessities.

Since we lived so far away -- at least in those days Canoga Park and Oxnard were considered distant from Thousand Oaks, it was not uncommon for my parents to shop every two months or so in those towns buying flour, sugar and chicken feed in 100 pound sacks. Thus before rationing was enacted, my parents bought several 100 pound bags of these items.   At that time with the war just beginning, my father was uncertain what government intrusion in private homes might be. Besides, in a small town everyone knew everyone's business.   Thus my parent's shopping habits were known, and who could perceive what desperate actions might arise in desperate times. He was willing to share, but he wanted a reserve cushion.

He now faced a dilemma. He had the flour and sugar, but where was he going to store it safely out of view. The solution was found in the chicken house, which by the way was as well built as our small home with a good roof and solid walls. There he had a sturdy storage bin with two compartments--one for purchased grains and the corn we grew and one for mash--a perfect place to store the flour and sugar, hidden under the chicken food. Throughout the war, we children were admonished to keep our friends out of the chicken house lest they find the secret store. In my opinion, no one least of all our friends had any desire to enter this smelly, dusty place, where ill tempered hens attacked with gusto as we tried to retrieve the eggs. Furthermore, we were told to scoop out the food gingerly to avoid tearing the cloth sacks. Fortunately, we never faced the need to use this emergency food source, but much to my father's chagrin, when he went to get the hidden food, he found the sacks decayed from time and the weight of the grains--thus his store was worthless, his efforts in vain.

Although food rationing had minimal impact on our lives, gasoline rationing proved to be more of a handicap. My mother's car was considered non-essential to the war effort, so she was given a black "A" sticker for her windshield with an allotment of four gallons of gasoline per week. My father was granted a green "B" sticker and allotted eight gallons a week.

Because of his employment, my father drove many miles each week and used part of my mother's portion. My elderly grandparents lived in Canoga Park and need assistance from time-to-time, requiring use of gasoline to reach them. In addition to these uses, our

family planted seven acres of corn each year, necessitating a gasoline powered tractor for tilling the soil and planting the corn. After some pleading, my father was able to convince the ration board to grant him a "R" non-highway ration of gas. With this additional provision and careful planning, we had sufficient fuel.

While the farming was never a lucrative venture, we did give corn to our community and sold some to affluent movie stars and other residents of the Lake Sherwood and Hidden Valley areas. My siblings and I thought our father farmed to provide us with the tiring chores of weeding, suckering, and harvesting the corn. We got very up close and personal with the dirt of those seven acres. One year my father either didn't have enough time or enough gas, but for whatever reason, he was unable to plant corn on his three-acre parcel. In those years Thousand Oaks was blessed with abundant rain; so on the untended plot, a beautiful field of mustard plants flourished with their yellow blossoms beaconing from lofty six-foot stalks.

Now the neighbors always curious about any deviation from the norm, asked my father about the mustard field. Well, either from vanity not wanting to admit any personal failure or from an attitude of "it's none of anyone's business," he told them, "Oh, I'm growing mustard for the government to make into mustard gas to use against the Germans and Japanese." One person told another and soon Johnny Beyer's mustard gas project was all over town. In reality, mustard plants are very hearty with deep roots; it was a labor intensive job to get the land ready for the next year's planting. However, the mustard gas saga was one of my father's favorite tales.

CARELESSNESS AND CONSEQUENCES

As I mentioned earlier, Thousand Oaks experienced heavy rains during the 1940's. Flooding was minimal because open land absorbed the overflow easily. There was a deep six-foot ravine just before the road reached Ventura Boulevard U.S. 101 (now Thousand Oaks Boulevard) that in a good rain flowed with a swift current of running water. Throwing sticks and other objects in the water on one side of the bridge and then running to the other to spot the reappearing items provided a fun diversion for us country children.

In those days, there was no home mail delivery. Our mail was delivered to a mail box two blocks away on Ventura Boulevard, one block was dirt which became mud when it rained; the other was paved. My mother frustrated by three lively children confined in a small house and against her better judgment sent us off to get the mail with a warning to stay out of the water and protect our rationed shoes. Overjoyed to be free of the house, we quickly put on our galoshes and went on our way.

Trudging through the slush, we acquired quite an amount of mud on our galoshes. Once we got on the paved road, we lost some of it, but there was still plenty left when we reached the ditch. We were compelled to clean our muddy galoshes . Of course we were going to be careful to protect our shoes just barely stepping at the edge of the water. But we stepped a little too far, or we slipped. The result was the same; the water went over the top of the galoshes. Well, we knew we had disobeyed our mother, but since the shoes were already wet, we might as well enjoy ourselves before we faced our punishment, so we spent some happy moments watching the sticks and other debris flow along the ditch. Eventually, we returned home with the mail.

Our mother didn't say much; we cleaned our shoes. Then she touched them up and placed them on the door of the wood stove oven to dry. Later she rubbed them with linseed oil to soften them. Her silence was a powerful rebuke much more significant than any scolding could ever be. Our shame in disappointing her and causing her extra work and worry was major. Yet, I am sad to admit but on at least one other occasion, we were lured by the rushing water and returned home again with the mail and soggy shoes. Rationing and our mother's burden just didn't surpass our desire for gratification. As the oldest, I bear the greatest shame.

My next act of carelessness centered on the chickens. As I reflect on this time, it appears that the chickens were a constant presence. Following the principle of division of labor, my parents determined that we children could assume the major responsibility of caring for the chickens. Thus it was our duty to feed them, collect the eggs, open the gate so they could roam free, and then secure the coop for the night--a simple chore with no requirements other than to be sure all the chickens were in the coop before we closed the door.

Along with rationing, the government imposed strict blackout regulations during the war. All windows had to be fully covered to prevent any stray beam, a possible beacon for enemy pilots, from escaping into the night. I remember my parents putting up blackout curtains and then my father walking around the house checking each window for any trace of light. Pleased with the results, my parents were proud to have done their bit for the war effort.

Ah, but thanks to their older daughter and the chickens, their satisfaction was short lived. As the oldest, my final chore of the evening was to close up the chickens for the night--a simple task just wait till the last chicken enters and close the door, preferably before dark. Several characteristics of chickens complicate the simplicity. There's always one, fearless explorer that delays bedtime until dark. Then there's the uncanny hearing of chickens. Instantly aware of my stealthy approach, they promptly made a mad rush for the exit in anticipation of a bedtime snack. Angry to be denied and further irritated by my vain attempts to shoo them into the coop, some of the roosters would claw my bare legs with their sharp spurs.

Closing the chicken coop door was never easy. I finally decided it was best to just wait until dark. But darkness brought its own problems--finding the chicken coop door and latching it. Normally, there were a few lights around, but in wartime, it was pitch dark unless there was a full moon. Listening to my lament, my mother took pity and gave me a flashlight with the admonition to focus the beam on the ground. At first grateful for this light, I carefully held the beam to the ground; but eventually I started flashing it a little farther afield. Eventually, I was aiming it to the distant trees or just swinging it back and forth as I walked along, intrigued by familiar objects featured by my spotlight. I still remember the power I felt walking through the dark night with my little light.

Unbeknownst to me, others were observing my swaying light. It wasn't too long before officers were at the door. It seems the neighbors had reported seeing lights flickering from our area. Ever vigilant against suspicious activity, they had reported us, certain that we must be in contact with the enemy.   My parents were stunned and very, very nervous.   They were really perplexed since they had taken such care with the windows. What could be the source of this mysterious flashing light.   Gradually, my mother remembered the flashlight. This time my carelessness had almost resulted in my parents being charged with espionage. From then on, it was either battle with the chickens at dusk or find my way in the dark.

CONEJO SCHOOL AND WARTIME

I was privileged to attend Conejo Elementary School from 1939-1945. It was an impressive mission revival building situated atop a knoll overlooking a large playground. Its thick walls provided insulation that kept us warm in winter and comfortable on hot days. Tall windows facing north gave us excellent light. A heavy partition separated the lower and upper grades and could be raised to create a large auditorium.   There was a rose garden with a rock edged fish pond. A playhouse for the girls and a workshop for the boys accented the garden. Unfortunately, the school was demolished in the 1950's because of earthquake liability.   Today, the large playground remains as does the rock wall that bordered the roadway.   The school now faces Conejo School Road.   Adjacent to the entrance is a crepe myrtle tree. At its base stand a memorial marker with the names of my parents, John and Myrtle Beyer "Friends of Children."

The principal of Conejo School, Mrs. Irene F. Scott, had always been an avid devotee of physical fitness. The war now gave her ample opportunity to promote her athletic regime.   A tennis/basketball court was installed; tether balls were added, the softball field was kept striped; a track course was established; and heavy mats were purchased for acrobatics. We dutifully used them all under her diligent supervision. She organized competitive "Play Days" with neighboring Timber (Newbury Park) and Santa Rosa Valley schools. We always won the most ribbons achieved not so much by ability, but by knowledge that if we didn't win, we'd be spending countless hours in training. Our fitness was her personal contribution to the war effort.

To keep us mindful of the American military, Mrs. Scott coerced some local retired soldiers into teaching us to march and perform some parade like drills. We were encouraged to dress in the uniforms of the Army, Navy, Marines, and Coast Guard as best we could. (The Air Force was part of the Army and did not become a separate service branch until 1947.) Somehow we got flags of each branch, which the best or tallest marcher was honored to carry. Mrs. Scott was most persuasive and somehow she got the Navy from Port Hueneme and the Air Force from Camarillo to send active duty personnel to evaluate our marching and to lead us in new drills--impressive for a small country school.

Our music lessons now included "Anchors Aweigh," "The Caisson Song," "The Army Air Corps," "Semper Parataus," and "The Marines' Hymn." We were assigned to memorize the words of all the songs and all the verses. I am not sure if the sailors and airmen were forced to listen to us, but I know our parents were. I remember feeling great pride in knowing these and other patriotic songs.

Conejo School teachers promoted the war effort through various programs. The community scrap drive was located at the school. One of our writing assignments was based on personalizing the fate of a piece of scrap. My essay was entitled "Cot in the Scrap," a tale of a child's former bed being converted into a gun. It won a prize in Ventura County competition. The teachers collected our dimes to buy War Bonds. It seemed it took forever to get the 187 stamps plus a nickel needed to buy the $18.75 bond to be redeemed for $25.

While our mothers gathered at the school to roll bandages, we girls were taught to knit scarves for soldiers to protect their necks from the cold. Needles and yarn were collected for our use. As luck would have it, I was given oversize needles and a thin gauge yarn. I valiantly knitted on in spite of the fact that my efforts produced a scarf with large gaps (holes) between stitches. I often wondered if some poor soldier got that flimsy scarf and if it did him much good. But I could proudly say I had completed my task for the war effort.

Nutrition was also important. The government provided the school with large boxes of premium oranges and apples for distribution to us students. They were simply delicious, and I still remember eating the juicy oranges and crisp apples on my walk home from school. The school served as a distribution point for government flyers regarding growing victory gardens, balanced meals, and a variety of topics related to winning the war.

The lookout program for spotting enemy aircraft was located at Conejo School. Adults and older students were trained to recognize airplanes and to record details such as description, time, and date of observation and then to submit a telephone report. We never spied an enemy plane, but we did our duty.

AFTERMATH

By 1944, it had become fairly obvious that the Allies would emerge victorious in World War II. Life returned to normal. Rationing restrictions were lifted. At school we weren't drilled so much physically. Studying to pass The Constitution test mandated by Ventura County for promotion to High School became the focus of our school days.

I remember one chilly spring day being called in from recess to be told that Franklin Delano Roosevelt had died. I felt a sense of sadness that this great leader would not live to see the end of the terrible war that he had united the country to fight. I later remember sitting in class listening to Harry S. Truman take the oath of office as the 33rd President of the United States. His high-pitched voice blocked my hearing his sincere pledge of dedication to serve our country. I thought he would be inept. It took me many years to appreciate what a remarkable leader and man of character he was.

By the time I began Oxnard High School in fall 1945, the war was over. By 1949, my parents were able to purchase a new car. Life was good. I met Kenneth Le Roy Warkentien in geometry class and married him in 1951. We have two sons, Stephen and Karl and four grandchildren Jonathan, Anna, Brian, and Nicole. Kenneth is patient, loving, helpful, and has graciously assisted and encouraged me to pursue all my dreams.

I have been blessed with good health, credited to my mother's fine cooking and all the pure, homegrown food we ate even if my siblings and I felt bitterly put upon in working to help produce it. I credit my love of nature to growing up in Thousand Oaks--it was a paradise--a ring of mountains surrounded a valley of open fields, full of spring flowers and majestic oaks. I credit my interest in government to my father, who was a citizen activist, speaking at almost every Thousand Oaks Planning Commission and Council meeting from 1964, when the City was incorporated until 1988.

How can one summarize the impact of an event such as World War II? It was frightening and horrifying. For a part of my childhood, I lived with threat of devastating invasion by a cruel enemy resulting in loss of all I held dear: family, home, school, and country. Out of this fear grew a great dedication to my country, The United States of America. The War, then, developed my sense of patriotism--love of the freedoms I enjoy, a feeling of equality, the right to learn, and the opportunity to choose my destiny. Without the War, I do not know if I would have felt such devotion, and thus the War gave me a great gift--appreciation for my magnificent country. I am indebted.

©Barbara Warkentien

APPENDIX

GOD OF CONEJO OFFICIAL SCHOOL HYMN 1940

God of Conejo, the morning light breaks.
Silver the meadow the mocking bird wakes.
Child of the valley, a clarion call
Ushers a new day within missioned walls.

Molten the gold flows down hillside's brown seams.
Noontime is weaving a pattern of dreams.
Here in Conejo, the dreamer rides high.
Each one an artist. His palette, the sky.

God of Conejo, the evening winds sigh.
Lull us to rest with their sweet lullaby.
Hold us real close to you velvety breast.
Nighttime is drowsing the sun in the west.

Chorus
God of Conejo, your green arms are swaying.
In tenderest rhythm, our lips softly praying.
We thank thee for sunshine that crowns the hillcrest,
For oak trees and peace in this vale of the blest.

Words and music by Marie de Winstanley Parks.
Arrangement by Harold D. Winegar.
Written for the Conejo School children, 1940
Declared the Thousand Oaks City Anthem the 18th Day of April, 1972 by Raymond Garcia, Mayor of Thousand Oaks, California

   Mrs. Parks lived in Thousand Oaks for over sixty years. She appreciated the natural beauty of the Conejo Valley as well as creating a sanctuary of trees and flowers in her own yard. She wrote about local people, Conejo Valley Days, trees, and any subject that caught her fancy. My mother asked Mayor Garcia to name "God of Conejo" the official city song. When he learned about Mrs. Parks and the many Thousand Oaks themed poems she had written, he officially recognized her as the Poet Laureate of Thousand Oaks, also effective, April 18, 1972.

WORLD WAR II MEMORIAL

In Memory of Those who gave their lives in World War II that Freedom might live:

C. Leon Biddle	Air Force
John Hays	Army
Roy Spain	Navy
Harold Wienke	Army
Richard Wienkler	Army

Erected by the Thousand Oaks
Chamber of Commerce 1951

For a few years after World War II ended, Thousand Oaks remained a small town with a strong sense of community. Development was coming, but the large influx of people that would follow the massive housing projects had not yet arrived. The Chamber of Commerce led an effort to memorialize the fallen of the war. Since most of them had attended Conejo School, the school grounds seemed an appropriate place for the memorial. A bronze eagle shield plaque with sheaves of wheat, engraved with the names of the honored dead was constructed and dedicated. Later the area on which the memorial is located was converted to a small park named after city activists, John and Myrtle Beyer.

© 2012 Barbara A. Warkentien

CHARLIE WAUGH IN WWII

Early in the spring of 1944, after a couple of years devoted to the war effort as an engineer with Lockheed Aircraft in Burbank, I found myself wanting to be even more directly involved. The Navy was agreeable, commissioning me as an Ensign in the Naval Reserve. In that same eventful spring the adorable, bright and lovable Lorraine Scott agreed to be my bride.

On April 3 the Navy ordered me to report to Oak Ridge, Tennessee. Having expected to be sent somewhere in the Pacific, or at least to a place nearer to water than Tennessee, and having never heard of Oak Ridge, with no idea of what my duties would be, I was surprised and not a little puzzled.

Lorraine and I decided that our wedding would be held at Oak Ridge in June and that she would join me there a few days before the ceremony. I went ahead, finding on my arrival there a massive complex of buildings, most of a temporary construction, nestled in a picturesque valley surrounded by forested hills. Nearby the Clinch River descended from the Clinch Mountains in Virginia to the northeast, flowing through Norris Lake and the Norris Dam of the Tennessee Valley Authority, to join downstream with the Tennessee River.

I was one of about thirty newly commissioned Ensigns, all graduate engineers, assigned by the Navy as a part of its assistance to the project. None of us, however, knew at the time the reason for our assignment, nor did we know the purpose of the facility or what our duties would be. Soon we learned that Oak Ridge was a part of the Manhattan District, headed by General Leslie R. Groves under the direction of the Army Corps of Engineers. We would be performing engineering work in connection with a process, the nature of which was highly secret and would not be disclosed to us or to anyone else. Any information whatever obtained in connection with our work was not to be disclosed to anyone, family members included.

A timely hint, however, led me to read a chapter in a physics textbook which described nuclear fission experiments performed in 1939. They confirmed a belief of Bohr and Fermi that an atom of a uranium isotope, U-235, would break apart when bombarded by a neutron. According to their hypothesis, the fission would produce additional neutrons, plus energy equivalent to the resulting reduction in mass. In the presence of an additional critical amount of U-235, the emitted neutrons would strike other atoms, causing a chain reaction and releasing a huge amount of energy.

The function of the Oak Ridge facility was to separate the tiny 0.7% of U-235 present in natural uranium from the slightly heavier U-238, a challenging task since the two are identical chemically. Two methods of separation were set up on a large scale, one a gaseous diffusion process and the other an electromagnetic process based on the principle of a mass spectrometer.

It was an eerie environment, in which the finished product, completely unknown to nearly all of the thousands employed, was measured in grams and was never seen except by a select few. In my experience, security was religiously observed. Wives of the naval personnel were all in the dark, often speculating among themselves and guessing at one point that a cure for cancer was being produced. Not until Hiroshima, more than a year later, did Lorraine have an inkling of what was going on.

I was assigned to the electromagnetic separation process, in an area designated as Y-12, managed by a civilian contractor, Tennessee Eastman Corporation. In addition to other tasks, I devised a simple detecting circuit for which a patent was issued, my first. Any moral aspects of the project scarcely entered my mind, or the minds of friends, to the best of my knowledge. No discussion of the subject was possible because of rigid security, but if it had been, I believe that the consensus would have been: "This is war, the bomb is a way to win it, and it is therefore good." Only after Hiroshima did I begin to reflect on the broader issues introduced into our lives by the nuclear age.

Lorraine had a long tedious trip from Los Angeles on trains that were heavily loaded with wartime traffic. Arriving a few days prior to the wedding at the Knoxville station, she disembarked amid cheerful goodbyes and waves from dozens of soldiers who had shared the final segment of her journey. She never appeared to go out of her way to make acquaintances, but through some undefined quality would invariably become a focal point in a new situation.

We were married on June 3, 1944, in the Oak Ridge Chapel, the ceremony and reception arranged in style by the small military contingent, delighted to have an excuse to brighten up the social life of that remote community. It was the first such event performed in the chapel, later recounted from time to time in Oak Ridge chronicles. Our brief honeymoon, concurrent with the June 6 landings in Normandy, was high in the Great Smoky Mountains of East Tennessee, at Gatlinburg, a charming village – so charming in fact that it has since become overrun with tourists.

To furnish our apartment on Waddel Circle in the residential area, we purchased, for $1.50 each, four ladder-back maple chairs from an oldster in the Smoky Mountains. He made his furniture on a foot-powered lathe under a tree beside his one room log cabin.

In March of 1945, the isotope separation process was performing well and fissionable material was being produced in a quantity sufficient to power the Bomb for the subsequent Trinity test at Alamogordo, New Mexico. The urgent need that brought the Navy to Oak Ridge being taken care of, we were all ordered to duties far and wide. I went to the Naval Air Technical Training Center in Memphis for three months of training as an Aviation Engineering Officer.

I looked forward eagerly to duty aboard an aircraft carrier in the Pacific, but it was not to be. Orders instead were to the Naval Air Materiel Center in Philadelphia, where engineering help was needed. The jet age was coming into being and tests were being made on engines that would power a new generation of Navy aircraft. I was assigned to develop a device to measure the torque developed by the turbine in driving the jet engine's compressor. After nearly a year of effort, a successful device was developed, for which U.S. Patent #2621514 was issued.

In April of 1946, some eight months after the surrender of Japan and nearing the time for a return to civilian life, an opportunity arose which was exciting enough to consider remaining on active duty for a few more months. From Washington came news of Operation Crossroads, the atomic bomb test to be performed that summer at Bikini Atoll in the Marshall Islands of the western Pacific. Having (like many others) thought and talked endlessly about what we would do after the war, Lorraine and I were looking forward to an early return to California and putting ideas into effect, but for the interim Bikini won out. I applied, was accepted, and shortly headed west to Oakland, reporting aboard the hospital ship Haven (AH-12) to Col. Stafford Warren of the Army Medical Corps, who later become the first head of the new UCLA Medical Center. Warren was in charge of the Radiological Safety Section, responsible for monitoring the extent and intensity of radioactive fallout, and for the radiological safety of the some 20,000 military and civilian personnel of Joint Task Force I, as the fleet was named. His group was staffed by several prominent radiologists, plus a larger number of young Naval Officers, of which I was one, who did the actual monitoring. The Haven, a hospital ship acting as a transport, carried us to Bikini and served as our headquarters while there. Air conditioning, a luxury offered by few if any of the other vessels in the fleet, gave us a privileged status in Bikini's tropical climate.

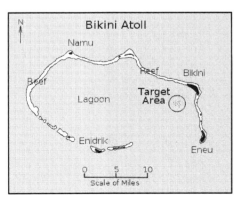

Bikini Atoll comprises a string of islands surrounding a roughly oval shaped lagoon, 24 miles long by 14 miles wide. The largest island, Bikini, is between two and three miles long and half a mile across at its widest point. In 1946 it was covered with tall coconut palms growing out of a low lying sandy surface a few feet above sea level. The palms were unharmed by our two blasts, but were completely destroyed by subsequent more powerful explosions. Most of the other islands are no more than barren reefs, barely rising out of the water. The lagoon, about 100 feet deep, is so clear that the bottom is plainly visible from the surface. A shelf outside the atoll extends from one to several hundred yards out to sea, no more than three feet deep over much of its span. It is populated with an endless variety of exotic sea life, a snorkeler's paradise. Although there was no snorkeling equipment on hand, the brilliantly colored fish could be seen fairly well while wading and peering down into the clear water. Beyond the shelf the bottom drops steeply, several thousand feet in the first mile or two.

Prior to our arrival Bikini's tiny native population had been evacuated to another atoll, where their fragile culture gradually disintegrated. Unable to return to their contaminated treeless homeland, they were, although physically unharmed, nonetheless unhappy victims of the nuclear weapons race.

In the weeks between our arrival and the first test there were meetings and instruction about the Geiger counters that we would use to measure radioactivity resulting from the blasts. There was also much leisure time, some spent on shipboard writing letters, playing chess or chatting, but more spent on the island, playing volley ball, swimming, looking at the sea life or patronizing the bar of an officer's club, a screened enclosure that had been erected in the center of the island.

The first test was made on the morning of July 1st, in the air above some sixty large target ships plus additional smaller vessels. The Haven was in an excellent viewing position, lying about

ten miles outside the lagoon. We were issued heavily darkened glasses to protect against the brilliant flash of which we had been repeatedly cautioned, so often in fact that I and others did not wholly trust the glasses, averting our eyes during the instant of the explosion.

My first reaction was one of surprise that it was over so quickly, but then I realized that all of the motion pictures that had been shown of the Alamogordo explosion had been in slow motion, exaggerating the duration of the flash. Within an hour following the explosion even the spectacular mushroom cloud had disappeared, leaving only a wisp of smoke from a burning target ship to indicate that anything had occurred.

Early the next morning our group boarded small boats which carried us into the lagoon, where we commenced our assigned task of measuring radioactivity levels, determined simply by reading the dial on a hand held Geiger counter. We were the first humans to view damaged ships at close range, one of which gave up, slowly turned over and sank while we watched nearby

In the second test, on July 25, the bomb was exploded underwater, producing almost instantly a huge inverted cone of a darkish color streaked with red, extending 2,000 feet in the air. In another instant the cone was obscured by a white hemispherical cloud which rose rapidly, revealing a cylindrical column of spray perhaps a quarter of a mile in diameter.

Once again we of Radiological Safety boarded a few of our thirty-foot long LCP's (Landing Craft, Personnel, Light). Each boat carried four or five persons, while all the rest of the thousands manning the tests stayed in ships outside the lagoon, waiting to learn from us if radiation levels were at a safe level.

At one point, in our boat, we ventured near to the venerable USS Saratoga, one of the earlier aircraft carriers, known the world around for actions, including many in the Pacific during WW II. She was well remembered by crews in the thousands and by the public as well. We few were alone, close by, within a few hundred yards, when it became apparent that she would not stay afloat for long.

The Saratoga went down while we looked on, a sad ending for that memorable ship. The bombs we tested did no damage to Bikini Island itself. In subsequent years, however, fusion bombs – thousands of times more powerful – utterly destroyed that tropical paradise.

WORLD WAR II IN FRESNO BY FRANK WELCH

The war began a year after my sister Harriette was married when I was twelve. I was visiting her on a sunny Sunday morning when we heard about the attack on Pearl Harbor on the radio. Needless to say we all were quite stunned.

Most of my adolescent years in Fresno were under wartime living restrictions. I lived in a modest but comfortable California bungalow-style house with my father, mother, and younger sister on the north side of town. Dad was a printer for the Fresno Bee and a veteran of World War I. Mother maintained a "Victory" garden during most of the war. Except for the inconvenience of shortages of many things and rationing of some essentials, my family was not affected much by the war. We learned to black out windows at night to hinder Japanese attackers if they came; we bought war bonds with our savings; and we collected recyclable critical materials, like tinfoil from cigarette packages, grease drippings (used to make explosives), and rubber.

I was in the Boy Scouts who participated in many patriotic activities. About this time I read about the Chinese "tong wars" that took place in the twenties in San Francisco and to a lesser extent in the large Chinatown in Fresno. Favorite weapons used in these clashes were hatchets that were thrown with deadly results. Since we Boy Scouts had hatchets and hunting knives, we practiced throwing them at every opportunity, and became quite proficient at sticking them in trees or other targets.

With the influx of soldiers and migrants from the "Dust Bowl" the population of Fresno grew substantially in the early years of the war. There were two military bases in Fresno: Hammer Field, a night fighter base north of town, and an army training center in nearby Pinedale. "Black Widow" night fighters and B-25 light bombers flew from Hammer Field along the coast on submarine patrol. Hammer Field is now Fresno's municipal airport. I don't think there was much crime in Fresno at that time, but there were occasional fights between GIs and Zoot Suiters from the West Side of town. Zoot Suiters were the "gang bangers" of that time.

We were careful what we said lest a spy might pick up secrets. Common posters proclaimed "Loose Lips Sink Ships." We were sure every Japanese farmer was giving their homeland the flight plans of the bombers from Hammer Field. After Pearl Harbor and the fall of the Philippines, feelings against the Japanese were very heated and it was probably good that the Japanese were removed from California before any "vigilante" atrocities were committed against them. It is hard to appreciate today our fear and hatred of the Japanese in California at the start of the war. Since the United States Pacific fleet was destroyed at

Pearl Harbor, we felt the next move would be an attack on the U.S. West Coast. Concerns eased as momentum shifted with the U.S. victories in the South Pacific.

Harriette's in-laws were of German extraction and had many friends of German heritage in the Fresno area. We were invited to many of their lively parties and barbecues where the men played pinochle and drank beer and the ladies prepared delicious dinners and pastries. At the end of the evenings, the rugs were often rolled back and the young people danced. When war was declared with Germany, they prudently ended these gatherings because of ill feelings toward the enemy. None had any problems during the war but they kept a low profile.

Harriette's husband Roy was drafted in 1943 but spent most of his service as a cook in camps in the U. S. Harriette lived with him most of the time. He was sent to France in 1944 and was there for the end of the war, but he never saw much, if any, combat. My uncle and several cousins were in the service, but all returned safely at the end of the war.

The only effects the war had on us were some inconveniences and restrictions: transportation was curtailed (gasoline and tires were rationed); some foods were rationed (sugar, butter, meats); and many household and clothing items (e.g. Levi jeans and the popular leather flight jackets) were in limited supply. We had "A" gas stamps that I believe allowed us four gallons of gas a week. We would save up our gas allotment to get enough for short trips. Those who were more dependent on their cars got "B" or "C" stamps that were good for larger amounts of gas. New tires were hard to come by, so retreads were a way of life. Needless to say there was a thriving black market in all materials that were in short supply or rationed. Since Roy's family had a meat market, we always had enough meat. To get Levi jeans, you had to know someone in the clothing business. Levis were always sold to preferred customers as soon as shipments were received and never made it to the store shelves. Nevertheless, we always had plenty to eat, a comfortable house, warm clothes, and a few luxuries. We lived quite well.

I learned to drive when I was fifteen, near the end of the war. Our family car then was a 1936 Nash sedan. I sat in it at every opportunity, learning to shift the gears. Then I nagged Dad to let me have the keys so I could move it back and forth in its parking place. Eventually he let me drive it from the front of our house around to the alley in the back to our garage where he parked it. Finally, I was parking it myself. I then bought a 1934 Ford coupe when I got my license as soon as I turned sixteen.

I always had some sort of job since becoming a teenager. The first jobs were brief and not very rewarding, but I had regular jobs continuously through the war years. Because of a shortage of farm labor, calls went out for volunteers to pick grapes for raisins. I lasted about one week doing this backbreaking work in the hot sun. I then worked for several years during high school in a men's clothing store that catered to working men. Everyone including me was able to speak enough Spanish to sell clothes to the many Mexican agricultural workers that patronized the store.

The war came to an end while I was in high school, but physical fitness was still a big thing. There was a military style obstacle course on the playing field, which all male students had to run, frequently. There were extensive calisthenics daily in gym class including a hand-over-hand rope climb to the ceiling. We all looked for ways to avoid these exertions. In addition, the usual interscholastic sports continued uninterrupted throughout the war years.

Jazz and swing music were very popular, and the high schools all had dance bands. Students and bands from all the schools often gathered together on Saturday nights in a central hall for larger dances. Added attractions were several of the famous "big bands" on tour that gave concerts in the Fresno Municipal Auditorium.

After the war ended, boys still had to register for the draft when they became eighteen. All able-bodied men were expected to put in at least two years of military service. Deferments for school or essential occupations became much easier to get, so fewer were actually drafted. Many still enlisted in one of the services for four-year hitches on active duty or seven-year commitments in the active reserves. My high school graduation class in 1947 was the first after the war in which the men could go on to college on a student deferment without going into the service first. I was fortunate to go directly to college and graduate without a stint in the military. The Selective Service System was not disbanded until the 1960's.

My uncle and cousins all returned safely from the war and resumed their careers. As far as I know, only my brother-in-law Roy suffered injury; he got frozen feet in the frigid winter of 1944 in Belgium, but came home to an active and long life. One cousin went to college and became an engineer.

CIVILIAN REMINISCENCES OF WARTIME BY ADINA WILSON

Almost everyone has mentally and emotionally locked away profound impressions of certain unforgettable events. I can vividly experience again a certain Sunday in 1941. I was doing homework in our Long Island living room with the radio on and heard the shocked broadcaster announce the attack on Pearl Harbor. As young as I was, my instant and almost fatalistic sense was that life as we had known it would be changed forever.

Our lives were impacted slowly as changes took place and the nation geared up for the war effort. I'm not sure I remember these changes sequentially or as an adult might, but the memories linger. Since we lived near the east coast and enemy attack was considered a possibility, everyone in that area was expected to have blackout curtains on all windows so that house lights were not visible at night. We also painted the headlights on our cars with black paint halfway down to diminish light radiating upward. These precautions made night driving both difficult and hazardous.

The only phones available were "party lines" with up to five different families using the same line. Each phone had a distinctive ring and we were honor-bound not to listen in on someone else's conversation. It also meant that often one had to wait one's turn to use the phone as the line was already in use. My parents took their turns as airplane spotters whose job it was to report any plane heard or seen overhead. In those days of prop planes, hearing and spotting was much easier than it would be now with the jets. At these times their reports took precedence over any other phone usage, and they were given access immediately.

Some commodities became increasingly scarce and everyone was issued ration stamps for certain foods and also for gasoline and tires. Items using oils and fats were in short supply. My mother had me carry some of the ration stamps with me so that between us we could comb the stores for scarce items, she on her weekly marketing trips and I on my lunch breaks. This way we could access markets in two different towns. A jar of mayonnaise or a box of Ritz crackers was a precious find. Meats and sugar were also hard to get and I learned then to drink tea and coffee without sweetening.

Who can ever forget our introductions to oleomargarine in lieu of our usual butter? At the time the law did not permit the margarine to be colored, so it resembled a big slab of unappetizing lard. Included in the margarine package was a capsule of bright orange coloring which was to be broken into the white oleo and kneaded in. Try as one might, it was virtually impossible to get the color even and smooth throughout. Our table spreads were often slightly striped or blotched and not too appealing. Embarrassed at having to serve margarine instead of butter, my mother had us hide in the pantry as we frantically massaged the margarine package to near perfection so guests "wouldn't know it was not butter."

Gasoline was another problem. Because we lived in the country with no public transportation available we were issued plenty of gas rationing coupons. The difficulty was that the service stations just weren't receiving enough gasoline to honor the coupons. We carpooled and shared rides as much as possible but it was difficult. At times, the only way my father could get home on weekends from his wartime job was to supplement the gasoline in his tank with some benzene, a procedure not recommended for an engine's health. Our local gas station proprietor would phone his regular customers when he expected a gasoline delivery. In the dark, without headlights, we would drive up to the station and he would fill our tanks. If we had not done this covertly, lines of cars would have materialized out of nowhere, and the station's tanks would soon have been pumped dry.

After Pearl Harbor, the war effort created jobs and my father, a World War One veteran, found steady work at the Brooklyn Navy Yard. Our financial situation gradually improved, and when the war was over Dad was finally able to live at home full time and reestablish a building business. Somehow during the bad times, we children never felt "poor" or "impoverished." We always had plenty of love and laughter and learned that one can cope, improvise and adapt to almost any situation when necessary.

Our home faced the main east-west highway on Long Island and was only a few miles from Camp Upton, a place made famous by Irving Berlin in his World War One musical "Yip Yip Yaphank." Day and night, army convoys rumbled past our house carrying troops to Camp Upton, in the town of Yaphank. (This site has since become that of Northern Brookhaven Laboratories.) From there they received their deployment orders for overseas. One lasting picture in my memory bank is that of my little grey-haired grandmother, clad in one of her bright smocks, standing on our front lawn and giving the V for Victory sign to the passing troop trucks. She was always rewarded with whistles and hoots from the soldiers being convoyed past.

At my high school graduation, a small class in a relatively small school, several classmates were not present for the event. They had been permitted to finish high school, but were whisked off through the draft before the actual ceremony took place. Most returned from service, grown up and impacted forever by their experiences. One of them, however, did not return.

National pride and national spirit were intense. Probably my most poignant recollections from that time in our country's history were the feelings of togetherness and common purpose - "All for one and one for all." Victory gardens sprouted up everywhere.

We cheerfully did without some of the amenities we'd been accustomed to. Flags flew and stars blossomed in windows. We avidly listened to the radio each evening as Lowell Thomas brought us the latest news. Many of us said goodbye to friends and loved ones. Women worked in factories and took over other jobs previously held only by men. Movie theaters did not charge service personnel for tickets, and no hitchhiking service person waited very long for a ride. Uniforms blossomed everywhere. Songs reflected the times, and "Don't Sit Under the Apple Tree With Anyone Else But Me' and "They're Either Too Young or Too Old" were big hits on the airwaves. Old patriotic songs were revived and new and inspiring ones were added. Do you remember "Coming in on a Wing and a Prayer"? Irving Berlin's "God Bless America" became and has remained the ultimate patriotic anthem.

We were all so proud to be Americans.

CHILDHOOD MEMORIES OF THE WAR IN ENGLAND BY JENNIFER ZOBELEIN

My parents emigrated from Australia and were married in England in 1933. After war was declared in 1939, my Uncle Malcolm, still in Australia, volunteered for the Australian Imperial Force and served as a signaler in the islands north of Australia. Uncle Brian served in the Royal Australian Air Force as a radio operator, also in those northern islands. My Auntie Vaux was an assistant in the Munitions Supply Laboratory where she worked on anti-gas equipment, testing filters for gas masks, and modeling hands for molds for making rubber gloves.

By the time I was born in England, it was January of 1940, just a few months after war was declared. At first, when my mother found out she was pregnant with me, she was dreadfully worried. The threat of war in Europe was very real, and the thought of bringing another child into the world at that time was appalling to her. She adjusted her thinking, however, and was able to find just the right home for us where I was born while my father was away on military service. In my mother's journal, I found these words, dated sometime in early September of 1939:

"We have had 2 weeks delightful holiday with the children at the seaside. At the end of the month, war clouds gathered. Immediately following the declaration of war (September 3, 1939) air raid sirens sounded, but proved to be false. We returned to a blacked-out London.

My father applied to the Air Ministry and was promised a position on the Camouflage Staff, leaving in October, 1939, to report for duty. He was an artist by profession and the British military made a conscious effort to assign people to positions that would make use of their skills. So, he became one of two camouflage inspectors, overseeing air fields all over England, Wales and Northern Ireland. An RAF pilot would take him aloft and he would snap photographs of air fields using a Hasseblad camera. Later, he would examine these photos and work with the commanders on the ground to correct any deficiencies in the aerodrome buildings by adding camouflage paint, fish net, and other materials, as needed. Interestingly, early in World War II, the Swedish military captured a fully functioning surveillance camera from a downed German plane. Realizing the strategic advantage of developing an aerial camera for their own use, they approached Victor Hasselblad to help create one. He began its design, and by late 1941 Sweden had a model which used a larger negative and could be permanently mounted to an aircraft. This was the type of camera my father used.

At regular intervals, he would take the train from our home in Purley, near London, to the nearest air base to perform his duties. During these train trips, it was his habit to spend this travel time in quiet thought, praying that peace and brotherly love would ultimately outweigh the horrors of war. On one such trip, he was standing in the crowded aisle of the carriage, holding on to the leather strap. He was deep in thought, but suddenly felt impelled to lean down and look out the window. It was such a strong intuition that he immediately bent over and peered outside. The train was approaching a high embankment. On the top was a church with a tall steeple. To his utter astonishment he saw what looked like a baby, on a crib mattress, firmly wedged at the bottom of the steeple against a small railing. In a moment, the train had passed. Nobody else had seen this amazing sight. Immediately, he signaled the train engineer. At the next station, they contacted the nearest police department, and a rescue team went out to the church. The child, still alive and well, was brought to safety. No one in the neighborhood had even noticed the baby's predicament.

Later, my father found out more details. There had been a bombing raid the previous night, and a row of apartments near the church had been demolished. The authorities surmised that the bomb blast had not only blown out all the windows, but had also lifted up the crib, with the baby in it, and carried it out the window. The crib fell away, and the baby on the mattress continued to fly through the air, until intercepted by the church steeple. The mattress cushioned the baby as it slid down to the base railing. Sadly, the parents did not survive, but the child was placed in foster care. I have often wondered what became of that orphan who was literally saved by the embrace of a church!

My father also attended a night class at a London college during the war, as time permitted, but was always ready for his military assignments. One evening, the class was abruptly halted and everyone was told to evacuate the building. A bomb had been discovered, in a suitcase, in the cloak room. As the students and teachers chatted nervously outside, waiting for the bomb squad to arrive, my father strolled over to the administrator in charge and said, "I can dismantle that bomb for you." The man looked surprised and asked my father what experience he had. My father replied, "None, sir, but I can tell you that it is _my_ suitcase you discovered, and it is _my_ alarm clock that is ticking inside!"

Early in the war, the bombing of London became ever more severe and our house, located in a suburb south of the city, was definitely in the flight path of many air raids. My mother felt impelled to move us to a safer location but had no idea where she could take us. We had no other family in England and nowhere to go that we could afford. She was led to contact someone, who knew someone else, who had a relative in Sussex who was willing to take us in - my mother and the three of us children. This dear lady welcomed the four of us into her home for several months. Shortly after we moved out, my father telephoned to say that our house had indeed been bombed. All the windows were blown in, and the roof blown off. But - we were not there!

Later, we returned to this home and made repairs. There were shards of glass stuck in all the beds, and the attic room which was my father's art studio was a roofless disaster. The house had contained many beautiful stained glass windows, but we could not afford to replace them and were forced to use plain glass instead. We were just grateful that the house was still standing and in livable condition.

Of course, my older sisters took great delight in teasing me at times. All of us slept together in the front bedroom so we could easily run to the little sheltered place under the stairs when we heard the air raid sirens. When we were huddled in bed, with the windows opened for fresh air, the blackout curtains would move eerily in and out with the breeze, and my sisters would tell me that Germans were walking outside in the garden and that I better be quiet and still! I wasn't sure what to believe, so I buried my head under the covers. (My mother soon put a stop to that foolishness.)

During the war years, our family received Care Packages from various sources. Some of these came from our grandparents in Australia. Some came from churches in Canada and the United States which sent over parcels of food and clothing to be shared with our congregation. We were surprised by cake mixes which we had never seen before. Since we did not have fresh eggs very often, we would mix in powdered eggs and add a bit more liquid. Sometimes we received squares of chocolate and tins of condensed milk. All sweets were severely rationed so this was a great treat. Also, in his work as a camouflage inspector, my father had opportunities sometimes to purchase a few fresh eggs and vegetables from farmers who lived near the airfields where he landed. Since our ration books did not allow for many of those foods, we were delighted when he brought them home.

Christmas time during the war was always a very frugal celebration. I don't ever remember having a tree, or any fancy decorations. I do recall the steamed plum pudding and other traditional foods my mother miraculously produced in spite of rationing. Somehow she also managed to provide one gift for each member of the family – usually something practical like socks. These presents were wrapped and placed in a white pillow case, tied with a brightly colored ribbon. On Christmas morning we would delve into this "bag" and open our gifts – happy to have anything that looked festive. On the evenings preceding Christmas we enjoyed the carolers who would walk by on the street, stopping at our front door to sing. My mother would thank them with a special treat she would dig out from who-knows-where.

I will never forget "queuing up" in long lines to purchase the items we needed. We didn't have a car, so I remember walking with my mother one day after we had shopped. We were crossing the street at an intersection when suddenly loud air raid sirens went off immediately above us. I was so startled that I dropped the small tin of tooth powder that I was carrying and ran for the sidewalk. My mother comforted me, but I have never forgotten the closeness of that frightening sound in my ears. We also had to practice putting on gas masks, but fortunately never had to actually use them.

King George VI and Queen Elizabeth were greatly admired for their stalwart patriotism and unselfishness during the war. They refused to leave London. Buckingham Palace received nine direct bomb hits and the royal family narrowly escaped injury and possible death, choosing to suffer the same hardships as their subjects. When asked if the two princesses, Elizabeth and Margaret, would be sent safely off to Canada during the war, the Queen firmly replied something to this effect: "The princesses will not leave without their mother. The Queen will not leave without their father. The King will not leave under any circumstances." Princess Elizabeth, age nineteen, took on the duties of a wartime auto mechanic and truck driver as a good example to other young British women, and the King and Queen often visited the severely bombed areas of London after a blitz, offering encouragement, smiles and handshakes to the beleaguered citizens who had lost their homes. I remember listening to inspiring radio addresses by the King and also one by Princess Elizabeth.

In 1942, my father made a visit to Bushy Park on the outskirts of London where a large U.S. base called Camp Griffiss was established as headquarters for a number of the Allied departments. He noticed the American and British flags flying side by side and was told that when Dwight Eisenhower made his first appearance at the base he saw that the American flag was mounted on its mast at a higher level than the British. He was outraged and demanded that both flags be displayed at the same height. He explained in no uncertain terms that our two countries were fighting together as allies and there was to be no indication of American superiority. In February and March of 1944, General Eisenhower moved his Supreme Headquarters Allied Expeditionary Forces to Bushy Park where the initial planning stages of the Normandy invasion took place.

Near the end of the war, I was a kindergarten student in a school where my mother taught. Often our classes were interrupted by air raid sirens, and the teachers would lead us quickly to the protection of an outdoor bomb shelter. We carried our schoolbooks with us and the lessons continued until the all-clear sounded. On one such occasion, I apparently wandered off across the school yard, fascinated and curious about the sound of a buzz bomb passing overhead. It actually exploded in the nearby houses a few blocks away. Frantically, my teacher had chased after me to bring me back to safety in the nick of time. Afterwards she chided me and asked why I had not gone immediately to the bomb shelter. With the childlike innocence and trust of a five-year-old, I replied, "But, my shelter is in my thinking!" She had no idea what I meant, so she asked my mother about it. Apologizing for my disobedience, my mother assured her that it would not happen again. Then she explained that whenever there was an air raid at home, she would gather the family together and lead us to a small storage closet under the stairs. There, she would reassure us that our true safety was in prayer, and if we filled our thoughts with the certainty of God's protection and power, we would always feel at peace. Then, huddled in the darkness, awaiting the all-clear siren, we would sing the familiar hymns that we knew by heart. I well remember those occasions, and these words by Isaac Watts still ring in my consciousness:

> ***O God, our help in ages past,***
>
> ***Our hope for time to come,***
>
> ***Our shelter from the stormy blast,***
>
> ***And our eternal home.***

Two years after the war, we left England for Canada, traveling on the RMS *Aquitania*. This Cunard Line ship had been used for troop transport during the war years and had only recently been changed back into a passenger liner for trans-Atlantic crossings.

As we steamed out of Southampton headed for Halifax, the white cliffs of Dover gradually receded, and we looked forward to a new adventure in a different part of the British Empire. We could not afford first-class, so my mother and we three girls were in a dormitory-type room with bunks for six people, while my father was in the men's quarters in a similar situation. We enjoyed meals together in the third-class dining room, marveling at the abundance of real butter, cream, chocolate, and other foods that we had not seen since before the war. We lived for seven years in Canada before moving eventually to California where I completed my high school and college education.

Many decades later, in the 1980's, my husband and I visited that house in England that had been bombed early in the war. It had been converted into a home for retired people, and we were graciously welcomed by the residents. I looked outside at the back garden and saw my father's greenhouse still standing in the far corner by the fence. It brought tears to my eyes. I remembered the rows of vegetables that we grew to supplement our meager rations.   I showed my husband the front bedroom where we all slept, with blackout curtains on every window.   I also looked again at the stairwell, seeing in my mind's eye our family huddled in the little storage area beneath the stairs during a nighttime air raid, waiting for the all-clear to sound.   The memories flooded back, but mostly I was reminded of my parents' reassuring words of comfort that always brought a sense of divine protection.

© 2012 Jennifer Zobelein

Made in the USA
Charleston, SC
11 November 2012